SIX MODERN AUTHORS AND PROBLEMS OF BELIEF

Six Modern Authors and Problems of Belief

PR
479
B44-
G7
1979

PATRICK GRANT

Associate Professor of English
University of Victoria, British Columbia

BOOKS
10 East 53d St., New York 10022
(a division of Harper & Row Publishers, Inc.)

First published 1979 by
THE MACMILLAN PRESS LTD
London and Basingstoke

Published in the U.S.A. 1979 by
HARPER & ROW PUBLISHERS, INC.
BARNES & NOBLE IMPORT DIVISION

Printed in Great Britain

Library of Congress Cataloging in Publication Data

Grant, Patrick
  Six modern authors and problems of belief.

  Includes bibliographical references and index.
  1. English literature — 20th century — History and
criticism. 2. Belief and doubt in literature.
3. Philosophy, English — 20th century. I. Title.
PR479.B44G7 1979   820'.9'38   79–14511
ISBN 0–06–492515–3

For
M. John Francis

Insofar as we think as strictly human beings,
we fail to understand what is below us no
less than what is above.
                Peter Boone in Aldous Huxley's
                After Many a Summer Dies the Swan

Et s'envire en chantant du chemin de la croix.

                Baudelaire

Contents

Preface

With the rise of science in the Renaissance, a crisis occurred for the literary imagination. My discussion centres on six modern authors who are explicitly concerned with this fact, and with relationships between language and reality affected by it. In a modern world where empirical philosophy promotes scientific progress while discrediting the literary imagination as a valid mediator between nature and God, these authors focus also on the symbol of the cross to make their statements about the uses of imaginative language. They suggest that literature concerned with theology in such circumstances can most effectively present the problem of belief itself.

My focus lies within the twofold arbitrariness of a historical claim and a selection of authors, but I have tried not to diminish the case by defining it too sharply. On the historical side I encourage the reader to look at a study of mine, *Images and Ideas in Literature of the English Renaissance* (London: Macmillan, 1979), which deals with the impact of empirical philosophy on literary imagery during the seventeenth century. That book offers a fuller discussion of positions I treat summarily in this one. On the critical side, I introduce to the main discussion figures such as Greene, Lawrence, Joyce, Carroll, Kipling and William Empson, sometimes to make a counter-case and clarify the central point, but also to suggest alternative directions which the argument could take. About each of my main authors – Huxley, Graves, Jones, Tolkien, Barfield and Polanyi – I attempt to say something new, and questions raised by my selection prompt an assessment of the critic's place in making the interconnections between literature, science and theology which the book discusses.

I acknowledge with gratitude the help of Charles Doyle, Laurence Lerner and Tony Nuttall, who read the manuscript and made numerous suggestions. I thank also Owen Barfield, William Blissett, René Hague and Henry Summerfield for their generosity and advice, and I extend special thanks to David Jeffrey, without whose encouragement the project would have faltered. I acknowledge with gratitude and respect the Izaac Walton Killam Trust and the Canada

Council, from whom I received a Killam Senior Research Scholarship for 1977—78, enabling me to write the book.

Permission to quote from a letter has been received from Mr Owen Barfield, and from the following journals to reproduce articles already in print: *The Malahat Review*, 'The Dark Side of the Moon: Robert Graves as Mythographer' (1975), pp. 143—65, and *Cross Currents*, 'Tolkien, Archetype and Word' (Winter, 1973), pp. 365—78. 'Arachne', from *Collected Poems*, copyright © 1949, 1977 by William Empson, is reprinted by permission of Harcourt Brace Jovanovitch, Inc., and Chatto and Windus, Ltd. 'For God While Sleeping', from *All My Pretty Ones*, by Anne Sexton, copyright © 1961, 1962 by Anne Sexton, is reprinted by permission of Houghton Mifflin Company and The Sterling Lord Agency.

October 1978   P.G.

1 Introduction: New science and the autonomy of signs

I. MODERN REFLECTIONS ON AN EARLIER REVOLUTION

On 30 January 1649 King Charles I stepped out from the Banqueting House of his palace at Whitehall. He had an orange stuck with cloves in his pocket, pearl rings in his ears and two shirts on his back. And he made his way to a scaffold improvised there for his execution.

When Sir Anthony Van Dyck several years earlier painted this king's head in three positions, the sculptor Bernini, commissioned to copy the portrait in stone, had said it was a doomed face, the most unfortunate he had ever seen.[1] Perhaps Bernini responded just to the melancholy countenance; perhaps also to rumours of civil insurrection carried to Rome from England in the late 1630s, and which he saw reflected in Van Dyck's interpretation.

Today we do not know what went on in Bernini's mind, but we have much less doubt about how the king himself would have taken the comment. The royal countenance of course would express a people's suffering, for was a king not head of their body, the 'earthly god, celestial man',[2] divinely appointed their representative? Indeed, the major difference between Charles I and his executioners was that they could not share such a way of looking at things. In royalty the regicides saw instead a parade of symbols which, posing as facts, were merely instruments of tyranny to prey upon the people's imagination. Facts for Cromwell were of a different order altogether: we will cut off the king's head with the crown on it, he had said, and *that* would be a fact.[3] Yet Cromwell also underestimated the real power of those conventions he dismissed as fictive. The last thing he expected was that within eleven years the crown should have fallen only as far as the head of the king's son.

An observer of the execution has left some words carefully gauged to have us measure these contending claims of time-honoured symbol against new political reality:

> *He* nothing common did or mean
> Upon that memorable Scene:
> But with his keener Eye
> The Axes edge did try:
> Nor call'd the *Gods* with vulgar spight
> To vindicate his helpless Right,
> But bow'd his comely Head,
> Down as upon a Bed.[4]

Marvell, master of the oblique, might mean that Charles I stood above common humanity because he *was* something special, a king. But the verse calls attention also to the king's plain humanity, and whether Charles was uncommon because of his inherited divine right or because he behaved himself well under stress we do not learn from these lines. One result is that our sense of the condemned man's predicament is shot through with extra pathos. Behind the belief with all its props (ear rings, pomander, the crown) stood a human being, a man whose dignity was enhanced by his sense of symbolic reality. We appreciate the nobility in his weakness, and it is a pity he should have suffered.

For modern readers, an ambivalent reading of this sort is likely to prove more satisfying than the attitude summed up in Cromwell's opinions about facts, and yet this is so partly because we have in many ways inherited Cromwell's legacy. We have come far enough along the road of secularism no longer to feel strongly that the world manifests the transcendent wisdom of a creator who organises it hierarchically, leaving vestiges of his wisdom in his works for man to read and thereby ascend, by a 'song of degrees', towards beatitude.[5] Such theories we allow to characterise the belief of a bygone age. For Charles I, however, they were still very much alive,[6] as we find from *Eikon Basilike*, his own account of the war which led to his defeat.

The royal person, the *Eikon Basilike* tells us, is sacrosanct according to 'all that is settled or sacred in religion and laws'. The king's rights subject him only to God, and his government is a prologue to the second coming itself.[7] Not surprisingly, Charles sees his own impending death as a crucifixion, and prays in Christ's words: 'O remember Thy great mercies toward them and forgive them, O my Father, for they know not what they do'.[8] It is as if Christ's passion is taking place at the present moment, for the king does not just recall the past event and look to it for strength. His quotation has no hint of irony or blasphemy, and the prayer implies a way of reading events as an embodiment of their exemplars. The blow struck at Charles's head, in short, does not betoken just an attack on a particular individual, or even on a certain type of government; it implies the rejection of a whole civilisation's way of reading things as signs of the transcendent and eternally fixed ideas which they embody.

In *L'Homme Revolté*, his study of modern history, Albert Camus combines the themes of revolutionary regicide and crucifixion to help clarify his argument that twentieth-century man, having abandoned the old gods of religion, now faces disillusionment also with the new gods of history and progress. Camus argues that the special plight of modern civilisation begins with 'the passion of Louis XVI':

> the condemnation of the king is at the crux of our contemporary history. It symbolizes the secularization of our history and the dematerialization of the Christian God. Up to now God played a part in history through the medium of the kings. But His representative in history has been killed, for there is no longer a king. Therefore there is nothing but a semblance of God, relegated to the heaven of principles.[9]

By dispensing with God, Camus tells us, man becomes free in a new way to determine his own future, and erects absolutes which now are placed not on the 'vertical' axis of a cross where man stands in relation to eternity, but 'horizontally', where he stands in relation to time. Without the traditional sanctions embodied in eternally fixed standards, 'All morality becomes provisional. The nineteenth and twentieth centuries, in their most profound manifestations, are centuries which have tried to live without transendence.'[10]

Taken together, Camus and Marvell remind us that secularism is a mixed blessing, but they also make clear that its advantages, whether in promoting constitutional government, European Enlightenment, or the rise of science, remain based on a general, widespread attack against the usefulness of divinely-appointed authority for organising or determining human knowledge. Certainly, the new thinkers, from Bacon and Hobbes and Locke to Sprat and De la Mettrie, denied consistently that the human mind can abstract from an object any such thing as 'substantial form' or conceive thereby some 'idea' of the object as part of a divinely-patterned hierarchy of perfections created according to a blueprint in God's mind, and therefore immanent in nature. The senses, simply, are not to be trusted to read Divine Ideas in the Book of the World.

This does not mean, however, that the scientific impulse was uniformly bent from the start on promoting secular progress. Although Bacon saw science as ameliorative, he had to carry out a strenuous public relations campaign to persuade others, and to disengage science from its association with magical élites and secret schemes of individual aggrandisement.[11] Paradoxically, his own strictures on experimentation without hypotheses, if adopted literally, would have impeded the very advances he recommended, because such strictures refused intuition any important part in organising evidence or experiments.

Nor is Camus's suggestion about God's 'dematerialisation' to be taken at face value. The whole of patristic and mediaeval theology had proclaimed God immaterial, and it was for the scions of the scientific revolution, such as Hobbes, to suggest otherwise. And if Camus means just that God became more transcendent, even that is not universally true of the great intellects most influenced by the new philosophy. Newton, for instance, makes the material universe God's *sensorium*, and Spinoza identifies God with nature itself ('*Deus sive natura*'). If anything, it was Calvinism, not science, which proposed most vigorously to separate God from the world, implying with the absence of human merit the incapacity of human reason to deal with notions of deity. No doubt such reasoning ultimately allied itself with a scientifically-based positivism, but, at first, Calvinist distrust of human aspiration could operate also to repress scientific enquiry,[12] a point well exemplified in *Paradise Lost* by Raphael's rebuke of Adam's astronomical curiosity.

Plainly, the currents cross in complex ways, but the variety itself confirms the main point: the new thinkers, whether in politics or science or philosophy, mounted a consistent attack on the mind's capacity to apprehend those transcendent patterns supposed to determine form in individual things. As I have argued at length elsewhere,[13] poets of the period cannot help reflecting the pressures placed upon literature in such circumstances to serve the interests of traditional piety. If transcendent ideas are no longer expressed truly (however partially) in images, and if words no longer reveal the fixed essences of things, the traditional function of poetry in helping us to interpret the world for our spiritual edification, is clearly under duress.[14] The new emphasis is clear if we look briefly at St

Augustine's theory of rhetoric, which remained as essentially true for Prudentius and Dante as for Peter Lombard and Thomas Aquinas.

Images in the mind and images in books, St Augustine claims, are co-extensive, and are described as 'spiritual vision'. The term indicates the peculiarly human status of mental imagery as a mediator between 'corporeal vision' (the experience of objects) and 'intellectual vision' (which is ideal, and imageless, the discourse of angels). As a condition of human existence in fallen time, spiritual vision is, by itself, incomplete, and our mental images give an indirect, if true, reading of intelligible reality.[15] Literature, itself a mimesis of spiritual vision, is consequently also an account of the human pilgrimage in time, directed towards heavenly ideals, but trammelled by the corporeal conditions of a fallen nature. Augustine therefore supposes that words, by enabling an understanding of the material world, turn the beholder's gaze heavenwards, in contemplation.[16] This sense of continuity between mental images and the realms of material and spiritual substance constitutes the essential difference between his view of reality and that of Locke.

We can see how readily, in criticising the Augustinian kind of theory on grounds that the mind does not apprehend substantial forms, the new empiricism helped to set along separate paths the modern careers of science, theology and literature. The first is concerned with the structure of material nature (corresponding to corporeal vision), the second with the world of spirit (intellectual vision) and literature, the third, uncertain now of its traditional position as mediator between the other two, displays increasing anxiety about the nature of its own subject matter.

II. THE IMAGE OF THE CROSS

In *Eikon Basilike* the monarch prays to God in the words of the dying Jesus, and implies that the past event of the cross on Calvary is present, re-enacted on the scaffold at Whitehall. But Charles is not merely remembering the crucifixion, nor following Christ's example. The suffering Christ is, in a particular sense, the suffering king. The identity is one of participation, and to appreciate what exactly Charles might have felt and thought on this subject, we need to imagine ourselves more fully immersed than is habitual for us, in the medieval, centrally Augustinian theory of spiritual vision.

The cross, Augustine says, is not merely the instrument of a physical maiming which took place at a certain date in history. It is a symbol of God's eternal willingness to suffer on man's behalf, and so symbolises man's predicament in fallen space and time. It is the pre-eminent sign of faith[17] and there is therefore a close analogy between the cross and the status of spiritual vision itself. Both show the imperfection of human beings, and direct men through the conditions of an earthly pilgrimage towards the contemplation of God. The *Itinerarum Mentis in Deum* of St Bonaventure, Augustine's foremost disciple in the Middle Ages, makes this point especially clear. Our prayer of meditation should centre on the cross until, at the apex of vision, it will be replaced by the ineffable experience of Godhead. But when meditation on the cross passes, so also do the author's words. At the moment of intellectual vision, images are surrendered. Words and the cross are, alike, signs of man on the way to eternity through time, of *homo viator* who submits to the trial of faith that he may see God. The cross is divinely ordained to invest our human situation with significance, while indicating our temporal limitations.[18]

In the *Vexilla Regis*,[19] Venantius Fortunatus expresses a similar insight. He describes how the cross cancels the effects of Adam's tree, how its march forth into time subsumes and abrogates the political triumphs of Rome, how it fulfils David's prophecy because a new king assumes the throne and how, above all, it is radiant despite the rivers of blood. '*Arbor decora et fulgida*' spoils the devil of his prey.

The cross as Venantius Fortunatus presents it is, so to speak, objectively significant. There is no poetic 'viewpoint' through which we struggle to make something of it. Observer and reader are, equally, everyman, the human race in the condition of pilgrimage and redeemed by Christ's saving blood. Just as natural signs, given in creation itself, can show man a way through this world, so the cross, pre-eminent sign of redemption, is given by revelation to show the true nature of the human situation. Man is a pilgrim, imperfect in time and waiting on grace, but with an eternal destiny, and we accept such a sign as the cross in order to understand ourselves.

With the Renaissance, this kind of interpretation begins to change. Not surprisingly, the period which saw a philosophic attack on the premises underlying 'spiritual vision' was also the heyday of iconoclasm, and in the debate between defenders of images and their destroyers, the crucifix became a point upon which argument was particularly heated.[20] Reasons are not hard to find. In the crucifix spiritual and material elements are dramatically brought together, and the question of how far the domain of the latter could represent the workings of the former is presented in a manner compact enough to focus a whole range of issues involved in the larger debate.

Even among the traditionally-minded, during the seventeenth century, there is a certain unease about the sign of the cross. Consider George Herbert's poem, 'Redemption':[21]

> Having been tenant long to a rich Lord,
>   Not thriving, I resolved to be bold,
> And make a suit unto him, to afford
>   A new small-rented lease, and cancell th' old.
> In heaven at his manour I him sought:
>   They told me there, that he was lately gone
> About some land, which he had dearly bought
>   Long since on earth, to take possession.
> I straight return'd, and knowing his great birth,
>   Sought him accordingly in great resorts;
>   In cities, theatres, gardens, parks, and courts:
> At length I heard a ragged noise and mirth
>   Of theeves and murderers; there I him espied,
>   Who straight, *Your suit is granted*, said, and died.

The tone of the speaking voice – clear-headed, competent, ruminative – suggests the attitude of the pilgrim pursuing his course in a not very Christian frame of mind, looking for his 'rich Lord' in all the wrong places. At last he stumbles upon a company of thieves and murderers, where the Lord, amidst the 'ragged noise and mirth', grants the suit, and dies.

The point is that despite his own great effort, the pilgrim is brought to the Lord by the imageless mystery of grace, and indeed despite his own knowledge or expectations. The legalistic understanding of the 'old man' has led him astray, and so when he does find the Lord, at last, the request ironically is granted before he has time even to make it. God's foreknowledge and the mystery of grace have sought him out.

The paradoxes of the pilgrim's situation culminate in the crucifixion. The 'theeves and murderers' are, presumably, the two thieves executed with Christ, and the soldiers, who in this case murder an innocent man. But it is doubtful if the pilgrim sees anything more than a public execution. Thieves and murderers would, indiscriminately, be for him the crucified criminals and perhaps the rabble, but hardly the soldiers. The very last words, 'said, and died', are therefore a masterpiece. The suit is granted because Christ dies: to a Christian, 'and' signifies causality. But to the pilgrim the relationship seems temporal: his Lord said these words and then died. The significance of the cross may not be understood, hardly even grasped, by the pilgrim as the poem ends, and the question of how his Lord, in such strained circumstances, knew who he was or what he had come for has not yet hit him.

On one level Herbert treats the cross like St Augustine and Venantius Fortunatus. The mystery of divine love is central, and the cross signifies our limited comprehension of it. We could say that the vertical arms mediate grace, and the horizontal indicate a historical passage from old to new law. The time is at once the moment of crucifixion, the pilgrim's strangely a-temporal realm, and also the reader's time. The poem tells us that God's love remains a mystery, however much we seem to know, and therefore implies that although we are separate from the pilgrim we are bound to be making the same kinds of blunders, the same confused pursuit of truth, because we too work in a world of fallen time and through refractions of images. Yet the pilgrim has faith and does his best: that is what we should all learn, and our means of discovering the pilgrim's predicament, no less than our own, is the cross.

There is also one main difference between Herbert and the earlier examples: as we read 'Redemption' it is essential to appreciate the separate viewpoints of pilgrim and poet. The cross is no longer objectively significant as in *Vexilla Regis*: faith now struggles to realise a meaning which may not be mediated by the sign itself. Much as Herbert seems to carry forward a sense of the cross common in the iconography of medieval 'spiritual vision', that way of looking at things is under pressure in his work. In 'Redemption' it is not clear that the cross as a sign as distinct from event is efficacious at all. The pilgrim may be redeemed, and know nothing about the sign. Herbert is, of course, the poet who can make poems out of this very distrust of images: [22]

Riddle who list, for me, and pull for Prime:
I envie no mans nightingale or spring;
Nor let them punish me with losse of rime,
  Who plainly say, *My God, My King.*

Here, in short, is the Reformation man doubting the usefulness for spiritual knowledge of profane images and questioning poetry's function in religious life. The chief difference between Herbert and his medieval predecessors is therefore not in their appeal to traditional materials, but in the degree to which Herbert feels a discontinuity between profane images and spiritual meaning. His more zealous Puritan contemporaries, believing faith to be even less ambiguously an unmediated act of the transcendent upon individual souls, simply smashed what images they could, even though at times half regretting their destructiveness.[23] But whether they saw it clearly or not, the iconoclasts were basically in accord with that consensus of opinion which denied the efficacy of material things for truly mediating transcendent ideas, and by their hand, though with similarly confused feelings, the king's symbolic and sacred temple was 'broke ope'.

Images in poetry and in the visual arts, however, are not the same, and the Puritans who smashed visual icons often kept up a devotional literature with plenty of 'visual' images.[24] Poetry seemed less creaturely and less public than painting or sculpture, and in literature the cross remained an important image for Protestant meditation. Its meaning merely had become more private, more interior than before: the cross was, historically, the occasion of redemption, but as a sign it now stood mainly for the inner drama whereby man struggles to free himself from the oppressions of a sinful, outside world. The sense of sacramental participation of all times and places somehow in that event, on the model of Venantius Fortunatus, or the *Eikon Basilike*, was by and large surrendered, and the century of Enlightenment replaced, in public piety, the crucified God by the conceptually easier notion of an intelligent if remote designer. The future of the cross as a literary symbol lay, thenceforward, in the hymnody of Isaac Watts, the Wesleys, and their Victorian followers,[25] where it stood more than ever in contrast to the iniquities of a secular, unbelieving society.

These changes may be reduced to a simple contrast. The artist of the Middle Ages looking at the cross felt that the sign was divinely revealed to show him what life meant. His modern counterpart is no less interested in life's meaning, but for him experience is the only reliable given thing, and by organising it in terms of a traditional sign, such as the cross, he seeks to achieve some satisfying sense of pattern and structure.

With this contrast in mind, we can see how an explanation like George Santayana's at once betrays his stance as a modern, without his being aware of it. Santayana claims that for early pagans on the verge of Christianity the cross was an 'objectification of an inner impulse', and became a religious inspiration when it ceased to be 'a historical fact'.[26] But the distinction between history and significance was not so clear either to the Middle Ages or to Santayana's imagined converts. The fact of the cross embodied its significance, and only with the seventeenth-century revolution in epistemology were these two so clearly separated.[27]

In his monumental discussion of the cross, Jurgen Moltmann is more careful:

> Since the Renaissance, the Enlightenment and the rise of modern technology, the relationship between man and nature in most fields has been reversed. Man is no longer dependent upon uncomprehended forces in nature and history, recognizing in this dependence his total reliance on the Gods or on God. Instead, nature and history have become increasingly dependent upon man.[28]

This has a good deal in common with the passage quoted earlier from Camus. Since the Renaissance, man the inventor of the secular state has become master of history, and the further development of his powers as master of technology threatens to destroy him. Man does not now read the inherent significance of nature, but instead tries to invest the nature he has usurped and rendered inert, with significance. So for Moltmann the cross is full of meaning because, among other things, it represents with unique economy our modern crisis of relevance and identity; because it criticises the self-glorification of dehumanised man; because it represents the perplexity and suffering of a humanity which can surrender neither the awareness of an unanswerable problem of pain nor the need to pursue righteousness.[29] Moltmann's drift is clear: on personal grounds we may believe the objective truth about God in Christ, but the cross will carry weight for us in our everyday world, in proportion to the amount of existential 'secular' experience we can bring to bear on it.[30]

This kind of argument is taken a step further by Paul Tillich, who draws from it an interesting conclusion about sign-making itself. Tillich first suggests that symbols are not reducible in intellectual terms, and so may strike us with the force of given (because not consciously achieved) meaning.[31] But the weight of his argument falls, in the end, like Moltmann's, on the adequacy of the symbol for representing experience. In this respect he suggests also that the cross is unique because it implies a self-negation which shows its own lack of ultimacy:[32] all symbols are incomplete, but the cross reminds us of this and so is the symbol of symbols themselves. Tillich does not deny an objective content to faith, but asserts that it is a mysterious and private matter, affirmed in the modern world by courage in face of formidable critical odds. The argument on symbols, on the other hand, makes their power to a much greater extent proportionate to the range of public experience they can subsume.

This emphasis on man's taking upon himself a special burden of interpretation is poignantly confirmed by Moltmann when he reflects on the execution of three Jewish prisoners in a Nazi concentration camp. 'It is necessary,' he says, after quoting a passage on the deaths of two men and a youth written by an eyewitness,

> . . . to remember the martyrs, so as not to become abstract. Of them and of the dumb sacrifices it is true in a real, transferred sense, that God himself hung in the gallows, as E. Wiesel was able to say. If that is taken seriously, it must also be said that, like the cross of Christ, even Auschwitz is in God himself.[33]

The point about the executions is their absurd horror. As a spectacle of degradation and human abandonment, Auschwitz poses with unavoidable, sickening force the question of righteousness, and Moltmann's way of facing it is to offer no explanation deriving from theological principles. He resists arguing from God down to man, but tries to look instead at the terrible event and still see God. This, he claims, is the necessary post-Renaissance emphasis: 'The point of reference and the purpose of the questions have changed. . . . Jesus is no longer understood against the background of discourse about God as "God-man", but as it were in the anthropological foreground as the exemplary and archetypal "man of God"' (93).

Faced with facts like Auschwitz, Moltmann suggests, we cannot avoid seeing that we inhabit a world where we are neither free to avoid the problem of unjust suffering, nor to be satisfied with theological answers to it. In such a situation, the cross alone is relevant, because the uniqueness and pathos of Christ's death similarly rebuke easy answers. Christ died abandoned, and his death protests against theology, while it shows also how he preserved a singular, existential openness to God. Consequently, all unjust executions, whether of Jesus or the men and the boy at Auschwitz, have in common that they are irreducibly scandalous, and the cross remains the only adequate Christian means of approaching them. 'To suffer and be rejected,' Moltmann concludes, 'signify the cross' (53), and his point neatly reverses the traditional, medieval emphasis that the cross signifies, and helps to explain, suffering. Moltmann's conclusion thus remains close to Tillich's; both men believe the cross is the supreme Christian sign because it shows the limitations of signs, urging us to carry our convictions courageously. In man's forsakenness lies God's potentiality.

Some of these theological preoccupations are reflected in a modern poem about the crucifixion by Anne Sexton.

For God While Sleeping

Sleeping in fever, I am unfit
to know just who you are:
hung up like a pig on exhibit,
the delicate wrists,
the beard drooling blood and vinegar;
hooked to your own weight,
jolting toward death under your nameplate.

Everyone in this crowd needs a bath.
I am dressed in rags.
The mother wears blue. You grind your teeth
and with each new breath
your jaws gape and your diaper sags.
I am not to blame
for all this. I do not know your name.

Skinny man, you are somebody's fault.
You ride on dark poles —
a wooden bird that a trader built
for some fool who felt
that he could make the flight. Now you roll
in your sleep, seasick
on your own breathing, poor old convict.[34]

In the opening line, the 'I' is feverishly asleep, and in the second to last line Christ is also asleep and seasick. The title therefore is ambiguous, for it means 'for God while I sleep' as well as 'for God while he sleeps', and, when we think about it, both meanings interpenetrate, for God's being and man's consciousness in this poem are delicately interconnected. Perhaps Sexton's most striking effect is the way she renders this ambiguity, for it suggests the viewpoint of the twentieth century itself. The 'I' who sleeps in fever, who is dressed in rags and feels a shameful complicity in the pitiful execution even while denying responsibility ('I am not to blame / . . . you are somebody's fault'), the 'I' who is bewildered and disoriented and 'unfit to know' is all of us living in the historical period when God sleeps.

One main difference between 'For God While Sleeping' and 'Redemption', however, is that the modern poem tries conspicuously to work with as little assumed 'given' meaning as possible. Rather, the 'I' faces its absence. At best there is some vague knowledge that there was once a theory behind this suffering (the wooden bird was built by a trader 'for some fool who felt /that he could make the flight'), but the central experience of the poem is on a consistently human plane, as human pity faces human suffering in bewilderment. There is shame that a human being has been treated in this way, for the indignity has nothing to redeem it. The nameplate, the word, is indecipherable, and the 'I' is as isolated as the 'poor old convict'. The speaker's extreme self-consciousness has the burden of interpretation therefore imposed upon itself. God and man dream the same fevered nightmare, for man's inability to know the name is both the cause and meaning of the eclipsed God.

Yet, although the speaker does not know the assumed meanings, the poet does. She knows that the execution is a central event in the history of Western culture, and she presents a disenchanted view which speaks deliberately for our era of that history. We have lost, she seems to say, the sense of transcendence which once gave the cross meaning. But there is not much nostalgia for what has been lost: the poem implies that when we look at what the cross actually is, to glorify it must seem like some kind of desperate expedient for escaping the absurdity of suffering, and the bewilderment of the poet is in the end akin to that of her persona. Here, the contrast with Herbert's 'Redemption' is clearest. Although both poems have in common a lonely and isolated speaker who knows less than the author, Herbert's pilgrim assumes that meaning can be found, and his speaker claims that man's experience in the world is made meaningful by God, especially through the cross. God in the end gives meaning to our lives. Sexton makes no such assumptions, but reacts with outrage to the man hanged, half despairing at the prospect of finding any meaning there at all. Although Herbert is the more profound and achieved poet (he lacks Sexton's egregious sensationalism) the differences have got to do not only with poetic merit, but with attitudes to the symbol itself. To Herbert it is the vehicle of God's grace whereby human life is given meaning; to Sexton the burden of making something of it is thrust upon the observer. Hers is a more extreme statement than Moltmann's about meaning's dependency on man, or Tillich's on the courage of faith, but her insight is akin to theirs. Tillich, after all, admired 'Guernica' as an expression of the modern face of human suffering from which alone faith could arise.[35]

III. RECONNAISSANCE

As the modern rise of materialist philosophy has helped to free imagination by challenging it to make significant an inanimate world, so also it has diminished the given meaning of traditional symbols. What, then, should art do?[36]

In a famous essay, T. S. Eliot had this to say:

Our civilization comprehends great variety and complexity, and this variety and complexity, playing upon a refined sensibility, must produce various and complex results. The poet must become more and more comprehensive, more allusive, more indirect, in order to force, to dislocate if necessary, language into his meaning.[37]

The answer is both a diagnosis and a prescription. The artist will select his signs because of their adequacy, and discover in so doing how he can imbue them, and the tradition from which he draws them, with meaning. His art, presumably, will be non-representational to show that it is neither simply imitative of the 'real' outside world or the 'real' inside emotions, but aware of the status of the work of art itself as a symbolic structure.[38] It will reflect a critical awareness that human language mediates imperfectly and indirectly what it describes, for images and analogies no longer reveal a divinely-ordained purpose for things, and the empirical tradition has insisted that transcendental ideas are not useful for the process of true scientific knowledge. Twentieth-century art therefore will assume its share of the burden of that broad divorce between empirical science and theology initiated by a revolution in thought three hundred years ago. In so doing, it will also face, in a particularly challenging form, some inconsistencies of the classical empirical approach to knowledge.

John Locke, we may recall, had proposed that we are ignorant alike of Divine Ideas and the real material world, but then countered the potential excesses of this theory by confirming what common sense has always demanded: there is a concrete reality outside us, and ideals do shape human lives.[39] In an Enlightenment society, likewise dedicated to the virtues of good sense, Locke's kind of empirical psychology and plain man's philosophy managed to strike up an acceptable common-law relationship. Until, that is, it became increasingly clear that the process which cut man off from transcendent ideas in order to give him knowledge of the world, had cut him off also from the world. In so far as art in the twentieth century dwells still in the heart of such a paradox, it has become stunningly self-aware as Eliot says. Yet the artist continues to acknowledge that man in some sense is concerned with ideals, for man is incurably metaphysical.[40] The question is then, 'What ideals?' And when he thinks about this for very long, the modern artist finds he must add also, 'What concrete experience?' Here he can only offer to submit what he thinks of as his own ideas to the test of what he thinks to be experience, for in the twentieth century difficulties arise from the peculiar historical fact that both 'experience' and 'ideas' have become hypothetical, the acts of faith basic to science and theology, respectively.

The central contrast in this chapter can be described in terms of two executions, one at Whitehall and the other at Auschwitz, each being concerned with the motif of the cross, and two poems from the same two periods, dealing with the same theme. The main object has been to clarify a modern attitude to the perennial problem of how words convey belief, and to propose that the advent of science during the seventeenth century raised with fresh urgency certain questions about the nature and status of imagination. Such a proposal needs to be distinguished, however, from another to which it lies uncomfortably close, and which suggests that the seventeenth century somehow unleashed forces entailing a gradual evolution towards literary modernism. History does not move with such pleasing uniformity, and, of course, the Augustans, Romantics and Victorians also have inspired works of modern art. But attention to the seventeenth century clarifies in a particular manner certain questions about religious belief in a scientific age, which can stand as paradigms because we appreciate better their distinctiveness by examining them at their historical inception.

The argument helps, finally, to explain the choice of authors, because each thinks that the scientific revolution gave rise to problems of belief which he encounters as a literary man today. Also, for each, the sign of the cross comes to stand for the kind of statement literature can make about religion in a scientific age. But the fact that there is such a pattern of shared concerns prompts yet a further question about whether or not personal taste, equally clearly reflected in my selection, can usefully illuminate a historical claim. Because such a point calls for an examination of the nature of criticism itself, the practice of criticism is, presumably, the best approach to an answer.

2 Belief in Mysticism: Aldous Huxley, from *Grey Eminence* to *Island*

I. INTRODUCTION: SCIENCE, MYSTICISM AND THE LITERARY MAN

When Aldous Huxley became interested in mysticism in the second half of his career, his concern for science also deepened. He became less a literary man and more a man of ideas, writing, among other things, on a variety of issues connected with science in the modern world. To Huxley it seemed increasingly clear that unless man rediscovered the Absolute he would be destroyed by his own technology. The only adequate guide, he kept repeating, lay in the perennial philosophy, that core of mystical teaching described through the ages in strikingly similar terms by the world's great religions.

As Huxley argued these opinions in print, he found himself preoccupied also by his own limitations as a man of letters having to work in the written word and through the medium of images. Yet the question of what kind of writer he should be was not new to Huxley, for it had always troubled him. In a letter he once described himself as not a born novelist but 'some other kind of man of letters',[1] and when asked in an interview about the rules a novelist should follow, he replied there were none, 'except *do it well*'.[2] Often his talent did not fit the mould of conventional forms, and he was always a curious searcher after new ways of writing, by means of which he achieved his own peculiar excellence.

Concerning his essay on Maine de Biran ('Variations on a Philosopher'),[3] Huxley once confided to Harold Raymond: 'If the thing comes off as I hope, it will be an example of what I think is a new literary form, in which philosophical discussion is enlivened and given reality by the fact of its being particularised within a

17

biography'. [4] The essay remains among Huxley's best pieces: a unique mixture of historical learning, psychological analysis and speculation, containing a central diagnosis of twentieth-century discontents. It is neither a novel, nor history, nor a philosophical discourse, but a kind of case study psychoanalysed by way of history, and in the context of mystical theology. It is an unusual, experimental mix, through which Huxley's mature voice speaks with authority. Other books in the same manner are the *Devils of Loudun* (1952), and the less known *Grey Eminence* (1941). About the latter, Huxley remarked that he would like to find another episode like it, because proper case histories seemed especially important for discussing the ambivalent subject of religious ideas in the modern world. [5] *Grey Eminence* can therefore tell us a good deal about the new kind of man of letters Huxley felt himself to be, and why he thought the attempt to produce something other than novels may be a salutory undertaking for a writer in the twentieth century.

II. *GREY EMINENCE*: THE WAY OF TRANSCENDENCE AND THE WAY OF HISTORY

Grey Eminence [6] is the story of Joseph du Tremblay, Baron of Maffliers (1577–1638), who surrendered his noble patrimony to become a Capucin friar. While living a life of austere self-denial, Fr Joseph learned the techniques of contemplative prayer, but by a turn of circumstance was drawn into political life. He quickly became influential as Cardinal Richelieu's right-hand man, chief of the French secret police and perpetrator, in the interests of Bourbon supremacy, of the Thirty Years War. From something close to a contemplative saint, Joseph du Tremblay became something close to demonic, as an anonymous graffito on his tombstone says:

> *Passant, n'est-ce pas chose étrange*
> *Qu'un démon soit près d'un ange?* (262)

For Huxley, the story of Richelieu's Grey Eminence is an example of powerful spiritual energies fatally channelled in the wrong direction: *corruptio optimi est pessima*. Father Joseph had once stood on the brink of divine enlightenment. In his preaching and ministering to the sick and poor, his counsel and writings on the life of prayer – in short, in a wide range of reforming activities conducted on the margin of society where, Huxley believes, they could do most good – Fr Joseph came close to sanctity, 'at peace and happy in the conviction that his true vocation had been revealed to him' (86). How, then, were these extraordinary energies deflected to ruinous worldly ends?

Huxley looks first for an answer to the methods of prayer in which Fr Joseph was trained. Joseph's spiritual master was Benet of Canfield, whose teachings are recorded in *The Rule of Perfection* (1609). Benet, Huxley argues, is in the main line of Christian mystical tradition which goes back to Dionysius the Areopagite, but, as Benet's contemporary Fr Augustine Baker was quick to point out, Benet departs from pure theocentric mysticism on an important point. Whereas the older mystics insisted that the use of imagination in contemplative prayer was an introduction to mystical ascent, they had also taught (as we have seen with St Augustine and St Bonaventure) that images must be abandoned as we pass into the full experience of vision. Benet, however, insisted that meditation on Christ's passion, especially the cross, be carried on at all times, and that the meditator should not relinquish it. Hallucinatory visions and ecstasies were a common result, but these, in the end, fell short of the calm fullness of unitive experience. Contemplatives trained in Benet's tradition therefore developed a kind of prayer in which image and personal will were allowed to impede, not assist, the soul's enlightenment, so that 'direct mystical experience' became subordinate to mere personalistic theology (81).

Accordingly, for Fr Joseph, whose hallucinations threw him into ecstasies on the spot whenever the subject of crucifixion was mentioned, meditation did not lead to 'complete one-pointedness, complete absorption in ultimate reality' (120). He settled, psychologically, for something less than the best, and when opportunity presented itself in the person of Cardinal Richelieu ('one of the great incarnations of the personal will' [140]), Fr Joseph was seduced into imagining God's glory could be served by the advancement of the material and political interests of God's country, France. The subsequent path towards criminal folly involving high statesmanship (228), collusion in the horrors of the Thirty Years War, and the eventual degeneration of Joseph du Tremblay into a universally hated and feared minister of persecution and terror are narrated with a logic and insight which hold the reader fascinated.

Huxley's attempt to reduce history to a particular instance of religious psychology based on devotion to the cross is bold and ingenious, and it does not stop at the Thirty Years War. In a passage which begins by warning us, with arch seriousness, that 'To over-simplify is fatal', Huxley links the upheavals of seventeenth-century France with a series of European catastrophes leading to the Second World War, then bringing his argument back to the biography of Joseph du Tremblay, and so to the flaw in Benet's *Rule of Perfection*:

> But in truth, as we shall find if we look into his biography a little closely, his thoughts and feelings and desires were among the significantly determining conditions of the world in which we live today. The road trodden by those bare horny feet of his led immediately to the Rome of Urban VIII. More remotely, it led to August 1914 and September 1939. In the long chain of crime and madness which binds the present world to its past, one of the most fatally important links was the Thirty Years' War (14).

On one level it is preposterous to imply that had Fr Joseph remained contemplative there would have been no world wars, and Huxley does not quite demand that we think exactly this, but he does ask us to consider that history might have taken a different course had Fr Joseph not placed his extraordinary will and energy at the disposal of Cardinal Richelieu. The story becomes, so to speak, a negative analogue of the old legend that there are twelve just men in the world on whose sanctity the survival of all depends. Of course, nobody knows who they are: the chains of cause and effect in human history are so complex that the good done by a single man may have incalculable consequences. Huxley thinks the same of evil, except that negative results are easier to trace than good. So he charts the spreading circles of consequence from Fr Joseph's biography, and with such narrative skill that we hesitate to deny there may be something in it. Against our sense that the thesis is preposterous stands the story's brilliant plausibility, leaving us with a work so well imagined and deftly organised that we appreciate it as a *tour de force* in which the fictive and historical stand in perilous symbiosis. Indeed, part of the book's purpose is to make us wonder at this very ambivalence, manifested both in Fr Joseph and the book itself as a piece of writing poised between fact and fiction.

On the historical side, Huxley's main point is that war makes history; saints do not, and if we can learn from Fr Joseph's story about the chain-reactions of evil, this can show us, negatively, how we need to believe in the equally far-reaching though essentially unhistorical (because God-centred) consequences of good. Huxley is, therefore, a pessimist about the achievements of man in time:

> It is a dismal and vaguely cautionary tale — cautionary, like all history, against the consequences of merely behaving like human beings, of existing unregenerately as natural men. We may wish sincerely to avoid the crimes and follies of past generations; but at the same time we wish to live that natural life which (along with its quota of goodness and beauty) produces the very crimes and follies we wish to avoid. That is why, to all but the saints, who anyhow have no need of them, the lessons of history are totally unavailing (165).

This clear opposition between sanctity and history remains almost rigid throughout the second half of Huxley's career. In history's record, he holds, things are unregenerate, and society will not be improved until most of its members choose to be theocentric. Meanwhile, the few saints there are will have to be content with mitigating 'the poisons which society generates within itself by its political and economic activities' (248). Here, in another form, we meet again Camus's opposition between two types of transcendence, horizontal and vertical, with Huxley insisting on the primacy of the vertical. Time, as he says in *The Perennial Philosophy*, is merely a 'perpetual perishing'[7] in which we are preyed upon by the accumulated habits and memories which confirm our separateness and egotism. He cites with approval the dictum of Eckhart that 'There is no greater obstacle to God than time',[8] and in *After Many a Summer Dies the Swan* the spokesman figure, Mr Propter, develops Eckhart a step further by asserting that since actual good is outside time, nothing within time can be other than potential evil. Hence, history and the study of history are merely 'Cataloguing bits of fossil evil' which can never be more than a negative lesson on the saving experience of eternity. 'If you carry your analysis far enough,' says Propter, 'you'll find that time is evil.'[9]

Never one to balk at analysis, Huxley follows his spokesman character's advice, deducing throughout his later works a series of consequences which become favourite motifs in his discussion of the perennial philosophy. Mainly, he is preoccupied with the idea that time confirms individuality and separateness, which impede the mystical ingodding experience. Consequently, he argues, the time-bound conventions of language, on which we depend so heavily to organise experience, often distort it. The true end of human nature is the silent contemplation of eternity, and language is merely another temporal process confirming our egocentric habituations.[10] Huxley does not ignore the importance of language to culture, but he deplores the readiness with which symbols, or images, are mistaken for real things, an error which he sees in historical terms as nearly always having criminal consequences.[11]

From here, the analysis easily extends to literature, and so to the arts in general, because they deploy images. The entire enterprise of art in a Godless world, Huxley holds, is an aggravation of the human craving for temporal distraction. His own turning away from literary subjects in his later career, and the attempt to find 'new forms', express directly this growing conviction that literature, like history, can do too little good in a secular, materialist world. Mr Propter is made to lament the 'wearisomeness' of an endless stream of plays and stories 'with no co-ordinating philosophy superior to common sense and the local system of conventions, no principle of arrangement more rational than simple aesthetic expediency.'[12]

But although the 'aesthetic expediency' and formal preoccupations of modern art put Huxley, like Mr Propter, out of sympathy with it,[13] his very reaction against art's self-serving interests paradoxically places him also in the modern camp. Because art has lost its subject-matter as a mediator between man and God, Huxley sees clearly that the writer must now more than ever attempt to discover what, exactly, words can say.

On this question conventional religion offers little guidance. Ritual, again time-bound and fraught with images, provides at best a predisposition to holiness. Dogma, which depends on words, is decidedly dangerous, and the history of dogmatic religions amply confirms that the tendency to mistake words for things is not just a secular aberration. Too often in religious societies the price of this mistake is exacted in the horrors of persecution. The entire psychology of conventional religious belief therefore is suspect, even at best. Huxley points out that Christian saints have often found themselves embarrassed at having to cast off articles of faith as relics of their progress towards enlightenment.[14] And if dedication to enlightenment is missing, then the creeds, and with them language, art, and literature, soon become idolatrous distractions: a process of 'God-proofing', as Sebastian Barnack discovers.[15]

During the period beginning in the early 1930s, when Huxley became interested in the perennial philosophy which led him to such a set of opinions, he became convinced also that saints are the most effective promulgators of enduring good in society.[16] Ordinary people, comfortably self-concerned, are capable only irregularly of good works, most often executed in random and accidental circumstances and trammelled by personal concerns.[17] Consequently, the aberrant psychology of a religious individual, such as Joseph du Tremblay, can tell us a great deal about the failures of history by allowing us to see the potential for genuine good distorted by the concerns of time. *Grey Eminence* therefore is important in Huxley's canon because, by examining a particular case of religious psychology to discover something of the course of modern history, it demonstrates the range of its author's main theories, and also because in this book we observe him in the process of exploring a literary form which itself helped his theory to develop.

III. THE SPIRITUAL FLAW: THE CROSS AND THE NEW MATERIALISM

It is now time to question Huxley's diagnosis of man in history, and first we should look at his account of the flawed spiritual teaching which left Fr Joseph so vulnerable to Richelieu. Huxley concentrates on the teachings of two figures: Benet of Canfield and his Oratorian follower, Pierre de Bérulle. Both men erred by sullying the traditions of theocentric mysticism with an over-personalistic spirituality relying on images and hence on cravings of the time-bound ego. Consequently, their wide influence caused an almost total eclipse of true mysticism in the Catholic Church until the end of the nineteenth century (80). The ill results of this development for our own time, Huxley says, are incalculable because the mystics 'are channels through which a little knowledge of reality filters down into our human universe of ignorance and illusion. A totally unmystical world would be a world totally blind and insane' (82).

Yet there is one odd omission in Huxley's account of the social and intellectual context within which Benet of Canfield and Pierre de Bérulle lived and worked. At the celebrated conference of M. Chandoux, Bérulle had met a remarkable young man whose intellectual brilliance and insight into scientific method had enormously impressed him.[18] This was René Descartes, and Bérulle's enthusiasm soon proved mutual. Descartes took the older man as his confessor, and in turn was encouraged by Bérulle to pursue his revolutionary philosophy.

Bérulle's good opinion of Descartes was doubtless stimulated by the fact that Bérulle felt himself also engaged in a revolution: his self-styled 'Copernican revolution'[19] in the life of the spirit. Partly, this consisted in a return to mystical theocentricism which Bérulle, like Benet, felt was ignored by the strenuous anthropocentric energy of the Counter-Reformation, and particularly by the Ignatian exercises promoted by the Jesuits. Bérulle felt a strong element of personal assertiveness in the *Spiritual Exercises*, and rather than struggle to conform to the will to God, his 'French school' recommended the relaxation of personal will and the absorption altogether of egocentric impulses by relinquishing them in abnegation.[20] Yet this re-emphasis alone hardly accounts for Bérulle's genius, which arises rather from two other sources: his peculiar ability with language, and his insight into the complex historical circumstances within which he worked.

On the question of language, Bérulle deploys an original terminology for describing the life of the spirit, and can move his reader through an elevated, impassioned rhetoric. Centring on a novel theory of *états*, he uses a vocabulary describing various degrees of *admiration, adhérence, élévation* and *capacité* to create a sense of the soul's coming to recognise its true identity in God's will.[21] He is indebted to the Flemish mystics Tauler and Harphius,[22] but does not, because of this, surrender his own distinctive, vigorous style, and by way of acknowledging Bérulle's peculiar gift for seeing spiritual activity in concrete terms, the Pope conferred on him the honorary title 'Apostle of the Incarnate Word'.

Throughout his writings Bérulle insists how the physical acts of Christ's life and particular devotions of his followers should be taken as examples of ways in which we can conform to God according to our circumstances and capacities. Bérulle's main work, the *Grandeurs et Etats de Jésus*, is an extended meditation on the life of Jesus along these lines, and pays devoted attention also to the Virgin. His favourite saint is Mary Magdalene, whose physical beauty and dramatic conversion he thought could be used effectively to mediate spiritual truth.

Although Bérulle replaces the Jesuits' spiritual combat with something more in the theocentric tradition of Dionysius, he does not eliminate, as Huxley points out, a fascination for carnal imagery. Yet Bérulle's personalism is present, not because he was so naively orthodox as Huxley suggests, and to find out why the 'Copernican revolution' needed a theocentricism so related to imagination, we must look to the second source of Bérulle's originality, namely his interpretation of the social and historical conditions he addressed.

Here we recall Bérulle's relationship both to Descartes and Benet of Canfield, for the concern to promulgate theocentric mysticism (one of the main influences of Benet) was directed at a society which Bérulle saw headed for a revolutionary kind of secular and materialist organisation, of which he thought Descartes a harbinger. The affair of Marthe Brossier neatly comprises both concerns.

In 1599 Bérulle wrote his *Traité des Énergumènes* to castigate the civil authorities for interfering with an ecclesiastical tribunal which had found a young woman, Marthe Brossier, possessed by devils.[23] By order of the king, the woman was arrested because she was subject to frenzies in which inflammatory remarks concerning Huguenots were a cause of embarrassment to the government which had recently extended a toleration to this minority of the French population. The Capucins, who had disagreed with the toleration and were particularly zealous to evangelise the Huguenot domains, thought it in their interest to prove an association between Marthe's demons and Huguenot politics. It was therefore to their advantage, when analysing Marthe's babblings (and attempting to reconstruct from them that she was really speaking Latin and Greek under Satan's influence), to hear the demon say upon being driven out, 'Alas, I have lost my Huguenots'. Faced with such devisings, the king shrewdly had Marthe arrested by civil order and examined by a group of medical doctors who found her not demonically possessed but physically ill.

The ensuing row between church and state is significant beyond the immediate occasion because it indicates how spiritual theories of affections and passions, backed by ecclesiastical tradition and authority, were threatened by a secular and materialist argument whereby the passions, as quantifiable and mechanical forces, could be said to determine moral aspects of human behaviour formerly the province of the soul and free will. Benet of Canfield had been a member of Marthe Brossier's ecclesiastical tribunal with Bérulle, and (because he was a Capucin) had insisted that Marthe was possessed and that the unilateral judgement of the secular authority was dangerously wrong. In consequence, Benet eventually was forced to leave Paris, and went to England where he was imprisoned. He occupied his days by writing the *Rule of Perfection*, the work upon which our knowledge of his spiritual teachings is chiefly based.[24]

Huxley nowhere mentions the Marthe Brossier episode, though he does describe a case peculiarly its obverse. Mme Barbe Acarie appears in *Grey Eminence* as part of the story of how Benet of Canfield came to Paris. The main context for Benet's operations was Mme Acarie's home at the Rue Paradis, a kind of spiritual salon where the influential lady gathered together some of the most spiritually zealous and intelligent figures of her day. They included François de Sales, André du Val, Joseph du Tremblay and the young Pierre de Bérulle. But closest to the centre of this community was Benet, for when Barbe Acarie was first smitten by ecstasies and raptures, he had been called in to discern the nature of the spirits responsible. The medical profession, in this case, had been summoned first, and their ministrations had all but ruined Mme Acarie's health. Benet, however, soon decided that her gifts were genuine, and explained to her how to deal with them, whereupon, her biographer tells us, a stone was lifted from her heart and she went on to a holy and productive life.[25]

The trend in such cases is, clearly, reversed with Mme Acarie, as the medical men yield to the priest, and Huxley's point in recounting the story is to show that there are theocentric saints whose gifts elude altogether the theories of simple materialism. But the story of Marthe Brossier, which he omits, makes plain that Benet and Bérulle were intensely preoccupied with the new medicine and the new science. Benet's career in Paris began and ended because of a direct conflict with medical practice, just as Bérulle's work was written with its author's full knowledge of Cartesian philosophy, wherein the determinist theory of the passions plays a part.[26] Such circumstances are reflected strongly in Benet's and Bérulle's attitudes to mysticism, and the technique which Huxley dismisses as a naive aberration or flaw was, we may now suspect, a good deal more complex. Huxley's omission, consequently, may provide a clue for appreciating the peculiar treatment of images in his own later work. But first, a few words on Fr Benet, and some further observations on the questionable flaw.

Briefly, there is one central technique of meditation advised and exemplified throughout the *Rule of Perfection*,[27] and it is invariably reproduced among Benet's chief disciples. It has to do with the way in which we use physical things 'in themselves' as a means of conforming our will to God. Throughout the *Rule* Benet insists uncompromisingly on theocentricism, and all he has to teach can reduce, he says, 'to one only point', namely 'this of the *will of God*' (2).

But, as Brémond points out, Benet's consistent appeal to the images of sea and flowing streams of fluid substances to express the ideas of self-annihilation and of a Godhead where there is no separate identity or multiplicity (6) might well have suggested also to his readers a leaning towards quietism, a heresy which in seventeenth-century France was increasingly to incur ecclesiastical disfavour. Consequently, Benet was concerned to affirm the creatures, 'that none may think the corporall to be lesse then the spirituall; and to touche the deceipt and common error heerin of many spirituall men' (67). The will, he says, should strive to 'digest, work, and metamorphose' the corporeal into another form whereby the physical passion is acknowledged but turned to spiritual affect, and eventually the veil of the image itself is put off and the object brought to a 'pure abstraction' (68). Benet's work is, in consequence, full of evocations of a sublime spiritual sensuality which exploits physical passion for spiritual ends, and which operates by so overwhelming us with sheer physical stimulus that we recoil, sated, and find a kind of relief in the purer atmosphere of spiritual meaning.

The same technique applies to Benet's treatment of the cross, a traditional subject of Capucin devotion which is, as Huxley says, central to the *Rule*. Benet advises us always to have the cross before us, because it reminds us of the painful doubts and unavoidable liabilities and sufferings of our earthly existence. Yet, although Benet's treatment of the cross is lavish and intense, he *does* insist (a point Huxley denies) that the image, like all other images, passes away as we enter the Godhead.[28] Benet simply says *we* must not relinquish the meditation on the cross, but that *it will be* absorbed as God calls us to the highest union.

This idea helps to explain the peculiar hallucinatory intensity which Huxley notices in Benet's imagery, and also to relate it to the contemporary emergence of rationalist thought and determinist theories of medicine. The connecting link lies in Benet's novel emphasis (I take this to be the sense of Augustine Baker's point on the departure from tradition) that we must not attempt to abandon the cross ourselves, because, even at the last moment, self-sufficiency may intrude and distort the unitive experience with a movement of self-will. Human autonomy, in short, is a serious concern for Benet because he sees clearly that man's autonomous and secular investigations of nature-in-itself have led to such illusions of self-sufficiency that men are prepared to make judgements on spiritual realities in material terms, as in the case of the medical authorities who passed judgement on Marthe Brossier. Benet, consequently, is attempting above all to write a book of spiritual advice for an age of science, and this is his most significant influence upon his followers, including Bérulle. Throughout the *Rule* we are warned time and time again against imagining the 'work' as a thing in itself. A man must realise 'it is not his will that doth the worke, but the *will of God*' (86), and Benet reacts to the soul's propensity to see the object 'in itself' by attempting to let us glimpse the emptiness and revolting inanity of a world perceived without God. Throughout the *Rule* this point almost tiresomely underlines the acute, and novel, awareness Benet has of things 'in themselves'. Over and against God he sees the world: not simply the creatures, but the realm of hard objects, the extended reality of the new materialists, which men so readily idolise and in which they can become disastrously engrossed. The dramatic exploitations of pleasure and pain, the insistence on not relinquishing the image of the cross, the appeals to astonishment and horror, are passionate assertions of a traditional spirituality stressing the theocentric in face of a modern materialist self-sufficiency already well set to ignore it. The mind's images of the material world are put under stress in Benet's writing because he sees how important it is that the old 'spiritual vision', the manifold of matter, image, and transcendent idea, be kept synthesised.

Such a diagnosis, though the reverse of Huxley's, still focuses, like his, on the kinds of images used in the *Rule of Perfection*. The difference lies in the suggestion that Benet and Bérulle were more aware of the problems of their contemporary society than Huxley allows. They attempted to counteract a materialism that would lead men away from God, and they felt that the way to do this was not by abandoning traditional images, but by finding a way to use them, however much their contours might be altering under the influence of the new science, in order to show that the matter of science could still reflect the image of its divine creator.

We might argue, in conclusion, that the modern world does not find it too hard to abandon the traditional images, as Huxley says: it finds it too easy, and Huxley himself is constantly on the verge of being a key example. The inclusion of the story of Barbe Acarie allows him to show that there is indeed a divorce between the empirical explanations of science and the ineffable experience of the mystics. The exclusion of Marthe Brossier shows that he does not take nearly as seriously Benet's plea that the best way to bridge the gap between science and God is by remaining faithful to the traditional images of the civilisation which itself produced the scientific revolution and had also managed to nourish the traditions of contemplative life. Benet would want Huxley to be a Christian because it is consistent with the long-standing European attitude to how images lead men to God. Huxley's refusal causes him instead to assume a negative attitude both to images and to the history itself of his own culture. Yet Huxley remains a man of letters, and he cannot simply expunge the complex of traditional evaluations implicit in his language and allusions. He faces this paradox head on in *Grey Eminence* by using the fruit of his learning, the historical data, as a negative analogue.[29] History is the vehicle of discourse, and Huxley stresses how strange historical facts can be:

> Every human being is an individual slice of history, unique and unrepeatable; but the majority of such slices belong to one or other of a number of familiar and recognizable classes. This is not the case with exceptional individuals. These represent the wildest improbabilities, such as only life can make actual; for life alone possesses the resources and the patience to go on playing the lotteries of heredity and environment until the necessary number of one-in-a-million chances turn up simultaneously, and an exceptional individual appears and runs his course. That is why truth is so much stranger, richer and more interesting than fiction (116).

Father Joseph, the real thing, is odder and more improbable than a character out of a book, and Huxley can capitalise on the fascinating quality of the man because the biography also fits his general theory of history so well. Fr Joseph's claim to fame is an almost perfect instance of the irrelevance of history to salvation, and Huxley can use historical learning to denounce history, and fact to replace fiction. Under such conditions he *can* accept the past, and it provides his book with a density of texture and richness of incident which give it body. Since history is mainly the catalogue of human folly, his satiric embellishment of the countless individual stupidities and scandals behind the received facts is entirely consistent with his general purpose, and the reader's irreverence for the past is constantly encouraged. Richelieu, we learn, had fits wherein he thought himself a horse (138); the king suffered from a fissure in his fundament (222); Marie de Médicis had her son birched every morning before breakfast for the previous day's offences (98), and there is a whole panorama of corruption and treachery, treated with dispassionate irony which would make it uproarious were it not disgusting. And, at the centre, stands the enigma of Joseph du Tremblay himself, with his trances and ecstasies, walking up and down and across Europe in his bare feet, fixated on the cross and dreaming of a new crusade, and all the time disguising from himself his profoundest corruption under a thickening cloak of righteousness.

We can hardly resist admiring the brilliance of Huxley's device. But since *Grey Eminence* relies a good deal on the strangeness of facts, these must be correct, and the facts as far as Benet and Bérulle are concerned are made to suit Huxley's own peculiar views. Benet was perceptive, not deficient, when he regarded images as a means whereby man as scientist and man as mystic are joined to the great body of humanity-makers-of-images, dwelling in their fantasies and attempting to structure their imperfect lives. Interestingly, Huxley's willingness to ignore this dimension of Benet's achievement reflects in the recurrent, general complaint about his own writing; namely, that it does not show sufficient sympathy for just such a body of ordinary humanity. The individuals with whom his books deal in detail are too often specimens of human imperfections examined from an ironic distance, and summed up in a general denunciation of 'the intrinsically unsatisfactory nature of actions performed by the ordinary run of average unregenerate men and women' (240). Huxley has little hope for these ordinary unregenerates, an attitude which caused Thomas Mann to charge that Huxley's writing could not succeed as fiction.[30] Yet Huxley is far from callous or indifferent, and it is impossible to deny in *Grey Eminence* or elsewhere, that he is passionately concerned for the injustice and cruelty which men have wrought upon each other.[31] The account in *Grey Eminence* of atrocities recorded by Callot moves us, admittedly not to pity for the suffering, but to a sense of outrage and indignation. The moral fervour, sincerity and willingness to grapple with pain and moral evil remain compelling testimony of a powerful, sensitive mind, and throughout *Grey Eminence* the historical format and biographical portraiture offer an especially fruitful ground for discussing such problems in the light of Huxley's basic contentions in the second half of his career. In varying degrees, the later writings continue to probe these same issues. The culminating effort is *Island*,[32] a book which has met with mixed reception among the critics. Huxley himself was disappointed that it was not taken as seriously as he intended, for in it he tries to summarise his main conclusions about man, especially man seeking God in a modern technological society, and to express these coherently in a complex manner.[33]

IV. *ISLAND*: UTOPIA AND THE ESSENTIAL HORROR

Because *Island*, unlike *Grey Eminence*, describes a society in positive terms, Huxley cannot look to history for his subject. History remains the fossil catalogue of human evil in time, and in *Island* everyone with a past suffers because of it. From the opening pages the central character, Farnaby, shipwrecked on the forbidden island and stunned by a fall as he climbs the cliff, is plagued by time and memory. 'Time to get up. Time to get dressed. Mustn't be late at the office' (7). As his consciousness begins to focus, Farnaby is haunted also by re-criminations about his wife's death, caused he feels by his own heartlessness and infidelity. Memories of his plunge into the 'Other World' of sensuality with Babs mingle with a growing sense of terror concerning the urgency of time and fear of death: 'Death, death, death' (19).

All this of course is the hallucination of a mind not fully conscious after being stunned, but the careful structure of the opening chapter in terms of clock time, of the outside impinging on the inside both in Farnaby's consciousness and in Farnaby the outsider coming to the forbidden island, shows Huxley carefully delineating his main subject – enlightenment in the experience of waking up to full human consciousness. The first word in the book is 'Attention'. We hear it simultaneously with the central character, and perhaps with as little comprehension: his stunned mind comes to stand for our ordinary unregenerate normality. The novel ends also with 'Attention', suggesting that within the circular structure we may learn something of the island-nature of ourselves, as Farnaby does, and about our potentialities and limitations. Also the circle indicates the a-temporal nature of enlightenment, so that the time which passes in the course of Farnaby's education is mainly a process of exorcising the past. As always, time and history are judged pessimistically, and especially by those in the book who know how to live by the enduring, timeless values: 'History and prisons', says Dr Robert, 'I discovered that they were closely related' (156). Sometimes the point is made with less than convincing obviousness: '"I took a course at Shivapuram in the history of Christianity." Susila shuddered at the memory. "What a horror"' (100). By contrast, the authoritative book for the Palanese (entitled *Notes on What's What* to show that it should not be taken too seriously, and certainly not dogmatically) is not historical: '"Does this give the history of the reforms?"' asks Farnaby. 'Dr Robert shook his head. "It merely states the underlying principles"' (38).

Yet Pala does have literature, even though books do not last long in the tropical heat. And here again we encounter Huxley's problem about the efficacy of written words. The point is raised by Dr Robert, explaining why English has become Pala's literary language: 'Every writer needs a literature as his frame of reference; a set of models to conform to or depart from. . . . Adopting English as our stepmother tongue, we gave ourselves a literature with one of the longest pasts and certainly the widest of presents' (136). In short, there has to be something to write about, as well as an audience to write for. In *Grey Eminence* Huxley had solved this problem by using the history of seventeenth-century France. But history is largely excluded from Pala, and one result is that Huxley's description of the ideal society lacks convincing density. As reviewers have pointed out, the islanders are not credible: it is hard to believe Huxley thinks theirs would be a viable society, or that he cares deeply about what becomes of them, and this mainly because he fails to invest them with a depth and concreteness which makes us feel their particular substance. They fail simply as probable fictions, and their virtue is mixed with a measure of cuteness and Hollywood south-sea island idyllism. We meet children whose skin glows like 'pale copper flushed with rose', 'how faultless, how extraordinarily elegant!' (13); bronzed statuesque men with delicate sensibilities (203); trite supermarket slogans and recipes for happiness ('thanks to MAC', and 'Take twenty sexually satisfied couples and their offspring; add science, intuition and humour in equal quantities; steep in Tantrik Buddhism and simmer indefinitely in an open pan in the open air over a brisk flame of affection' [93]); a great deal of sensible virtuousness that is often complacent and sober (' "Eternity," ' says Farnaby reaching for profundity, ' "Believe it or not it's as real as shit!" ' 'Excellent!' says his instructor, with unperturbed professional approbation [276]).

Faced with this, Frank Kermode has condemned *Island* as among the worst novels ever written.[34] But another distinguished critic, Wayne Booth, praises it, and, different as these opinions at first seem, they are not really inconsistent, for Wayne Booth is careful to state that he does not think *Island* is really a novel at all.[35] Booth's caution is

correct, because Huxley in *Island* clearly remains intent on developing the intellectual positions we find informing *Grey Eminence*.
Because *Island* is a positive vision, Huxley surrenders the historical
focus, and so needs to create some kind of fictional world in order to
mount his discussion of the ideal society. Admittedly, we are not
carried very convincingly by this novelistic component, and the most
moving aspect of *Island* lies elsewhere. Mainly, we discover it in the
author's struggle to find peace with the convictions which led him to
write the book in the first place.

Huxley's sense of organisation is the key to *Island*'s special strength.
His descriptive, novelistic passages are carefully paralleled throughout by discursive sections wherein the complementarity of image
and idea is probed and tested. The inside of ideas is, as it were,
scrutinised in terms of outside criteria. The inner sanctuary of the
island stands symbolically against the outside world of hard modern
facts which threaten to destroy it. ('And meanwhile the outside world
has been closing in on this little island of freedom and happiness' [59];
'"Are you that man from Outside?" she asked. "Almost infinitely
from the outside," he assured her. . . . "We're all very sorry for
you," she said' [251].) Likewise, the main character's personal inside
is challenged by the world of other people and objects in which he
will find divine enlightenment or demonic isolation. ('By what
sinister miracle had the mind's natural state been transformed into all
these Devil's Islands of wretchedness and delinquency?' [273];
'William Asquith Farnaby – ultimately and essentially there was no
such person. Ultimately and essentially there was only a luminous
bliss, only a knowledgeless understanding, only union with unity in a
limitless, undifferentiated awareness. This, self-evidently, was the
mind's natural state' [273].) The opposites are balanced deliberately,
and Huxley's concern is never to allow advantage to the side of
eternity or personal wish-fulfilment without presenting a case which
checks our enthusiasm. The positive utopian ideas are forced
repeatedly to make concession to an anomalous, alien reality which
seems to confute them, and the most compelling single effect of *Island*
is the sense that emerges of Huxley absorbedly and painfully
wrestling with himself to be honest before his own theories.

An analogy is Plato's *Republic*. Despite the specious logical turns,
the mixed attitude to art, the impossible discussion on eugenics, there
is a ground bass repeated throughout, asking whether or not the best
we can imagine could ever be made concrete. As a measure of Plato's
honesty (again, the most moving thing in the work), Socrates is

forced gradually to lose ground, making concessions to the irrational in human nature. Thrasymachus, the violent anarchist who stormed out near the beginning, never really leaves, and the dialogue moves from psychology to politics and finally to eschatology as the hopes of realising the Idea in temporal circumstances slowly yields to the hope of a just city, maybe, in life after death.

Though Huxley is not Plato, his work is moving for the same broad reasons. Farnaby reads in the *Notes on What's What* that 'One third, more or less, of all the sorrow that the person I think I am must endure is unavoidable. . . . The remaining two-thirds of all sorrow is home-made and, so far as the universe is concerned, unnecessary' (88−89). Yet the irreducible one-third, like the spirit of Thrasymachus, makes its presence felt increasingly, and emerges more and more clearly as the book's central preoccupation. This 'Essential Horror' persistently haunts Farnaby and afflicts even the most saintly of the Palanese: ' "How can anyone take yes for an answer?" he countered. "Yes is just pretending, just positive thinking. The facts, the basic and ultimate facts, are always no" ' (244). You are always alone, Farnaby observes. 'Alone in your suffering and your dying' (244), and 'what about the presence of cancer, the presence of slow degradation? What about hunger and overbreeding and Colonel Dipa? Are *they* Pure Suchness?' (246).

These passionate arguments are dramatised resolutely and consistently because Huxley sees that to validate in human terms his belief in the imageless transcendent, he must force himself to return again and again to the facts of suffering, and so to the horizontal timedimension where suffering belongs. In so doing, he makes of his ideas − literature, and in the process he embraces not only the fictive image, but the cross itself more fully in the spirit of Fr Benet than his own theory approves. Near the beginning of *Island*, for example, we have Nurse Appu's elevating lecture to her patient Farnaby on preventative medicine: ' "So whether it's prevention or whether it's cure, we attack on all the fronts at once. *All* the fronts", she insisted, "from diet to auto-suggestion, from negative ions to meditation" ' (69). But Nurse Appu's idealism is offset by an account of how she could not prevent her own irrational infatuation for the nasty Murugan. Likewise, the elevated teachings of the Raja's *Notes on What's What* are countered by the bookmark happening to be a poem of Susila's which reveals her recent bereavement (88−89). So the extended account of the idyllic and scientifically advanced Pala is qualified by the 'senselessly evil' (240) facts of death. Farnaby recounts his memory of Molly's cancer, while Dr Robert's wife dies from the same disease. 'Only God,' says Farnaby, 'can make a microcephalous idiot' (242), and even the 'occasional islands of decency', such as Pala, are 'always totally surrounded by the Essential Horror' (242).

Huxley of course intends us to compare Molly's despair with the more dignified and mature 'art of death' practiced among the Palanese, which makes Lakshmi's death more endurable. Two-thirds of Molly's suffering, the account implies, is home-made as a result of deficiencies in the society in which she lives. But the Horror is not absent from Pala either. Susila's husband died in an 'incomprehensible' (167) mountaineering accident, perhaps by suicide, and Lakshmi's cancer is also reasonless. Even Farnaby's blissful vision under the influence of the drug is compromised by his watching the lizard devour the preying mantis couple just as the female has bitten off her mate's head. Farnaby is terrified, and the bass-theme returns: '"No escape", he whispered, and the words confirmed the fact, transformed it into a hideous certitude that kept opening out, opening down, into depth below depth of malignant vulgarity, hell beyond hell of utterly pointless suffering' (285). Here we are most fully inside Farnaby's experience, and most fully apprised also of the extremes of ecstasy and horror within which he attempts to make his choice of a final attitude. The moment is crucial to his personal development, and Susila at last convinces him that compassion is the only road to take in the face of evil which somehow has to be accepted along with the clear light of eternity. Farnaby for a moment seems to open out towards her in total recognition, but, as he does, the first sounds of invasion reach his ears as the troops from Outside advance along the road beneath them to murder Dr Robert, pronouncing through loudspeakers their takeover of the Island. The symmetry is exact: as the personal inside seems at last to awaken, the outside again introduces Horror in the form of violence and destruction. Farnaby is left holding Susila, and we do not know what either of them thinks.

The entire structure of Island expresses Huxley's misgivings about his own utopian vision, and the result is less that we are convinced by the novelistic vitality of the characters than by the poignant spectacle of a man remorselessly putting to the test the best ideas he has and finding them wanting. The slogans, cheap idyllism, and so on, are not redeemed by this kind of defence, but they become less important because self-indulgence is offset by a more significant, argumentative rigour. Here Huxley's technique is opposite to that, say, of Graham

Greene, an author also concerned with religious vision in a world made sordid by violence and materialism. A jacket blurb describes *The Power and the Glory* as a 'modern crucifixion story', and in this tale of a forlorn whisky priest pursued by revolutionary Mexican state police we observe a man hounded to death by secular authorities and, paradoxically, by heaven. Greene, however, unlike Huxley, *is* a born story-teller, and an example can show the kind of difference this makes to the way ideas are presented in their work.

At the beginning of Greene's novel, Mr Tench, the dentist, is at the quay to pick up an ether cylinder. He watches a girl on board the ship, and remarks vaguely to himself that she is pretty.

Mr Tench swivelled round. 'You English?' he asked in astonishment, but at the sight of the round and hollow face charred with a three-days' beard, he altered his question: 'You speak English?'

Yes, the man said, he spoke English. He stood stiffly in the shade, a small man dressed in a shabby dark city suit, carrying a small attaché case. He had a novel under this arm: bits of an amorous scene stuck out, crudely coloured. He said, 'Excuse me. I thought just now you were talking to me.' He had protuberant eyes: he gave an impression of unstable hilarity, as if perhaps he had been celebrating a birthday . . . alone.

Mr Tench cleared his mouth of phlegm. 'What did I say?' He couldn't remember a thing.

'You said my God a pretty one.'

'Now what could I have meant by that?' He stared up at the merciless sky. A vulture hung there like an observer. 'What? Oh just the girl I suppose. You don't often see a pretty piece round here. Just one or two a year worth looking at.'

'She is very young.'

'Oh, I don't have intentions,' Mr Tench said wearily. 'A man may look. I've lived alone for fifteen years.'

'Here?'

'Hereabouts.'

They fell silent and time passed, the shadow of the customs house shifted a few inches farther towards the river: the vulture moved a little, like the black hand of a clock.

'You came in *her*?' Mr Tench said.

'No.'

'Going in her?'

The little man seemed to evade the question, but then as if some explanation were required: 'I was just looking,' he said. 'I suppose she'll be sailing quite soon?'

'To Vera Cruz,' Mr Tench said. 'In a few hours.'[36]

The suspense comes from us not kowing the stranger's identity while picking up the ominous signs. The priest cannot quite disguise himself, or the fact that he is fugitive. But he is vulnerable because so open to inadvertent self-betrayal: 'my God a pretty one' might possibly sound devotional, but to take it that way is off the mark — the response of a man wearied by vigilance, at once too finely-tuned, yet dulled in his perception of normality. Also there is a hint of recklessness in his caution ('unstable hilarity'), as if he wants to give the secret away in order to be free of the strain, and not alone. His hinted moral admonishment, 'She is very young,' ironically draws from Tench the ecclesiastical term 'intentions' (good and bad intentions as a way of examining one's conscience), suggesting that Tench unconsciously picks up a clue, but does not focus it. His own, different kind of aloneness dulls his interest, and he records impressions of people without being wholly alive to them. The too inconspicuous attaché case and the too conspicuously crude novel (the jacket conceals a breviary) mean nothing to Tench, but to the reader they suggest some barely adequate disguise. To be allowed to look more carefully for a moment, we feel, would uncover everything, and for the stranger to count on Tench's kind of enervation for getting by is too dangerous a game. But the reader in part must share Tench's viewpoint, and so is kept guessing, and the unsettling effect is heightened by the passage's being so full of menace. The predatory vulture looms while the shadow of the customs house (secular authority) grows longer, and the stranger seems already a corpse, stiff, with his face wasted. These details we, not Tench, feel are premonitory but indefinitely so, and a final, ambivalent clue is Tench's seemingly casual information that the ship is bound for Vera Cruz, true cross. The stranger will miss it, but arrives at its destination in another sense, by another route.

Greene's art depends very much on indirection. Two characters, each with his own complex fears and oddities, meet, and through their encounter we sense the book's main themes, which are the same as those of *Island*: the human experience of abandonment and desire to escape, the unavoidable fact of death and the challenge of religion, the ambivalence of human motivation. But such general concerns are implicit in the suspense and characterisation throughout *The Power and the Glory*, whereas with Huxley the reverse is the case, for he is first of all a thinker, and then a man of letters seeking a story to embody his ideas. Robert Nichols, writing in 1931, already drew attention to the shortcomings of Huxley's fictive imagination while also admiring his characteristic courage and honesty: 'A.H. hasn't the technical resources of T.S.E. − but he's *game* which T.S.E. isn't. He wrestles with his despair. . . . The spirit − and the will to pay − in Aldous is making a desperate battle. . . . He has terrific courage and formidable mental integrity − he is a hero: one of the few heroes among the writers of our time.'[37] This quality remained in Huxley's writing, and perhaps especially in *Island*, where the historical facts which provided body for *Grey Eminence* find their counterpart, not in the non-history of Pala, but in the author's own biography. Huxley's favourite avocations, such as hypnotism and drugs, Taoism and the *Tibetan Book of the Dead*, are all discussed and examined. Events in his personal life appear thinly disguised, for instance the death of his wife (the model for Lakshmi) and of his brother Trev (Duglad), or the suggestions of his own early self in Farnaby, so clever and able and avoiding commitment.[38] To read the biography and *Island* together is to have the impression that *Island* is a curiously private book, a kind of personal *reprise*. It is not, as Sybille Bedford says, to be read simply as the author's last testament, for Huxley intended to go on and write more.[39] But the fact that she needs to warn us off is to some extent prompted by the quality of the book itself, and by the unusual cirumstances of its composition. The manuscript was rescued from the flames which destroyed Huxley's house and library in 1961, and was being written when Huxley knew he had cancer. Clearly, we do not judge aesthetic merit by such extrinsic criteria, but neither is such evidence irrelevant for indicating how we should take the work as an example of the craft of fiction. It is fair to conclude that, as history and biography in *Grey Eminence* provide a medium for examining a theory about the nature of man, so in *Island* Huxley's experimental technique has not changed, but the medium is now, tacitly, autobiographical.

As *Grey Eminence* describes the crisis in Western spirituality which accompanied the birth of modern secularism and modern science, *Island* describes a personal solution to this crisis, preserving the gains of secularism and the advances of technology. We should not look here for the rich texture of the novel, but read *Island* instead as the testimony of a man debating with himself his own most cherished ideas. The aspiration for eternity, as we see, had entailed for Huxley a negative attitude to images, but this remains crossed by his re-cognition that the way we are rooted in our past is part of us, and a precondition of our sympathetic understanding of our fellows. That Huxley preferred to castigate the foolishness of temporal concerns rather than celebrate the world of images stems from his conviction that if people are to be happy they should settle for nothing but the best. In a world with no coherent religious commitment, he held that the images of art divorced from the conviction of eternity are too often distractions only, just as the techniques of science in the same situation become instruments of human self-destruction. Yet the world of images is also the world of suffering humanity — the realm of faith and the cross which Fr Benet had insisted must be recalled in a civilisation increasingly bent, with the advent of scientific mat-erialism, on the reification of objects and people alike. The cross, after all, signifies compassion for suffering, and although Huxley lamented the negative historical results of the Christian worship of a slaugh-tered God, in a way he did not refuse the cross himself. In some sense throughout his later career, the intellectual and mystic who held the cross in special abhorrence had also to be the suffering participant, willing to carry it.

3 Belief in Anarchy: Robert Graves as Mythographer

I. MYTHOGRAPHY IN THE MODERN AGE

In the latter part of the seventeenth century an obscure but learned English parson described for his readers a pleasant garden. Walking in it, a sequestered *homo beatus* may, unawares, activate a hidden device and, to his delight, watch an elaborate machinery depict mythological characters and events before his eyes. He is charmed and appreciative of the ingenuity and pleasant digression.

The devout author of the book in which this description occurs was John Norris of Bemerton,[1] a reclusive Cartesian philosopher dedicated to promoting in England the new critical method which was fast providing for Europe a persuasive, mechanistic interpretation of nature. At the same time, as a sincere country parson, Norris sought earnestly to demonstrate how the human soul remained mysterious, thereby distinguishing mankind from all else in the lower creation, and how the soul's intuition of divine ideas is necessary to all that we know of nature. Predictably, Norris' epistemology left him easy prey to the more sanely rational community of political arithmeticians headed by Locke and Newton, whose emphasis fell not on transcendental philosophy, but on empirical descriptions of human experience.

This out-of-the-way passage on John Norris' garden puts clearly the problems facing any modern and post-Cartesian mythographer. The crucial point is Norris' separation of mythology from nature, and his presentation of myth as a pleasant digression dictated and controlled by technology. Even an acute spiritual sense such as Norris enjoyed can find no real place for myth in nature regarded primarily as object and machine. Not surprisingly, the twentieth-century authors of *The Rise of Modern Mythology, 1680–1860*[2] begin at the period when John Norris was writing, for in England between 1600 and 1680 mythography turned decisively away from a universe of poetry (to adapt Robert Graves's distinction) to a universe of prose. Today, if he is to speak with authority, the mythographer must first face the critical world of scholarship and seek to epitomise his materials in relation to the findings of archaeologists, historians, etymologists, folklorists, antiquarians, and sundry experts whose technical vocabularies are the fruit of patient research based on scientific methods. Conscious of so much expertise, scholars have grown generally suspicious of the diverse universal theories and 'exciting' interpretations of myth which have burgeoned so variously in this century. Even the simple reporting and collection of myths, they point out, can reflect a compiler's latent theoretical prejudice.[3] Consequently, a rigorous scholar who puts a premium on fidelity and accuracy will tend to favour the 'reliable' account trammelled with circumspection. A good example is the influential work of H. J. Rose, *A Handbook of Greek Mythology* (London: Methuen, 1925: 6th ed., 1964). Rose claims his book supplies 'an accurate account of Greek mythology, in accordance with the results of modern research' (Preface, vii), and his careful weighing of evidence and tentative conclusions (stories of Triton's body perhaps concern 'large dried sea-beasts of some kind, probably improved by the addition of artificial parts' [75]) are a model of positivist restraint and discrimination. Yet to maintain his stance as critical assessor, Rose must be content merely to 'wish well to those who study the imagination' (10), for he cannot himself indulge in speculations upon its workings.

In a brief but sharp review of Robert Graves's *The Greek Myths*, Rose clarifies his position by complaining that Graves includes 'sentimentalities of his own devising, legitimate enough in a work of the imagination, but quite out of place in a handbook of mythology, where a story should be told as the authorities tell it, or epitomised from their account.'[4] Although the word 'imagination' recurs here, its use in this and in the earlier passage is not quite identical: in the first instance Rose means by 'those who study the imagination', psychologists, and in the second, artists. Graves and Rose disavow psychologism in mythology — one of the few views they share — and maintain that the sublimed yet persistent spiritual, banished from nature by the scientific revolution, has nowadays reasserted itself widely as 'archetype' or interior drama, but remains uncomfortably separate from the world of nature outside the waking mind. Rose dislikes this because it is not objective, and Graves because it separates the world of history, in which myth is based, from the world of artistic imagination, which is mythopoeic.[5] The question, therefore, of what has become of mythography since the rise of science is, for Graves, vital for understanding the situation of poetry itself in the present century.

The predicament can be summarised simply: the contemporary mythographer inherits a formidable equipment of technology and scholarship, and can no more ignore it than he can ignore the modern prose in which he expresses himself and which is no less a fruit of the same soil. To treat myth, in this light, as object for study is to provide a useful service of one sort, but it robs the story of its affective and noumenous dimension without which it does not remain mythic. But to treat imagination in myth without the context of historical analysis is to run the risk of divorcing the story from the lived experience which engendered it.

Although the theorists have made presentations of great sophistication, proponents of ritualism, of euhemerism, and of psychology have found reconciling these contraries extremely difficult. The analytic mind, its force bound by its own strength, finds in mythology the infuriating paradox (and rebuke) of a whole meaning which existed prior to the divisions of speech by which the very sophistication of analysis is achieved. In such a predicament, claims Graves, the artistic imagination is singularly powerful, and by its means we can focus afresh on the old stories to experience them new and whole – as poetry undivided, not as prose analysed into sober familiarities.

Consequently, though he will adapt the modern skills and sciences, Graves does not aim to reproduce their results, and to criticise him for not doing so is to fall into a trap, as he scornfully expects we will. Not surprisingly, he provides no final answer to the problems of modern mythography, though he perceives these problems with clarity, and enjoys unusual gifts of imagination and scholarly talents of a high order by means of which he effects a distinctive solution. The most illuminating historical context for assessing Graves's originality, however, is not the prehistory to which he so tirelessly alludes in *The White Goddess* and elsewhere, but the late Renaissance in England. This is so because he repeatedly singles out the Puritan revolution as the historical event which most distinctly heralded the modern world, and thereby engendered an entire spectrum of attitudes and prejudices which he believes antipathetic to myth and poetry alike.

II. ROBERT GRAVES AND OLD EUROPE

Mainly, we are told in *The White Goddess*, the Puritan revolution established in England a 'purely patriarchal'[6] culture. Previously, between the Crusades and the Civil War, the 'Queen of Heaven with her retinue of female saints had a far greater hold in the popular imagination . . . than either the Father or the Son' (*W.G.*, 406). This enhanced sense of female power endured into the reign of Elizabeth, 'the last Queen to play the Muse' (*W.G.*, 407), but the Puritan revolution was essentially 'a reaction against Virgin-worship', and the 'iconoclastic wantonness, the sin-laden gloom and Sabbatarian misery that Puritanism brought with it' (*W.G.*, 424) wrought a division between poet and priest and, by forbidding devotion to the Virgin, established the puritanical Thunder-god in sovereignty. This occurred mainly in the Commonwealth period, which, as a result, is 'the most remarkable event in modern British history' (*W.G.*, 406). The Thunder-god has, since the days of Cromwell, had his ups and downs, but, according to Graves, we still live in 'an Apollonian civilization' (*W.G.*, 458) dominated by rationalism, technology and a vain (predominantly male) desire for autonomy and self-sufficiency which leads to 'sentimental homosexuality' (*W.G.*, 446) and eventual self-destruction. Moreover, we dwell in a culture where, increasingly, the myths 'are wearing thin' (*W.G.*, 459), and this not least because poets themselves have turned so resolutely away from nature in their consideration of myth: not 'one English poet in fifty could . . . distinguish roebuck from fallow deer, aconite from corncockle, or wryneck from woodpecker. Bow and spear are antiquated weapons; ships have ceased to be the playthings of wind and wave' (*W.G.*, 458–59). Mythology, in short (even among poets), has lost its roots in natural processes. The drama of sunrise and sunset was once felt directly as a mimesis of human passion, and expressed in, say, Apollo's pursuit of Daphne, or the stories of Tithonos and Eos and of Samson and Dalilah. Now such 'whole meanings' are sacrificed to the comprehension of these stories by the differentiated Apollonian functions of modern scholarly mythographers who aim at an accurate statement as remote from the observer as John Norris' statues are from the trees and shrubs of his garden. Here is H. J. Rose on Tithonos and Eos:

> She has a comparatively well-marked personality and appears as

the heroine of three love-stories, in all of which she appears, not as pursued, but as pursuer. The most famous of these represents her as mated to Tithonos. . . . The author of the 'Homeric' Hymn to Aphrodite tells his story in full (*Handbook*, 35).

Rose abstracts the story, and concludes with an account of how Tithonos was changed into a cicada.

Graves, dealing with the same myth, repeats much the same outline, but gives it a twist by resorting to a far-fetched etymology and a piece of curious learning. Tithonos 'is likely . . . to have been a masculine form of Eos's own name, Titonë – from *titō*, 'day' (Tzetzes: *On Lycophron* 941) and *onë*, 'queen' – and to have meant 'partner of the Queen of Day.' Cicadas are active as soon as the day warms up, and the golden cicada was an emblem of Apollo as the Sun-god among the Greek colonists of Asia Minor' (*G. M.*, 1, 150).

Rose has delivered a precise no-nonsense account which follows consistently from his deadpan first sentence. Graves uses his learning with a different emphasis, and if he runs more risks than he ought, we are enlivened by his confrontation of night and the Queen of Day, and by his suggestion of human participation in the ritual of nature by being told of cicada-worship in Asia Minor, which, linked back through etymology to the myth itself, provokes in us a fresh perception of the means by which human language belongs in the cycle of nature's rhythms. This approach is poetic rather than prosaic: Graves is much closer than Rose to the impulse of, say, Edmund Spenser, who uses the same story with profound poetic effect in Book III of *The Faerie Queene*, despite the curious unscholarly habits of his authorities among the Renaissance mythographers.

As is well known, the complementary opposite to the modern Apollonian and prosaic is, for Graves, the lunar White Goddess. She is the muse of poetry, representing the female in her three roles as mother, lover and layer-out, and she ensures that the enskied imaginations of mankind aspiring to spiritual autonomy stay rooted in the mysteriously cyclical and complexly passionate conditions of human nature. She reminds us that language is a remote declension of the flights of cranes and the beauties of trees. She tells us that science is not the only means of describing phenomena, and warns that 'as soon as Apollo the Organizer, God of Science, usurps the power of his Mother the Goddess of inspired truth, wisdom and poetry,' then, inevitably, 'negatively ethical' (*W.G.*, 479) behaviour follows.

In one way the White Goddess is a highly syncretic figure such as only a sophisticated Apollonian mind could conceive, but she is also, in more conventional terms, the Muse, for 'Poetry began in the matriarchal age, and derives its magic from the moon, not from the sun' (*W.G.*, 448). The poet's 'inner communion' with the Goddess is therefore the source of the poetic truth he utters, and from her worship 'emerges the single grand theme of poetry: the life, death and resurrection of the Spirit of the Year, the Goddess's son and lover' (*W.G.*, 422). Graves also goes on to conceive language itself on two models reflecting this opposition between Apollo and the Goddess, applicable by extension to the cultures of pre-Commonwealth and post-Commonwealth England: 'There are two distinct and complementary languages: the ancient, intuitive language of poetry . . . and the more modern, rational language or prose, universally current. Myth and religion are clothed in poetic language; science, ethics, philosophy and statistics in prose' (*W.G.*, 480).

Graves, however, does not think of the Catholic Middle Ages as an ideal to be admired, except in a limited way, and insofar as the Middle Ages retain much that is healthfully pagan, with the cult of the Virgin providing an antidote to an otherwise firmly patriarchal culture. But Graves's attitude to mythography is more firmly rooted in pre-Commonwealth traditions, let us say in the traditions of 'old European' mythography, than in their modern counterparts, even though in language and technique Graves adapts the habits of modern scholars, for he believes that the facts of history must not be sacrificed in the study of myth.

It is difficult to assess briefly the hallmarks of an 'old European' mythography, and yet there are some basic attitudes which remain constant in the main line of such a tradition, extending through such figures as Fulgentius and Macrobius to Isidore, Pierre Bersuire, John of Salisbury, Natales Comes and Boccaccio.

First, in dealing with pagan materials, the old European mythographer characteristically assumes that a tacit kernel of Christian meaning is bodied forth in the story. This theory often leads to allegory, but it is not so simple as the literary techniques of simple allegory imply, for the outer expression and pagan colour are held to be a manifestation of religious mysteries to which the poet gives his full assent. Admittedly, the relationship of pagan to Christian is not one of equivalence, but subordination (which Graves deplores). Yet the survival of the pagan gods in the Middle Ages was achieved without strain primarily because myth and religion, whether pagan or Christian, remained clothed in the language of poetry, and because the language of critical prose had not yet, in the Cartesian fashion, separated out nature from supernature, or divided idea from image and extension. Thus Boccaccio argues that poetry (and here he includes mythology) 'proceeds from the bosom of God,'[7] and encloses 'the high mysteries of things divine' (44) lest they fall into contempt by being objects of common knowledge (44). He confirms Aristotle's precept that the first poets were theologians (46), examines etymology (*poetes* and *exquisita locutio* [40–41]) to find the original meaning of poetry as inspired song which has 'streamed forth' upon souls 'while even yet in their tenderest years' (41). Moses' 'poetic longing' (46) was an original gift of the spirit, revitalised by gentile poets whose myths share, in a garbled and impure fashion, the original secrets imparted to Moses and the prophets. At any rate, some few ancient seers such as Musaeus, Linus and Orpheus had performed a priestly function 'under the prompting stimulus of the Divine mind' and 'invented strange songs' (44) in rhyme and meter for the praise of God. To continue in their tradition, a poet now needs to 'behold the monuments and relics of the Ancients, to have in . . . memory the histories of the nations, and to be familiar with the geography of various lands, of seas, rivers and mountains,' and to find encouragement in 'the lovely handiwork of Nature herself' (40). Mythology, in short, concerns the mysteries of human nature, and contains a true message connected to sacred history through Moses, but involves no contradiction between historical fact and psychological abstraction. Euhemerism co-exists readily with spiritual interpretation, for 'these myths contain more than one single meaning. They may indeed be called "polyseme", that is, of multifold sense.'[8] Prometheus, for instance, may have been a distinguished teacher, a student of the Chaldaeans who taught astronomy to the Assyrians, but he also represents God's creative action and Adam's prelapsarian power.[9]

In Boccaccio, as in his main instructors from Petrarch to Macrobius, Lactantius, Jerome, Rabanus, Fulgentius, Isidore of Seville, and (Graves's own favourites) Suetonius and Apuleius, one still feels powerfully the experience of language and of history as representations of the human condition, not descriptions of it. These mythographers wrote in a pre-nominalist framework, and, as his modern editor explains, Boccaccio speaks 'at once as poet, critic, and scholar. Nor does he from time to time exchange one function for another, but all three powers of his mind are coactive throughout his discussion, if indeed they are not really one and single'. He 'regards poetry, classical antiquity, and mythology, as pretty much one and the same thing, a deep and abounding source of civilisation and spiritual energy; and his task is to defend, explain, and revive this regenerating power.'[10]

Much of this assessment – and the description preceding it – can be applied directly to Graves, who, as a mythographer, insists that he is not to be understood by the analytic means of the literary critics. They 'can be counted upon to make merry with what they can only view as my preposterous group of mares' nests' (W.G., 25), and Graves claims instead that his presentation of the single variable theme of poetry and myth rather 'commits you to a confession' (W.G., 14). He insists, moreover, that at the centre of poetry (and ultimately of language, and of the alphabets in which the insights of poetry were first recorded), lies a secret. Poets are essentially preservers of the ancient knowledge from which civilisation increasingly departs as its powers of articulation develop. Much of the eccentricity and monomania of the moderns is simply their 'concealing their unhappy lack of a secret', and Graves laments that 'there are no poetic secrets now' (W.G., 462), as there were among the ancient bardic colleges of pre-Christian Britain or among the early Christians, though the Athanasian creed has since made them disastrously explicit (W.G., 463). Indeed, much of The White Goddess is taken up with solving the riddles of two ancient Welsh poems, the Hanes Taliesin and the Câd Goddeu, in which the secret of the single poetic theme was concealed to evade the demands and impositions of Christian orthodoxy.

Graves insists also that the origins of myth are in religious ritual – in 'ritual mime performed on public festivals' (G. M., I, 12) which celebrate the birth, fruition and death of the year. The modern rift between poet and priest is therefore baneful for literature, and especially since the Puritan revolution 'It has become impossible to combine the once identical functions of priest and poet without doing violence to one calling or the other' (W.G., 425). Graves claims, however, that true poetry, whether modern or ancient, remains an inspired initiation: however disguised the 'secret' by accretions of history and trite verbal commonplaces, the sense of it still can be given in a 'strange song', as Boccaccio says, and which, in Graves's description (derived from Housman [W.G., 21]), makes the hair stand on end and the blood pulse. From his earliest critical writings On English Poetry, to his Oxford lectures, Graves has consistently argued for this primacy of inspiration, but insists (again like Boccaccio) that a true poem must be cast in meter, and must preserve the full meaning of every word.[11]

The poet's contact with original meanings is, therefore, of special importance, and the power of the secret is closely connected with etymology: '*arcana*, "religious secrets"' we are told derive from 'the Indo-European root *arc* — meaning "protection,"' and are connected to 'such Latin words as *arceo*, "I ward off" *arca*, "an ark"' (*W.G.*, 145). We are then required to imagine complex connections extending through the deflecting processes of riddling metaphors, leading us to see afresh the acacia wood ark, sacred to the Moon-goddess Astarte, and to consider the lore of trees and their letters which furnish significance alike to the plastic artifact and the rhythms of poetry. For the artist, learning and love of nature are equally desirable, and Graves affirms that 'the poet's first enrichment is a knowledge and understanding of myths' (*W.G.*, 30) wherein learning and nature combine.

One result of such an approach to myth is a fresh appreciation of language as 'polysemous', but this, according to Graves, is in the teeth of modern nominalism which threatens to reduce scholars and divines to zombies (*W.G.*, 223), unable to 'think poetically' and 'resolve speech into its original images and rhythms and re-combine these on several simultaneous levels of thought into a multiple sense' (*W.G.*, 223). For an example of multiple sense, Graves points to the cycles variously representing the 'Apollo-like god on whose behalf the inspired poet sings' and which are 'types of one another'. He tells us that there are 150 cypher alphabets, all mastered by the bards, and the perplexing figures of Hercules may have forty-four different meanings (*W.G.*, 124). Trying to follow Hercules in such a fashion from Egypt to Wales, however, soon leaves us performing in our attention the maze or labyrinth dance itself, a ritual basic to the progress of heroes and the technique of artisans, most familiar in Daedalus. But we belong *in* the maze, Graves implies, and do not simply observe. The facts established by logical definition are never final. If we try, for instance, to pin down Gwion, author of the key riddling poem, *Hanes Taliesin*, we are left with a provocatively elusive set of conclusions, themselves difficult enough to isolate. Gwion, hero of the *Romance of Taliesin*, the provenance of which is itself complex and doubtful (*W.G.*, 27), is a miraculous child, also called Taliesin, but not to be confused with a sixth-century historical Taliesin, some of whose original poems survive in *The Red Book of Hergest*. There is a further 'paganistic cleric with Irish connexions' (*W.G.*, 75) of the ninth century, as well as a twelfth-century Gwion who revived Druidism. Finally, there is a North Welsh cleric, a Gwion of the late thirteenth century who based his writings on the ninth-century original. Gwion, we note with relief but perplexity, is 'probably . . . more than one person' (*W.G.*, 77).

Plainly, by this method we approach Boccaccio's kind of polyseme structures, and from Graves's mythography we should not expect apodictic consistency. Nor, in the most engrossing parts of *The White Goddess*, do we ask it: the explication of the partridge dance, for instance, is full of startling suggestion and insight which find justification in a power to command our attention and wonder. It is so with all language at the beginning, and part of Graves's aim is to have us rediscover this fact in our experience of his book. He attempts, furthermore, to goad us into it, often by mocking at scholarly timidity and even with an adolescent 'you don't dare . . .' (see *W.G.*, 348), so that it is frequently hard to gauge how much, in all this, he enjoys just playing the ogre. Yet his remarks on historiography[12] reveal that he does believe in a necessary coalescence of imagination and history, and takes seriously the challenge of stimulating his sceptical and scholarly readers to appreciate the consequent dramatic or 'physiognomic'[13] character of myth, as Cassirer calls it.

The equivalences between certain of Graves's attitudes as a mythographer and the mainstream of European mythography until the seventeenth century can now be summarised. There is a common conviction that (1) myth is the fountainhead of inspired poetry; (2) myth, like true poetry, contains the profoundest cultural secrets; (3) by inspiration and formulation in stirring meters these secrets find most valid expression; (4) the poet's task is priestlike; (5) learning and love of nature are indispensable poetic tools; (6) etymology reveals the full and original meaning of words to be 'polysemous', and prior to reductive conceptualisation that distinguishes historical fact from imagination; (7) such conventions find expression in an almost perversely disorganised and digressive style. In all this, Graves appears 'old European' rather than modern.

Where, then, does Graves depart from this model? Mainly, as is well enough known, in an obdurate and consistent refusal to acknowledge God the Father as the source of true poetic inspiration. The mystery for Graves resides with the mother, and in all his study of mythology Graves reverts to the hypothesis that patriarchy, and the patriarchal gods, were regrettable results of schism from a prior matriarchal order wherein woman, as mother, lover and crone, was worshipped as the Great Triple Goddess, the power of the waxing, full and waning moon, and of the three-season year of spring, summer, and winter. The poet remains dedicated to the Goddess, his muse, so that 'The test of a poet's vision, one might say, is the accuracy of his portrayal of the White Goddess and of the island over which she rules' (W.G., 24). The single theme of all poetry and living mythology is the identification by the poet of himself with the waxing year, and his inevitable fate is that of the king whom the Goddess Queen of the ancient matriarchy took to herself and ritually sacrificed to ensure fertility: 'every Muse-poet, in a sense, die[s] for the Goddess whom he adores, just as the King died' (W.G., 489). The poet is, in short, crucified by his love of the muse, and according to the rules of her game.

Graves remains sympathetic to pre–Commonwealth mythography, then, only in so far as it allows the muse a place in a usurping hierarchy of all-male deities (the Christian trinity). He acknowledges the Virgin of the nativity scene, and the woman celebrated by troubadour poetry, as well as those native traditions readily assimilated, or at any rate tolerated in the celebrations of 'Candlemas, Lady Day, May Day, Midsummer Day, Lammas, Michaelmas, All-Hallowe'en, and Christmas' (W.G., 24), together with the secret doctrines of witch cults which were, by and large, also tolerated until the Reformation period. Against all this, and forcing its subordination (especially at the hands of Commonwealth puritans) are two religious concepts borrowed at first by Gentile Christians from the Hebrew Prophets and extrapolated by way of the newly patriarchal Olympian religion of the Greeks and by Socratic reason: 'that of a patriarchal God, who refuses to have any truck with Goddesses and claims to be self-sufficient and all-wise; and that of a theocratic society . . . in which everyone who rightly performs his civic duties is a "son of God" and entitled to salvation, whatever his rank or fortune, by virtue of direct communion with the Father' (W.G., 475). From the beginnings of Christianity, Apollo has therefore claimed ascendency by usurping the mother, and Jesus remains dedicated to the remote sky-God of the Hebrews. With the Civil Wars in England, 'won by the fighting qualities of the Virgin-hating Puritan Independents' (W.G., 476) the world of modern science and technology confirmed these attitudes, and brought the patriarchal principle to unprecedented ascendency. True poetry, nourished by contact with the Goddess, was eclipsed by the pseudo-poetry of Milton and the Enlightenment, and during the Romantic period and in the present century genuine poets have had to struggle to re-affirm the rights of the Great Mother in a society founded on principles which deny her.

This, we may agree, is all very well and interesting, except that of course the entire, perversely learned reconstruction of pre-Pelasgian matriarchy itself shows Graves's decidedly Apollonian talents. His debt to scholars such as Bachofen and Briffault is clear, and behind them sound the strains of Nietzsche and the German romantics, while the contributions of Sir James Frazer and Jane Harrison are well documented.[14]

On the one hand Graves's mythography therefore depends on a 'logic of myth' (W.G., 321) founded on a pre-nominalist, partici-patory consciousness; on the other, his *White Goddess* is the product of an enormously sophisticated post-Cartesian self-conscious mind. Such a mixed attitude then suggests a further ambivalence, for it is hard to reconcile the vast subtlety with which the figure of the Goddess is often presented with what seem to be frequent yearnings on Graves's part for the archaic and simply primitive. As 'the ancient power of fright and lust — the female spider or the queen-bee whose embrace is death' (W.G., 24) the Goddess exerts more power on Graves's imagination than in her aspect as lover. He is fascinated by the cruel rites which accompany her worship or characterise her nature:

Why the cat, pig, and wolf were considered particularly sacred to the Moon-goddess is not hard to discover. Wolves howl to the moon and feed on corpse-flesh, their eyes shine in the dark, and they haunt wooded mountains. Cats' eyes similarly shine in the dark, they feed on mice (symbol of pestilence), mate openly and walk inaudibly, they are prolific but eat their own young, and their colours vary, like the moon, between white, reddish and black. Pigs also vary between white, reddish and black, feed on corpse-flesh, are prolific but eat their own young, and their tusks are crescent-shaped (W.G., 222).

This combination of violence, blatant sexuality, treachery, can-nibalism and perversion of normal patterns of maternal nurture is not uncharacteristic of Graves's ruminations on the subject. Of course, we should not avoid acknowledging what such passages point to —

namely, the anomalous in nature – or the interesting way in which they do it. But an uneasy relationship exists between this side of the Goddess, and the other, sophisticated production, where she appears under a host of animal disguises and a litany of paradigms of complex interrelated cultural significance. Among the Celts she is Cerridwen, Blodeuwedd, Olwen, Bridgit and Maeve; among the Greeks, Euryonome, Danaë, Io, Leucothea and Hera; among the Hebrews, Eve, Salome, Dalila, Michal and Mary. Her effective portraits include that of Isis in *The Golden Ass*, where Apuleius, himself a sophisticated writer, draws upon a variegated array of cult figures. In this aspect, the Goddess expands in significance (and in *The Greek Myths* Graves tells us he has brought to bear for her elucidation the apparatus of modern anthropology and historical scholarship [I, 20– 22]) until she seems to represent more even than the flux of the material world, suggesting almost an anhistorical and timeless matrix against which consciousness itself finds definition; in 'Through Nightmare,' there is 'no way in by history's road' to the journey read 'In your sleepy eyes'.[15]

The Goddess suggests, in the end, the ground itself, always a mystery to us, from which we focus in the act of conscious attention. Our besetting illusion, Graves insists, is that logical structures are within our control, whereas in fact they emerge from an unfocused field which always exerts its own influence on them. His mythographic technique, consequently, forces his readers to appreciate that the bright centres of the major myths at the fountainhead of Western culture, with the values they imply, can alter in significance if attention moves (as in the well-known optical configuration) from vase to faces. The snag is that the habitually conceptual mind cannot readily focus on the 'secret' ground of language which must remain veiled by words rather than revealed by them. In his own prose, consequently, Graves works by paradox and irony because he knows the Goddess cannot be *proven* by Apollonian methods, though these have to be used and must not be falsified if the prose argument is to carry conviction. In one passage he indicates his fascination with this paradox of a shifting, yet coherent focus:

What interests me most in conducting this argument is the difference that is constantly appearing between the poetic and the prosaic methods of thought. The prosaic method . . . has now become the only legitimate means of transmitting useful knowledge. . . . And from the inability to think poetically – to resolve speech into its original images and rhythms and recombine these on several simultaneous levels of thought into a multiple sense – derives the failure to think clearly in prose (*W.G.*, 223).

The White Goddess begins by stating this problem in a deliberately provocative fashion when Socrates is castigated for rejecting mythology and for trying to make the male intellect spiritually self-sufficient. Yet the tone of Graves's writing, its challenge to the conventional and complacent reader, and its ironically assumed modesty ('No, my brushlessness debars me from offering any practical suggestion . . .' [*W.G.*, 15]) are themselves entirely Socratic.

Such technique, itself Apollonian, leads us logically to envisage the Goddess in philosophic terms as the unformulable ground of our rational certainties. Yet, in her own capacity as 'the ancient power of fright and lust' the Goddess remains an anomalous power in nature, the destroyer of certainties, and we must learn to accept her without explanation. But these two sides of Graves's mythography, which now may begin to seem separate, are in fact not so, because they polarise each other. For the self-conscious and sophisticated scholar who is critically aware of the divorce between literature and life, awareness of the Goddess as crucifier, as unexplained malignancy in nature, is apt to appear especially acute. So it is with Graves himself, whose deliberate archaism betokens a highly Apollonian pre-occupation with the problem of pain, and in this his sensibility is entirely modern. The paradox is evident in *King Jesus* (1946), the most important book after *The White Goddess* (1948) for understanding Graves's attitude to myth, and which tells the story of Christ from an inverted perspective.

III. *KING JESUS* AND *THE MAN WHO DIED*

Jesus, Graves proposes, is son of Miriam, a temple virgin secretly married to Antipater, and he inherits the right to succession after a series of abdications and political murders has annulled the claim of those closest to the aging and mad Herod. Jesus returns from Egypt literally to claim his kingdom, but his intense devotion to the God of Israel makes him want also to break the cycle of life and death which binds human history. He consequently refuses to marry his bride, Mary of Cleopas (the third Mary present at the crucifixion), and enjoins celibacy on all Israel. In his confrontation with Mary the Hairdresser (Mary Magdalene) he denounces the pagan matriarchal mystery cults on grounds that to conquer the female is to defeat death. But Israel will not hear, and Jesus, feeling his own impotency, looks to the prophet Zachariah and deduces that only after his own death by the sword will his message be heard. Judas detects the plan and conspires with Nicodemus to have Jesus arrested. But the plan is bungled: the disciples misunderstand Jesus completely, thinking the swords he has given them are to protect him, not kill him. As a result of further political corruption involving Pilate, Jesus is crucified, and in his ritual death (which he never expected) ironically becomes the maimed and hanged god of the waxing year, re-absorbed by the matriarchal powers he had denounced but within which his career was both instituted and developed. The three Marys who watch him die represent the White Goddess in her three aspects as mother, lover and layer-out. It seems there is a desperate, ironic battle between Christianity and the cross, and the cross is not, after all, a Christian symbol, but a kind of nemesis: a violent and unexpected reversal of Jesus' Apollonian aspirations and ignorance of women.

For Graves, however, such dedicated Apollonians as Jesus are not condemned alone to suffer at the hands of the Goddess. The poet's fate also is crucifixion, even though poets, unlike Jesus, reject the Apollonian and enjoy women. It therefore appears that the Goddess will be avenged on men in general, though poets acknowledge their fate and accept it, as it were, with open arms. For an entire civilisation which has, beginning with puritanism and the rise of science, ignored the hegemony of the female and the inevitability of the cross, Graves claims that some massive retribution, as unexpected as the crucifixion for Jesus, lies in wait, and this is one of the chief lessons of *King Jesus* for modern readers. Our civilisation, we learn, has ignored the *true* poetry of Jesus' life and death in order to stress the 'prosaic', doctrinal elements.

We might conclude that, despite his polemics, Graves's mythography like his poetry is about reconciling man to the inevitable fact of human suffering. Of course, for Graves to say this directly would be prosaic, and so a falsification, even though he does not recommend anti-intellectualism either. On the contrary, he insists on the need to pursue historical accuracy (even though the Goddess is the crucifier of history) and expends endless pains on his historical backgrounds. For instance, he execrates George Moore's *The Brook Kerith*, a work which we might expect would appeal to the author of *King Jesus*, on grounds that Moore is ignorant of history. ('Study it carefully, Sunday School children, and see how many factual errors you can detect!'[16]) His own position, poised between such devotion to history, and yet denial of it, can become clearer if we consider for a moment a better-known fictional version than Moore's of Jesus' death. D. H. Lawrence's *The Man Who Died*, like *The Brook Kerith*, argues that Jesus survived the cross, and Lawrence, like Graves, also makes Jesus the victim of a damaging ignorance of women.

Despite the fact that Graves disapproved of Lawrence as much as he did of Moore ('sick, muddle-headed, sex-mad'),[17] there are strong similarities in their diagnoses of Jesus' character. Both make him the victim of his own unlived life, and both share the sense, in more general terms, that the development of modern Christian civilisation has confirmed European man in a fatal divorce from his deepest roots in nature. Christian society, both agree, lives out the personal deficiencies of its founder.

The Man Who Died opens by describing a cock tied by the leg, his glorious energies trammelled by the peasants whose economy he serves. The bird's predicament is analogous to that of the maimed Jesus, who has suffered for man and who rests at the farm after surviving the cross and escaping the tomb. As he recovers, Jesus buys the bird, redeeming its physical glory.

The strength of Lawrence's opening lies mainly in the electrifying sense he gives of the bird's energy, 'resplendent with arched and orange neck by the time the fig trees were letting out leaves from their end-tips,'[18] and then in the correspondence between this imprisoned splendour and the figure of Jesus: 'on the same morning, a man awoke from a long sleep in which he was tied up' (127). Lawrence develops his parallels firmly but unobtrusively by allowing the man's sympathy for the bird to grow with his own reviving body. But Jesus' recovery is not just physical, for it stands in contrast to the peasants who are so close to the earth that their existence is not fully human. At one point Jesus is moved by the 'soft, crouching, humble body' of the peasant woman, but is repelled also by her narrowness: 'it was her thoughts, her consciousness, he could not mingle with' (139). Like the slaves later in the story, with their 'ruddy broad hams and their small black heads' (159), the peasants know little of 'the greater day of the human consciousness' (155), and are simply re-absorbed by the earth to which they belong 'overturned like the sods of the field' (134). Rather, a sensitive and highly self-conscious nature, which also acknowledges and realises the potency of the stirring animal, constitutes the truly human. Lawrence, despite his dark gods, is driven continually by his sense of the human struggle for consciousness, and it is a vexed question, how we should relate this impulse in his work to his interest in the irrational. Although Paul Morel in *Sons and Lovers* trembles at the great orange moon and sways in the womb-like fecundity of the cherry tree, both of which exclude the spiritual Miriam, it is she who brings out the artist in him. And at the opening of *The Rainbow* the church spire stands above ploughed fields; the true destiny of men, we deduce, lies with both together, just as the man who died discovers himself alive between the peasants and the shrill purity of his own past life.

It is therefore less than totally disarming to point out the paradox of Lawrence's deploring sex in the head and yet, in writing novels about it, putting it there.[19] Such a predicament corresponds exactly to Graves deploring the Apollonian and yet using the results of recent anthropological and historical research. The problem in both cases is characteristically modern: the artist deploys his technique partly to explore the nature and limitations of the technique itself.

Still, there are differences between Graves and Lawrence, and Graves is first to insist on them. In Lawrence, notably, the Apollonian does not take a historical form, and the pseudo-historical archaism of *The Man Who Died*, compared to Graves, is flimsy and artificially rhetorical. It provides local colour just sufficient to sustain the central psychodrama, but not quite to conceal Lawrence's indifference to the details of dress and daily occupation of the first century AD, never mind the kinds of cultural attitude which attend them. We have slave girls with jars on their heads, a man in a toga, 'probably' an overseer 'or' a steward (160), women washing linen on stones ('chock! chock! chock!' [160]) and slaves picking fish out of nets. But specificity is too easily won: the fish remain a 'tray of fish from the sea' (161), the washed garments remain 'wet linen', the peasant puts on nothing more particular than his 'day-shirt' (125). Likewise, in the dialogue there is a good deal which is meant to evoke the fabulous and remote but is merely stilted with portentous over-sincerities betraying again a deficiency of concreteness:

> 'Will you not look at Isis?' she said, with sudden impulse. And something stirred in him, like pain.
> 'Where then?' he said.
> 'Come!'

Against the rich sense of social actuality of, say, *Sons and Lovers* or some of the short stories, Lawrence's background in *The Man Who Died* is a mere theatrical flat. This may be all he requires, and Leavis for instance argues for a deliberate use of 'frame effect'[20] in the late stories to create a sense of carefully calculated distance, heightening the effect of fable. Still, to point out this quality in *The Man Who Died* shows us how differently the weight of emphasis falls in *King Jesus*. Here are Graves's two opening paragraphs:

I, Agabus the Decapolitan began this work at Alexandria in the ninth year of the Emperor Domitian and completed it at Rome in the thirteenth year of the same. It is the history of the wonder-worker Jesus, rightful heir-at-law to the dominions of Herod, King of the Jews, who in the fifteenth year of the Emperor Tiberius was sentenced to death by Pontius Pilate, the Governor-General of Judaea. Not the least wonderful of Jesus's many feats was that, though certified dead by his executioners after a regular crucifixion, and laid in a tomb, he returned two days later to his Galilean friends at Jerusalem and satisfied them that he was no ghost; then said farewell and disappeared in equally mysterious fashion. King Jesus (for he was entitled to be so addressed) is now worshipped as a god by a sect known as the Gentile Chrestians.

Chrestians is the commoner name for Christians, that is to say, 'followers of the Anointed King'. Chrestians means 'followers of the Chrestos, or Good Man' – good in the sense of simple, wholesome, plain, auspicious – and is therefore a term less suspect to the authorities than 'Christians'; for the word Christos suggests defiance of the Emperor, who has expressed his intention of stamping out Jewish nationalism once and for all. 'Chrestos', of course, can also be used in the derogatory sense of 'simpleton' '*Chrestos ei*' – 'What a simple-minded fellow you are!' – were the very words which Pontius Pilate addressed in scorn to Jesus on the morning of crucifixion; and since the Christians glory in their simplicity, which the most sincere of them carry to extravagant lengths, and in receiving the same scorn from the world as King Jesus himself, they do not refuse the name of 'The Simpletons'.

Because he uses a first person narrator Graves must duplicate the kind of things Agabus the Decapolitan might actually have thought and known. The writing concentrates our attention on how different such knowledge is from the way we are accustomed to see today. The passage is therefore packed not only with historical information, but with a historical sense that interprets this information in a manner sufficiently coherent to make us think twice about what we had always taken for granted. In this, Graves's writing is a *tour de force* of historical imagination, and requires a great deal of learning to bring off. As we see, there is no such learning evident in *The Man Who Died*, and the reason is that Lawrence wants to show us how the traditional story of Jesus is incomplete because it ignores a dimension of human nature we all share. Historical fact is beside the point: we are simply asked to feel something of Jesus' human need, and in so far as we feel it, we acknowledge ourselves his heirs. Graves, however, wants to show that *in fact* we have got the story of Jesus wrong, and in consequence of trying to live according to it, we risk being as incomplete as Jesus himself.

But if Lawrence has scarcely any interest in historical background, Graves may have too much. *King Jesus* is often tedious, and sacrifices the sheer energy of living things, the deadliness of physical exhaustion, the peculiar ambiguous intermittences of the heart that run between people, as for instance between Lawrence's peasant woman, or Madeleine, and the wounded man. At this kind of description Lawrence remains unsurpassed. Yet Graves in the best of *King Jesus* can give an equally unusual sense of pagan terror and bitterness, and of violent, archaic political intrigue which cause his story to be gripping in a different way.

The differences I am pointing to perhaps can be summed up in the figure of the cock. For Lawrence it is an orange and black bird, full of life and energy and strutting, undaunted male splendour. *King Jesus* does not feature a cock, but George Moore's *The Brook Kerith*[21] does, and Graves discusses it disparagingly:

> If Herod Antipas, a very rich man, sent his servants out for the best cocks in the Eastern Mediterranean, they must have brought him Delian, Tanagran, or Alexandrian birds, not the breeds invented by Moore: Cappadocian and Bithynian.[22]

Lawrence wants present vividness, Graves wants historical accuracy. Lawrence wants us to feel the pain that accompanied Jesus' wrongheaded, merely spiritual desire to save the world and deny the flesh, and then to feel also the warmth of Jesus' renewal in the body as a complete man when he encounters the young priestess of Isis. Lawrence therefore makes the cockfight a violent physical event.

Graves, however, wants us to appreciate how our denial of a complete humanity, promulgated through false ideals and consequently through a false attitude to history, will cause the sufferings of Jesus to fall upon our own heads. By means of his learning we are provoked to see things in unconventional ways. Graves is concerned that we know which cocks are which, lest we back the wrong one.

Yet these very differences confirm a preoccupation which compels both authors equally: they are haunted alike by the central, singular fact of Christ's death. Neither would have a story were there no cross. Lawrence begins *The Man Who Died* when the cross is finished, and, like Jesus, tries to forget; the suffering has been outlived and wounds can be healed. '"There are destinies of splendour," he said to the night, "after all our doom of littleness and meanness and pain"' (164). But the pain is not forgotten and becomes part of the saving knowledge of the reborn man: 'There was a beauty of much suffering' (154).[23] The author of *The Man Who Died*, we recall, also knew himself dying as he wrote.

Graves's narrative, by contrast, leads up to the cross, and his most brilliant turn is Jesus' undoing of himself, and the ironic horror of his execution. Graves, in a sense, gloats on the suffering as Lawrence wishes to evade or absorb it. But for both the key concern is the extent to which such suffering can be alleviated by a proper attitude towards love. Lawrence's crucified man is healed by love of woman. Graves's man may also love, even though woman will, inevitably, crucify him.

IV. THEORY AND PRACTICE

If Jesus is bold in rejecting the matriarchal and runs the risks of nemesis, so by analogy does Graves run risks in himself taking on so boldly the world of specialised scholarship and daring to show it up as incorrect, while also claiming the need to interpret it accurately. Organised scholarship, asserting its rights on this question, has been less than convinced that Graves has indeed honoured the facts as he claims he ought. *The White Goddess* is, in particular, problematic. It is without footnotes or bibliography, a fact which has caused recent scholars, even when directly concerned with matriarchal mythologies, to ignore it (as does E. O. James in *The Cult of the Mother Goddess*). The omissions also render almost impossible the confirmation, and sometimes even the application, of particular arguments and suggestions which Graves makes. Why, for instance, rely on the old and apparently inaccurate version of the *Mabinogion* in Lady Charlotte Guest's translation without at least introducing to the discussion the work of T. P. Ellis and John Lloyd,[24] or the French scholar J. Loth?[25] Why cite Professor MacAlister, but not the work of Thomas Francis O'Rahilly, in particular *Early Irish History and Mythology* (Dublin, 1946), or William John Gruffyd's study of the Mabinogi?[26] Why claim the Picts are from Thrace when their origins are so notoriously problematic, and not least because their name is a historical concoction, and, as a single race, they never existed?[27] Why state that St Ambrose lived in the third century and that Fortunatus, instead of Remigius, was Clovis' bishop in the twelfth?[28] Why treat Tuatha De Danaan as a historical people in the naive manner of such nineteenth-century scholars as O'Curry and O'Donovan, when the compilers of the pseudo-historical *Book of Invasions* seem so clearly to modern scholars to be engaging in euhemeristic fantasies to adapt the old supernatural deities to the interests of Goidelic solidarity?[29] And how can Graves be expected to decipher complex etymological riddles without a scholarly knowledge of the languages? Where is the archaeological evidence to be found for the imagined 'iconotropic' reconstructions of familiar mythological materials? And so on.

Although Graves's 'handbook of Poetic myth' is best appreciated on an old European model, the constant goads at scholars and the aversion Graves genuinely seems to feel from the subjective interpretation of mythic materials do render such scholarly-based questions pertinent. And with *The Greek Myths* the issue is even clearer because the confrontation is more direct. For a start, Graves's ordering of materials seems as random as the argument in *The White Goddess*. The freely indulged exercises in etymology have been classed as 'Howlers',[30] and Graves seems to ignore important modern efforts similar to his own, for instance the work of Rose, Kerenyi, and the *Oxford Classical Dictionary*. His preference for late commentators, such as Dictys, leads him, furthermore, to syncretistic interpretations in which conflations of such late sources are made without due regard for tradition or authority. Often he omits earlier sources while citing late ones, and the claim to 'assemble . . . all the scattered elements of each myth' (*G. M.*, I, 22) can hardly be upheld. For Prometheus he omits Horace, *Carmina*, I, 16, 13ff; for Antiope, Ovid, *Metamorphoses*, 6, 110; for Endymion, Plato, *Phaedo*, 72c and Cicero, *De finibus*, 5, 55; for Oedipus, Aeschylus, *Septem Contra Thebes*, 842. Add to this his postulating unidentified but imagined icons to demonstrate that the stories, for instance of Paris and Heracles, are misinterpretations of original graphic representations of the Goddess, and the credibility of most readers is strained. H. J. Rose adds the following sample of details: 'he seems to have read Hyginus in Micyllus's edition, confuses Callimachus and Epimenides (i. 165), cannot see a Platonic joke (ibid., p. 172), nor even an Aristophanic one (ii. 315), repeatedly quotes the *Parallela Minora* and *De Fluviis* as by Plutarch, and, perhaps the choicest specimen of all, informs us (ii, 344) that "Sophocles in the *Argument* to his *Ajax*" says thus and so.'[31] Small wonder Rose said that this would be acceptable in a work of imagination, but not in a handbook of mythology.

The question that now looms up is to what extent Graves's writing is affected as literature by these deficiencies, and by his crankiness as a historian, or even, how much of the crankiness is deliberate provocation by the *enfant terrible*, the literate anarchist mocking at the limitations of scholars by using their own tools to turn their findings inside out — the Irish in him, as George Steiner says. The question is especially relevant for Graves's poems, for poetry he considers his primary calling, and *The White Goddess* is subtitled *A Historical Grammar of Poetic Myth*, a kind of primer for his own poetic practice. The dedication poem, later reprinted with minor changes in *The Collected Poems*, begins:

> All saints revile her, and all sober men
> Ruled by the God Apollo's golden mean —
> In scorn of which I sailed to find her
> In distant regions likeliest to hold her
> Whom I desired above all things to know,
> Sister of the mirage and echo.

The main drift of the poem is to show us how the devotee of the Goddess rebukes the prudence of conventional reason and virtue: that of 'saints' and 'sober men'. Instead he pursues the Goddess into a violent and beautiful nature where she belongs. This main line of argument is not difficult, and its poetic force comes from a combination of supple meter with the contrast of violence and wistfulness in the images. The careful irregularity of meter and rhyme suggests a departure from the strict 'golden mean' without sacrificing resiliency that comes from a sense of structure. Thus the iambic pentameter is sufficiently clear that we detect departures from it, and the rhymes are carefully slanted ('men'/'mean') or unemphatic ('her'/'her') to suggest, through artfully imperfect regularity, the free movement of the lover against conventional restraint. To turn one's back on the god Apollo does not entail either mindless absorption by the Mountain Mother or licence to ignore the gifts of form and clarity Apollo provides. The last stanza makes clear what this oblique verse-craft implies. The sap springs up and the birds sing according to their season. But, line 18 insists, man is different: because of his self-consciousness man's devotion to the quest transcends the seasons, and here resides the Apollonian element without which Graves, or any author, could not write at all.

The central fructifying tension between careful artist and reckless lover is indicated further in the contrast between the opening line, concisely divided with a pattern of strong syllables falling symmetri-cally on each side of the caesura, and the opening line of the final stanza, metrically its duplicate but with a free movement suggested by the unimpeded grace of the words. We might catch also an echo of the Renaissance lyrics Graves admired in the archaic 'a-stir', or in the birds which 'shout awhile', sturdily Elizabethan, and there is a hint of the 'Good-morrow' in the allusion to seven sleepers, Donne's poem being also about headstrong love in the teeth of convention. In the imagery, furthermore, is a kind of indefinite wistfulness, the perpetual lure of the *femme fatale* contrasting a sudden sense of actual presence. The extremes of delicacy and destruction, spring and November, firmness and freedom, tradition and recklessness, somehow have to be contained by the hero, lonely in his self-consciousness and driven to seek love, but knowing he will find death as well in the 'broad high brow' as 'white as any leper's'.

Now suppose we look at the poem again, having read sufficiently in Graves's mythography to have a sense of his theories. We would at once appreciate the cultural significance of the opposition between Apollo and the White Goddess, and how the Goddess is destroyer as well as lover. We would learn of the contradictory emotions aroused by 'white' as purity or horror (*W.G.*, 67), how the white barley Goddess is also worshipped as a white sow, 'the snatcher' (*W.G.*, 67), and how sow's milk was held to cause leprosy (*W.G.*, 188). We would find that Leviticus, Pausanias, Strabo and Old Goidelic deal with the ambivalence of the Goddess' leprous colour (*W.G.*, 434) which is connected with the fertility of fields and the ancient lore of trees. We may also appreciate more fully the presence in the poem of rowan berries, for the rowan, or quick beam, is associated with the Goddess (*W.G.*, 185) and its berries heal the wounded (*W.G.*, 167). It wards off lightning (*W.G.*, 167) and so stands in opposition to the 'next bright bolt', the destruction introduced by the dying month of November from which the lover is protected during his season in favour. The further connection of trees to the alphabet and the cypher language of celtic bards in turn could lead us to consider the nature of poetry itself in relation to language and the mysterious nature it attempts to represent.

Graves has said about poetry that 'There is one story and one story only,'[32] but if we follow his allusions in this fashion back into *The White Goddess*, our pursuit of poetry's single theme through the rich tapestry of extended meanings will soon dissolve *this* poem's distinctiveness. It is to some degree the experience of submitting poetic diction to analysis by way of an etymological dictionary. Our reading is enriched, but the extra knowledge may not enhance our sense of the artistry, or the quality of a poem's particular statement.

Yet there is one point where the mythography may make a real difference. The allusion to the seven sleepers does remind us of Donne, and of the seven young men who awoke after centuries of miraculous sleep to find their faith vindicated: the pagan world which once cast them out had itself become Christian. Read in this light, Graves's line would mean, 'even further back than the earliest Christian times, when the pagan knowledge of nature fell asleep.' But in *The Greek Myths* (I, 354) Graves tells us that the cavern's original use was as a shrine to Artemis, in which case the line would mean, 'further back even than the earliest recorded pagan worship.' Still, whether we know about Artemis or not, the sense of penetrating back to a prehistoric reality remains, and although there is a certain difference here, there is not much.

A critic has written of Graves's Goddess poems that they

> are certainly original, and usually brief, but they are seldom very simple. Although their language and imagery are as precise and clear as anything Graves has written, and although the reader who is uninitiated into the Gravesian mysteries will still be able to receive almost the full emotional impact of the strange stories told by the poems, a complete understanding of them almost invariably requires a careful study of both *The White Goddess* and *The Greek Myths*.[33]

We might ask if we ever do have a 'complete' understanding of a poem, and, indeed, suggest that reading one of Graves's poems in light of *The White Goddess* leaves us with the impression that we do not understand fully at all. Sometimes it seems even that we understand the poem better *before* we introduce the Goddess, and in going through the mythography and the *Collected Poems* together, what is striking in the end is the sense of an extraordinary gulf between the bizarre complexities of the one and the lyric purity of the other. They overlap, indeed, and it is enriching, certainly, to explore the poetry through *The White Goddess*, but Frank Kermode's observation, after all, remains compelling: Graves is a poet who has gone to enormous pains to acquire an epic scholarly knowledge and then has written lyrics where very little of it is evident.[34] It is the major conundrum of Graves's career. Perhaps in nurturing it with such care he dramatises, finally, the width of the gulf about which he tirelessly complains (while protesting the uselessness of complaint), between Apollo and the Goddess in the civilisation in which we live. At any rate his attempt, Apollonian itself, to bend history to the service of the Goddess indicates how our minds may have to puzzle themselves into humility by way of the toilsome pedantries of logic simply to discover the infinite, further complexities of life upon which logic, like history, depends. It would be better, of course, if Graves's own history were accurate, for historical claims underpin his mythography and most of his novels. To find his learning suspect, as we found with Aldous Huxley, diminishes the force of his case. But the degree of that diminishment varies; Graves's poetry, even when it builds upon the 'historical grammar' of his mythography, is less vulnerable to scholarly refutation than, say, the historical speculation of *The Greek Myths*.

In a novel set in the period when John Norris lived and wrote, Graves captures the essence of problems involved in studying myth objectively and yet giving a sense of it as a mimesis of living nature. In *Wife to Mr Milton* (London: Cassell, 1942), Graves shows us Marie Powell, named for Queen Henrietta Maria, growing and thriving in a Royalist family which celebrates Twelfth Night, approves of Mayday festivities and the country customs of old England as well as of stained glass and images in the local chapel. But Marie's easy-going, hearty way of life is disturbed by the Civil War, and, to save her father from financial distress, she becomes wife to Mr Milton, a self-castigating, pedantic hair-fetishist, severe, callous and cold-hearted, a disastrous lover and ironically a victim of his own astonishing intellectual gifts and Puritan principles. Yoked to him, Marie loses her vitality, does not love her child, and dies never having consummated her life-long passion for Edmund Verney, a young cavalier treacherously murdered by Cromwell's efficient police. Yet the most interesting part of the book, and most pertinent here, is not the thorough disapproval which Graves expresses for the Puritan revolution, or even the monstrously irreverent portrait of Mr Milton, but the suggestion in the love relationship between Edmund Verney and Marie that life is full of pre-logical and vital 'correspondences' which do not submit to the logic and order of rational thought. Edmund ('Mun') and Marie experience each other's love by sympathy which is sometimes telepathic, and in secret language fraught with 'influence' – much as the experiments with weapon-salve by Sir Kenelm Digby (which the novel discusses) drew upon the vital sympathies of nature to effect cures. At the end, Marie's intuition of Mun's death, and the coinherence of the two souls of the parted lovers, suggest a dimension of human knowing which is 'poetic' (and its vindication in this novel is simply that we are moved by it) rather than 'prosaic' (we cannot hope to prove it to the iconoclasts of the new order). Such knowledge is of course lost beneath Independent pragmatism which breaks the images and imposes sobriety on merrie England. 'Merrie', says Graves elsewhere (W.G., 396), is the same word as 'Marie', and the story of Marie Powell thus becomes an allegory for the course of modern English and European history, as well as for the predicament of Graves as mythographer living within it.

Although Graves abjures the failures of Christianity, therefore, he has remained nonetheless faithful to Western thought and tradition in probing the roots of those failures. Consequently he belongs, in one sense, among the mythographers of the mainstream Western tradition, prior to the Puritan revolution which inaugurates the modern era of technology and scientific nominalism. Also, he is a product of a highly articulate and 'prosaic' post-Renaissance culture, and his perspectives and techniques are highly self-conscious and sophisticated. Certainly he realises the dimensions of experience he desires to uncover and revitalise cannot simply or prosaically be demonstrated: he appreciates the need on the one hand not to turn myths into objects for study, and also to avoid purely subjective interpretations. The facts of history themselves must yield the secret, as the earlier mythographers knew, and Graves undertakes to show how they may. His technique is ironic, his method proleptic, and his focus the White Goddess. She is not, and cannot, by definition, be understood by prosaic means, though the persuasiveness and factual accuracy of prosaic logic may lead some readers indirectly to her, and by Graves's process of arguing from focus to ground he ironically uses the light of the sun to reflect the phases of the moon and its triple female deity.

But the goddess does not represent only the richly unformulated in human experience: she is also the anomalous, the crucifier, and as such she holds a peculiar power over Graves's imagination. He had seen, especially in his trench experiences of the Great War, the massive violence which he later interpreted as a nemesis overtaking a lopsidedly developed civilisation. 'What has gone wrong?' he asks. And then gives an answer, vigorous as usual: 'The supersession of matriarchy by patriarchy led to the supersession of patriarchy by democracy, of democracy by plutocracy, and of plutocracy by mechanarchy disguised as technology. Technology is now warring openly against the crafts, and science covertly against poetry.'[35] The poet in such a situation cannot solve the problem of violence represented by the cross, but he can have us accept ourselves as victims by showing us the meaning of love, thereby helping to correct the one-sided, prideful self-sufficiency which has developed out of hand in our modern technocracies, and which sows only the seeds of a terrifying retribution.

4 Belief in Religion: the Poetry of David Jones

I. JONES AND JOYCE: LANGUAGE AND THE VARIETIES OF REALISM

David Jones's modernism has a good deal in common with that of James Joyce: 'affinity' is Eliot's carefully chosen word.[1] Both see the artist in a late culture phase as a kind of Ishmael,[2] and for both a similar Celtic complexity and intricacy express strikingly individual interpretations of the 'universum' of Western European civilisation.[3] Both share a Catholic respect for the sacramental: the awesome means by which a material world, properly dedicated, can become the vehicle of grace and illumination. Both draw on a similar kind of recondite erudition, not sparing the reader but drawing on curious etymologies, fragments of languages dead and living, popular sayings, folklore, slang, and curious patternings of dialect to create a sense of how, in an age of specialisation and intensive self-consciousness, even the peculiarities of one man's store of learning and experience must be fashioned to transmit the riches of his culture's past. 'Every word so deep, Leopold,'[4] says Bloom to himself; the same sense of language recurs everywhere in David Jones, who speaks of Joyce frequently and with admiration.[5]

Nevertheless, these two men are also opposites: one is a convert to Catholicism, and the other a renegade from it. Their shared inspiration has, clearly, little to do with their explicit commitment to a body of doctrine. Rather, it resides in their common way of looking at the nature of words and reality. In this context, Aldous Huxley tells an anecdote about Joyce,[6] who once explained an etymology concerning the name of Odysseus. It was as if Joyce, having found the derivation of the word, had discovered the true significance of the story – what 'Odysseus' must really mean. Huxley goes on to deplore this kind of total commitment to words as purveyors of meaning, and labels it the 'magical' view of language.

The anecdote of course oversimplifies Joyce, but there is truth in the notion that he never gave over his Catholic sense of words as efficacious signs, and this, pre-eminently, is shared by David Jones who says plainly that signs 'are themselves, under some mode, what they signify.'[7] What Huxley labels 'magical', Jones, in the spirit of Joyce and the language of Neo-Thomism, would instead call 'realist'.

St Thomas maintains that there are three types of knowledge: angelic, human, and sensible.[8] As humans, we know by means of 'participation' in the higher divine light which is seen directly by angels, and in which belong the essences of created things (215). But the proper object of human knowledge is a 'quiddity' (218); that is, 'nature existing in a particular corporeal matter', showing forth incompletely, though truly, the principle of its being. The world of objects therefore shares in immateriality to some degree, or else the physical universe would be totally opaque and formless (225), and in the act of knowing by which humans gain an imperfect idea of form by abstraction from quiddities, the concept does in some sense really resemble its object (230). In human knowledge, a universal, intelligible element joins always with the particular material thing (218), so that we may glimpse, however fleetingly, the 'splendor of form' in its intelligible reality. But in aspiring for higher knowledge it is prideful for man to despise the creaturely, which is necessary to cognition itself – 'nihil in intellectu nisi prius in sensibus.'

When Jacques Maritain, the Neo-Thomist commentator to whom David Jones is most indebted,[9] interprets this epistemology in relation to art, he resorts to the same notion of 'participation' to indicate how the artist truly discovers, through the intelligent working of his medium, the intelligible reality which his material is raised to reveal, and in which our reason dwells to our edification and delight.[10] Beauty, in short, gives us a scattered reflection of God's face, and shows how mind working upon matter can disclose something of the principles upon which nature is created. Yet beauty, in human experience, is never enough: however real, it remains an imperfect participation in that fullness of being which is not for us to know in this life.

Maritain's account of art according to scholasticism does not so much distinguish the artist's cognitive activity from that of ordinary humans, as show how the artist celebrates man's ordinary status as discoverer of significance in the material world. 'Art,' says Maritain, 'is a habit of the practical intellect' (11): it needs both the material element which belongs to sensible knowledge, and the intelligence to make something of it. Though the artist's aim is, as not always in human activity, the good of the work itself (this distinguishes art from prudence), nevertheless 'art is . . . a man's work, stamped with the character of a man' (7).

Maritain claims that his theory should also be understood historically, for only at the Renaissance, with the decline of scholasticism and the widespread rejection of the view of language Huxley calls 'magical', did art become self-conscious in a manner which encouraged the artist to see himself occupying a special role as self-sufficient and semi-divine creator (22 ff.). A consequent inflation of ego has, in modern times, threatened the artist's sanity. By contrast, his medieval counterpart was protected by unself-consciousness, for he worked primarily as artisan (104), and the more wholesome – more human – result was 'an ingenuous folk . . . educated in beauty without even noticing it' (22).

David Jones's opinions on man-as-artist are based on this broadly Neo-Thomist scheme. The forms that artists discover, Jones argues, are 'typic' of 'archetypal form-making' (*E.A.*, 160), and the artist's activity brings the 'splendor of form' to shine upon his material (*E.A.*, 156), thereby disclosing something of the higher mystery (*A.*, 33). But though he works *sub specie aeternitatis* (*A.*, 24), intuiting and attempting to render intelligible the beauty of creation, the artist must work 'within the limits of his love' (*A.*, 24), in terms of what he 'actually' (*A.*, 25) knows, the unique '*res*' (*A.*, 11) which is his own physical and intimate knowledge of a locality. Jones's word is 'contactual' (*E.A.*, 244), and means that the artist contains, in a valid work, something which shows his special knowledge of a particular thing (*E.A.*, 210). Here, again, human understanding is placed between pure intelligence and the senses, and the valid sign is religious because it impinges upon the divine mystery of form (*E.A.*, 158, 177). Jones feels intensely the continuity which this theory implies between transcendent mystery, mediating sign (the poetic image) and material ('contactual') fact.

Like Maritain, Jones also looks nostalgically upon a past culture when the artist was integrated with, indeed at the centre of, his community at large (*E.A.*, 97, 100). Even if cultural conditions today have led artists to see themselves as special, isolated figures, Jones argues that they still perform best when unself-conscious: 'the workman must be dead to himself while engaged upon the work, otherwise we have that sort of "self-expression" which is as undesirable in the painter or the writer as in the carpenter, the cantor, the half-back, or the cook' (*A.*, 12). René Hague says that for Jones this idea became a kind of maxim.[11] Certainly it is based on Jones's sense of the *ordinariness* of art as a human activity, and upon his understanding, derived from Neo-Thomism, of the boundaries within which it is properly human to work.

If Maritain is important for Jones's general theory, his influence is supplemented by that of Maurice de la Taille, who confirms Maritan's central assertions while also providing a theme which becomes a main preoccupation of Jones's poetry, namely, the relationship in the ritual of the mass between Christ's cross and the last supper,[12] and how this is a mimesis of the process itself of human sign-making.

De la Taille's main idea in *Mysterium Fidei* is that the supper and the cross are parts of a single sacrifice. At the supper, Christ symbolically dedicates himself, and so is committed to the actual suffering of the cross whereby oblation is completed by immolation, and symbol ratified by fact (10, *et passim*). As the supper room looks forward to Calvary, so the mass looks back upon it (10, 18, 36). Neither offering is complete without actual crucifixion, though at the mass Christ is not immolated anew, for his state of victimhood was established once and for all by his death (16, 311). Rather, the mass, by symbolically recalling the cross through the same words of dedication uttered at the supper, shares in, and renews the real, single sacrifice. This *anamnesis* (the word is also a favourite of Jones), is an effective recalling because the sign is efficacious of the sanctifying reality it suggests (23). 'That which belongs to the order of signs,' de la Taille writes, 'necessarily involves the presence of that which is signified' (206), and because signs are the the chief means of human discourse, God's central revelation to man was made by God placing himself for us in 'the order of signs' (212), which is to say, on the cross.

By combining de la Taille and Maritain, Jones can argue that the mass, like the entire liturgy, is a work of art. 'No artefacture,' he concludes, 'no Christian religion' (*E.A.*, 19), and in *Epoch and Artist* he claims that human culture itself is 'nothing but a sign' (88). All the sign-making of human history and art is therefore significant, because adumbrating the one most significant (because most richly symbolic yet concretely actual) event of history — the sacrifice of Christ. Even pre-Christian art and culture shared in the merits of the cross, and attained something already Christian (69), and Jones sees his Catholicism as an explicit statement of principles to which all men are, by their nature, already implicitly committed (*E.A.*, 177).

Jones, therefore, did not derive this theory of language from Joyce. Maritain and de la Taille provide the important formulations, and Jones tells us how, as an art student in 1920–21, before he knew Joyce's works, it had already come to him that post-Impressionist theories of art as a thing in itself and not an impression of some thing were 'analogous to what the Catholic Church maintained in her dogma of the Mass.'[13] He also denies that Joyce had a direct influence on *The Anathemata*.[14] We should, consequently, read Jones's admiration in terms of a more general Joycean attitude to modernism. For instance, both men felt how hard to earn are the desirable artistic qualities of 'wholeness, harmony and radiance' (*E.A.*, 306) in an age enervated by cultural rootlessness. The artist above all in such circumstances must speak out for beauty, *id quod visum placet*, while continuing to acknowledge the complexity of cultural conditions in which he lives. But where Jones is prepared to carry this into a commitment to religious dogma, Joyce is not, even though Joyce's very parody of belief in a way re-affirms it. The denunciation of the religious fiction he once took for fact is best expressed in the morally fervid idiom imparted by the religion he rejects. Throughout *Ulysses*, the pleasures of deliberate desacralisation thus become a means of sanctifying the profane, bathing it in a light which the dead forms of conventional religious practice no longer mediate. The drowned corpse, the dead dog, the decayed ritual, are revitalised, transubstantiated in the unlikely, profane ordinariness of Henry Flower, Mr Bloom.

Clearly, Joyce's art cannot be reduced to his opinions on Roman Catholicism, even though these are not irrelevant, and the affinity with Jones remains, despite the fact that Jones's faith commits him 'in the most explicit manner possible' (*E.A.*, 177). Jones centres his main work on the mass, which celebrates what he claims to be the most significant event in history. 'For the imagination of Jones,' says a critic, whose words can be taken as a summary of the main contrast in ideas between Jones and Joyce, 'Calvary is the supreme fact, not the supreme fiction.'[15] The difference is real. Yet in poetry, fact and fiction often interpenetrate to surprise expectations based on such conceptual distinctions alone.

II. POETRY AND THE SIGN OF THE CROSS

Jones sees art as holy because, like religion, it is an *anamnesis*, a recalling, a binding back to our origins. He stresses also that art is an ordinary human activity; it is beautiful, but reminds man of his limitations by binding him to the creaturely and particular, the proper orbit of his love. Humility is, in consequence, an important virtue, and in Jones's writing it appears both as a precept and a pervasive quality. The artist must be dead to himself as he works, and yet, Jones says, must not underestimate 'the almost insuperable difficulties of how to make the signs available for today.' 'Vulnerability' is essential, otherwise we may miss that special 'wedding' in man between the utilitarian world of fact and the holy (*E.A.*, 177–78).

The main catch with such a theory is that if it remains divorced from the 'contactual' it contradicts itself, and for this reason Jones is uneasy about writing didactically at all (*E.A.*, 17). But as a quality of his work, humility is less easily defined. Reviewing *The Heritage of Early Britain*, Jones concludes by admiring the techniques of modern scholarship: 'The Angel of Truth is nothing if not exact, so the more exact the researchers the more the findings should be on the side of that angel' (*E.A.*, 201). In a subsequent learned article on *The Arthurian Legend*, he closes a criticism of Charles Williams with a question, followed by the sentence, 'Fr. D'Arcy's *Mind and Heart of Love* should help us here, but I have not it with me' (*E.A.*, 208). The effect is to render an impressive display of learning disarmingly tentative by way of a personal touch which unself-consciously discounts the importance of Jones's own learned contribution. There is a sense that the author does not really see himself as the peer of professional scholars, even when he addresses their problems with diligence and acumen, often producing illuminating and learned conclusions. And there is no hint of perverse pride disguised as self-effacement: rather, a kind of surprisingness, an affirmation of open-endedness (Fr D'Arcy *should* help us, not *would*: it is a matter of conjecture, for discussion).

The poetry also shows this unassuming quality, often accompanied by wry humour. Everywhere is a sense of how vulnerable is human knowledge, combined with an evidently painstaking scholarship and craft which, despite its grandeur, never dispenses with the author's sense of his own human nature as nothing special.[16] Here is a description of cave paintings at Lascaux:

> And see how they run, the juxtaposed forms,
> brighting the vaults of Lascaux; how the linear is wedded
> to volume, how they do, within, in an unbloody manner,

under the forms of brown haematite and black manganese on
the graved lime-face, what is done, without,
                    far on the windy tundra
at the kill
that the kindred may have life.
                    O God!
O the Academies!   (60)

The vocabulary is learned: the technical languages, of art criticism
('juxtaposed forms', 'linear', 'volume'), of geology ('brown haematite', 'black manganese'), and Catholic theology ('in an unbloody
manner'), suggest that the sign-making of these early men is,
however obscurely, a sacramental act. Thus the phrase, 'that the
kindred may have life' is carefully ambivalent. It may mean that the
kill is for the kindred's physical sustenance, or that the community
survives by expressing in paint the spiritual bonds which keep it
together. The play on 'haematite' (the Greek root *haema*, for 'blood')
and 'unbloodied', helps to confirm the inherence of matter and
symbol, and the following 'O God!' is also ambivalent. It has the high
tone of jubilation ('How glorious are the works of God . . . '), as well
as the colloquial sense of the phrase used to register surprise or awe
('this primitive ritual is also how God stirs in men . . .'). But to have
the passage end just with 'O God!' would be to suggest high
seriousness courting the pretentious. 'O the Academies!' reassures us.
'O God!' can stand because the poet, picking upon the offending
nuance, mocks at it, nipping it in the bud. It is as if we listen to a voice
in three registers. First a learned, almost hieratic, formal voice
describing the cave rites; then 'O God!', which is still elevated but
implies a speaker jubilantly and awesomely aware of what the cave
rites imply; finally a voice we feel is aware of the artificial 'academic'
vocabulary it has been using, and how far 'Academies' fall short of
what 'God' might really mean. The wry twist is wholly typical,
modifying the tone of a learned passage towards something humanly
less certain, yet without sacrificing strength.

But more profoundly rooted in the poetry is Jones's manner of
combining this tentative quality with his theory of language through
the cross. For Jones, as for St Augustine,[17] the cross is the sign of faith,
representing, as it did throughout the Middle Ages in Books of Hours
and specula, on rood screens and tapestries, carvings, murals and
statuary, the conditions of man's journey through fallen history. As
lignum vitae it spreads its branches back in time, linking the old

dispensation to the new. As Adam's tree it foreshadows Christ's as Eve foreshadows Mary, Synagoga Ecclesia, and the fruit of death the fruit of life. Manned by Christ, it is the ship upon which the faithful ride, and the key by which they attain heaven.

> *Regnum quaeritis?*
> *Non intrabitis*
>   *Sine crucis clavi;*
> *Portum petitis?*
> *Non transibitis*
>   *Sine crucis navi.*[18]

Ship and key and live branches alike indicate process, and by dwelling in the spirit of such traditional iconography and building on it, Maurice de la Taille was able to argue that Christ's placing himself upon the cross is a sign of the process itself of human knowledge seeking salvation. The cross therefore stands for all the partial signs by which God reveals himself, until, at last, we are safely gathered in.

We can see how readily Jones, who was steeped in mediaeval learning,[19] could find in de la Taille a way to link his own 'realist' view of language with his sense of a 'modernist' predicament in which the artist's humility is called upon as a special virtue. He does so by claiming that just as valid signs bear a real relationship to each other, so they do to the cross which stands for all of them, especially in a culture where uncertainty is stronger than the edifying influence of tradition, and where a saving sense of beauty is closely associated with the artist's willingness to be vulnerable and compassionate.

This attitude persists throughout Jones's career: the *Vexilla Regis* became his subject in paint, verse and prose,[20] and the cross intrigued him even from his early engravings for *The Ancient Mariner* (1929), where he uses Coleridge's repetition of the 'cross-albatross' rhyme[21] to suggest the drama of Christian redemption. In one illustration the albatross, its wings spread, is pinned against a cross-shaped mast, with an arrow lancing its side (No.2). In another, the mariner, his arms outstretched as if crucified, carries the dead bird around his neck (No. 5). The tailpiece shows a pelican wounding itself, symbol of Christ the redeemer, and in the introduction Jones cites with approval those patristic writers who 'saw . . . amidships the image of the same salvific Wood.'[22] The mariner's journey clearly duplicates Christ's redemptive suffering.[23]

The cross also emerges **with** increasing firmness throughout Jones's main written work. It is present, if implicit, in *In Parenthesis*, more clearly a *leitmotif* in *The Anathemata*, and a central preoccupation in *The Sleeping Lord*, which deals mainly with events at the time of Christ's passion.

Section 7 of *In Parenthesis*,[24] 'The Five Unmistakable Marks', describes the climactic battle of Mametz Wood, in which Pte John Ball is wounded. The battle is a crucifixion, a harrowing and a judgement. The range of allusion extends from scriptural resonance ('you can't believe the Cup wont pass from /or they wont make a better show /in the garden' [158]), to hinted iconography, for instance in the seemingly occasional command, 'and don't bunch on the left /for Christ's sake' (160). Throughout, suggestions of the cross help to evoke a pervasive sense of human suffering in the 'interminable ways between' (7), and Jones deploys a complex of images, often involving wood and iron. There is a noise of carpenters hammering as for a scaffold (138), an apse bared in 'cross section' (149), and a cryptic shape of 'iron and wood and iron' (19). The 'Mother of Christ under the tree' is asked to pray for us (177), and in groves 'men come both to their joys and their undoing' (66).

Still, the cross is less the focus of *In Parenthesis* than suggestive of the general truth spoken by soldiers who feel in the trenches 'only the mazelikeness of all their goings' (87), and that 'You live by faith alright in these parts' (87). Each man 'masks the inward abysm' (109) of doubt and fear that accompanies trench warfare, but in so doing, each is sustained by small events made significant by our perception of a higher beauty in them. There is an 'unnamable nostalgia of depots' (28), and routine commands can appear heightened as devotional refrains: 'the liturgy of their going-up assumed a primitive creativeness, an apostolic actuality, a correspondence with the object, a flexibility' (28). The most powerful effects come through such scenes evoking separation, loss and perplexity – 'the stumbling dark of the blind, that Breughel knew about' (31) – illuminated by some small event through which the sordid and the mean brighten to significance. The mazy crossways become enigmatically beautiful, linking us back into history and helping us to discover how 'a whole unlovely order this night would transubstantiate' (27). In the trenches is that peculiar fellowship which grows from affliction, suggesting that suffering and self-sacrifice bear their own kind of fruit. Jones's repeated description of the trenches in terms of traverse and circle suggests the sign of the cross itself, made up of intersecting arms upon which men are stretched, yet intimating wholeness and restoration.

In Jones's final collection of poems, *The Sleeping Lord*,[25] there is again a preoccupation with soldiering, this time mostly among the ranks of the Roman army at the time of the crucifixion, and the cross is now, deliberately, made the measure of events. The ironies, for example, spoken in 'The Wall' by the Roman soldier stationed in Palestine who asks whether or not the whole imperial enterprise was undertaken just for commercial gain, are answered by the crucifixion in the background, which we recognise as significant, but he does not. In 'The Fatigue', the soldiers are again treated ironically, because the reader sees in the cross an event which will come to direct Rome itself. Likewise, in 'The Hunt', Arthur's pursuit of the boar suggests for the reader a re-enactment of Christ's passion. And in 'The Tutelar of the Place', the entire world's activity becomes a dance around Calvary, the new Tree of Life:

> Gathering all things in, twining each bruised stem to the swaying trellis of the dance, the dance about the sawn lode-stake on the hill where the hidden stillness is at the core of struggle, the dance around the green lode-tree on fair-height where the secret guerdons hang and the bright prizes nod, . . .(61)

Throughout *The Sleeping Lord*, the cross is a controlling concept, and the images of traverse and circle continue, along the same lines as in *In Parenthesis*, to suggest our mixed experience of wandering and intuitions of wholeness. 'We don't know the ins and outs / . . . / from the circuit of the agger /from the traverse of the wall,' as we go, enduring faithfully, appreciative of small mercies, brief epiphanies.

III. THE *ANATHEMATA*

Between *In Parenthesis* and *The Sleeping Lord*, Jones's writing in verse and prose describes, unsystematically but with increasing clarity, his convictions about man as signmaker, and about the artist's predicament in the twentieth century. Jones's main achievement in this period is *The Anathemata*. It combines the rich sense of European history which we find in *In Parenthesis* with an exploration of how the cross can focus the poet's concern as a man thinking seriously about religion at a time when mass utilitarianism has separated him from what is sustaining and beautiful in his culture. The result is difficult reading, but the effort of cracking the husk never fails to reveal a nutmeat, fruit of careful nurture. A brief *précis* of the poem's eight sections will show how each impinges upon the cross.

'Rite and Foretime' begins by establishing an analogy between prehistoric man and the Roman Catholic priest celebrating mass in today's wasteland. Both make signs and set them apart, and in so doing confirm their humanity in common. We then move back to the hill upon which Christ died, for the crucifixion links most meaningfully early man to man of today. In this light, we review some of humanity's earliest discoveries (fire, painting, pottery), and then come forward again through the painfully emergent contours of human civilisation, through an ice age that shaped the hills, to the central hill at Jerusalem, and so to the priest's celebration of the Eucharist.

'Middle Sea and Lear Sea' focuses again on the crucifixion, and uses it to examine the Greek and Roman contribution to western culture. Hector's suffering foreshadows Christ's, and Rome, like Greece, has a share with Israel in the divine inspiration which anticipates Christ and the Virgin. We see a ship, on the day of the crucifixion, hoving in sight of a Greek sculpture of a woman, from which it takes a bearing. The hard-drinking, pagan captain is in some ways like Christ, and his ship suggests the cross. Another, separate voyage into northern waters is now described,[26] and there is a list of questions and conjectures about the captain's perilous journey around the coast of Cornwall and up the Thames.

'Angle Land' continues the theme of voyaging in uncharted waters, but the journey is now moved forward in time, and the captain witnesses the fear and uncertainty of an Anglo-Saxon Christian after the Roman departure from Britain. A catalogue of place names and rivers links the unrest caused by ancient migrations of peoples to modern anxieties of a similar sort, caused by wars and nationalist sentiment in our own times. Clearly, 'Angle Land' develops from 'Middle Sea and Lear Sea', and although it does not directly evoke the crucifixion, it takes as its point of departure the ship which is analogous to the cross in the previous section, developing the motif of suffering and uncertainty which attends human destiny. The questions, which are so important to the tone of 'Middle Sea and Lear Sea', continue here.

'Redriff' brings the voyage-theme to nineteenth-century England, and to the poet's own ancestor, Eb Bradshaw. Bradshaw is a craftsman, and will not work quickly on a vessel which has come damaged into port. He announces that he would not hurry had he to prepare the holy cross itself, and thus the theme of the voyage is brought round once more to the cross, relating it to the activity of the craftsman as artist.

'The Lady of the Pool', the longest section, is mainly a monologue by a cockney woman whose identity merges with the Goddesses of the ancient world and with the Blessed Virgin. The poet asks if a visiting sea captain talked to her in London, and then her monologue begins. She starts by listing churches on local sites, some of which were dedicated to pagan Goddesses, and later to the Virgin Mary, through whom Christ was able to redeem mankind. She talks of some of her lovers, and then recalls a voyage described by the captain of a ship called the *MARY*. She tells how the ship was given up for lost, but, wounded like Christ, came to port safely. The ship in the storm was like the sacrifice of the mass, but the Christian sailors were assured of safety by mermaids. The lady then tells of other voyages of which she has heard, including one to Jerusalem where Christ was crucified, and, finally, she resumes the catalogue of churches, pointing out that these ancient celtic sites now celebrate redemption by the cross. This section, which is long and complex, combines an atmosphere tinged by the magical with a rich colloquialism, as the lady speaks for the sustaining and nurturing female principle which has its own part to play in redemption. Again the cross is central, but the redemptive act was made possible by a woman, and a powerful complementary principle is evoked here to balance the predominantly male enterprise of the voyaging sea captains in the previous parts.

'Keel Ram and Stauros' begins by saying that answers regarding the sea voyages in the last section are uncertain, and by way of a brief series of questions about the captain of 'Middle Sea and Lear Sea', the poem returns again to the crucifixion. This leads to a discussion of the kinds of wood and skill which have prepared the cross and the ship, both signs of man's salvation.

'Mabinog's Liturgy' centres on Guinevere, who resembles Mary. Despite her sinfulness, Guinevere draws men to her in devotion, and the poem describes the lavishness of her dress and her beauty at midnight mass, celebrating Christ's birth as, out of war-torn lands, bread and wine are laid aside in memory of Christ. At Christmas, the poem suggests, even witches pray in honour of the God who died and was reborn. Three Welsh witches then discuss Christ's redemption, and out of sympathy for Mary who suffered with him, decide for this night to offer their thanks. The concern for the female in this section develops the Lady of the Pool's monologue, and the celebration of nativity offsets the suffering image of Mary standing by the tree.

'Sher Thursday and Venus Day', the final section, centres on Good Friday, and begins by describing Christ as a knight who has come to Calvary to slake the thirst of the Waste Land. The actual suffering of the cross is compared to the Mass, where there is no renewed immolation, and where people are inclined to forget what the pains of the actual death were. Yet in Christ's desolation is a fullness of meaning for all such people, and for the different kinds of dedications and offerings that various cultures make. The drama of crucifixion and *anamnesis* thus leads back to the mass with which the poem began, and this final section confronts us most clearly with the complex unity of supper and Calvary.

Jones's practice in *The Anathemata* affirms that signs, as Maritain says, are the special and peculiar means of human understanding. Because the cross is the supreme revelation of this truth to man-the-signmaker,[27] Jones's central use of the symbol enables him to achieve a richness of texture, surrendering neither the clarity of mature conviction nor the humane appreciation of the signs other men have made, whose convictions and cultures are different from his. Like the mediaeval *lignum vitae*, the cross buds and sends shoots through the difficult courses of our human enterprise:

> The virid shoots precarious and separate as yet on the
> fronding wood.
> You can see: One, two . . .
> I can see three . . .
> Five!
> . . . .
> Can mortised stakes bud?
> Flora! Surely you know?? (190)

There is suffering here: the shoots are 'precarious and separate', the number five suggests Christ's wounds, and 'mortised' tells how the wood itself is tormented, so that the tree becomes a sign, foreshadowing Christ's pain. Nonetheless, the passage describes a budding in springtime, and Flora ensures that the shoots are alive to 'tendril and galloon' (191). Soon after she becomes the Virgin, whom the poet pictures in a rose arbour. Delicacy and gentleness, essence of beauty, are shot through with memories (or anticipations) of suffering and the effect is enhanced by the echo of *The Corpus Christi Carol* ('the trickling blossoms /by the ancient stone' [192]), as the poem draws us through a pattern of images comprising the pagan goddesses, Christ's tree, Mary, and the mediaeval song, centring in the paradoxical inherence of joy in suffering, and, so, on the mystery of the cross.

Throughout *The Anathemata* we appreciate such play of analogies, themselves carefully mortised by rhythm and syntax, and drawing on the traditional types of mediaeval usage. The cross is a winepress (156), or a ship in a storm ('but /sweet Christ's dear Tree! /her cordage!! /how does it stand /to stay?' [138]). Hector anticipates Christ crucified, as a fragmentary sixth-century marble figure on the Acropolis foreshadows the good shepherd (91), and as Korê, Selenê and Helen, like the splendid Athena of Phidias, foreshadow Mary:

> tower of ivory
> in the gilded *cella*
> herself a house of gold.   (94)

In these lines, allusion to the litany implies an unconscious aspiration in the pagan sculpture towards a higher, more complete, form. We apprehend such a meaning both conceptually, and through rhythm and the juxtaposition of terms suggesting the two cultures, separate, yet bound in a single meaning by the beauty they intimate together, just as they are by the syntax of the poem containing them in a single sentence.

Yet the difficult truth about human nature expressed by the title of *In Parenthesis* is not surrendered in *The Anathemata*, for the cross, though it blooms, signifies the doubt against which human knowledge and culture are never final proof. Such knowledge produces Jones's characteristic gentleness and sense of vulnerability, and helps to create also a certain swelling, subsiding, but continuously sombre undertone. In 'Rite and Foretime', the ice-age men make artifacts while witnessing all around them extinction intermittently relieved by interglacial phases until the last of them dies at the cave mouth. The language is redolent of commemoration, singing a requiem for us all:

> Now, Januarius brings in the millennial snow that makes the antlered mummers glow for many a hemera.
>   The *Vorzeit*-masque is on
> that moves to the cosmic introit
> *Col canto* the piping for this turn.

Unmeasured, irregular in stress and interval of interior
rhythm, modal.
                    If tonic and final are fire
the dominant is ice
                    if fifth the fire
the cadence ice.   (63)

The ice-age rhythms are themselves a kind of offering, sung with the
purity of plain chant even though the pattern of emergent forms is
unclear and irregular, as the breaks in rhythm of the closing lines
indicate. The deepest kind of plangency comes not from an outright
cry of complaint, but, as here, from sorrow emptying itself in praise.
Jones does not shout against unrighteousness, but commiseration is
clear. In face of abandonment suggested by 'diriment' (a form of
'diremptive', which means 'cutting off', the reverse of 'redemptive'),
and of extinction and encroaching cold, faith celebrates without
giving over uncertainty. Questions remain everywhere:

Who was he? Who?
Himself at the cave-mouth
                    the last of the father-figures
to take the diriment stroke
                    of the last gigantic leader of
thick-felled cave-fauna?   (66)

Not even the anchorite escapes violence, but lives, terrified, in a land
abandoned by Rome and defenceless before invasion.[28]

Past where the ancra-man, deeping his holy rule
in the fiendish marsh
                    at the *Geisterstunde*
                    on *Calangaeaf* night
heard the bogle-*baragouinage.*
                    Crowland-*diawliaidd*
Waelisc-man lingo speaking?
                    or Britto-Romani gone *diaboli?*
or Romanity gone *Waelisc?*   (112)

Uncertain questions, elliptical fragments of polyglot confusion and
the jagged arrangement of lines describing how he hears the speech of
Celtic survivors, suggest estrangement and terror underlying the

fragile order of civilisation itself. In our own times, 'the fratricides /of
the latter-day' (115) present a no less edifying spectacle: 'O Balin O
Balan' in 'the last pháse /of our dear West' (115).

Yet Jones's wry, unassuming ordinariness eases us through such
difficult passages, while the rhythms of colloquial speech, nursery
rhymes, carols, and his own kind of idiosyncrasy, leave a characteristic touch of the familiar and creaturely, which are cause for
celebration. There is never Olympian reserve or chill. The captain,
type of Christ, is Ischyros with sea boots; Eb Bradshaw's prejudice has
a pungency which the verse both parodies and makes humorous; the
sergeant gunner's wit, after the clerk blows up the pirate vessel with a
chance shot, captures a variety of attitudes:

> You old· God's arlot! well argued, that makes clear, that re-
> distributes their middle for 'em – now where's their premises? Ask
> of the strewed sea! (147–48)

There is relief, yet amazement and a hint of pique, that the clerk has
pre-empted the trained professionals. The sergeant's aggressive
profanity, yet subsequent agility in phrasing his compliment in the
clerk's learned language of syllogisms, helps to re-establish the
sergeant's self-esteem, while his quick address and tone of common
speech provide amusement to relieve tension.

The cross therefore focuses a pattern of wandering, suffering and
uncertainty, but the cross-tree also buds and flowers: witches kneel,
carols celebrate, Guinevere shines radiant, and the hills raise up their
'help heights' against the other 'anguish-heights' (55, 57). Images of
brightening abound and 'bright' as a verb is a characteristic usage:
'Brighting at the five life-layers' (74); 'As, down among the palaeo-
zoe / he brights his ichthyic sign / so brights he the middle-zone' (74).
A circle of light consistently irradiates the cruciform image by
suggesting redemption, shining from the crossed arms. The 'rejoicing
candles' attend with spheres of light our 'latria /to the Saving Wood'
(165), and circular shapes are described through the voyages themselves, and by the poem's circular action. About his design, the author
writes: 'If it has a shape it is chiefly that it returns to its beginning' (33).
This can indicate both the poem's circular structure, starting and
ending with the mass, and also the attempt to represent, by signs,
those beginnings which have made us man.

The Anathemata, to summarise, draws upon history and seeks in it a
pattern. It claims, mainly, that man as signmaker leaves his mark

everywhere, and his signs bring splendour of form to shine on material things. Man does not, however, transcend space and time, and human knowledge remains incomplete, dependent upon faith and signified by the cross. But faith is not just penitential; Jones's cross, like the Celtic version, bears the circle within its arms, and upon its surface the intricate designs of spiralling forms and subtle typologies. Interlacement and analogy themselves correspond to the underlying, complex truth about how human discourse is symbolic; a truth to which the poem, like the cross, bears witness.

IV. DAVID JONES AND WILLIAM EMPSON: SCIENCE, POETRY, AND THE PERSONAL IDIOM

Jones's attitude to the cross entails, once more, the 'magical' view of language Huxley describes, but this does not explain how Jones, any more than Joyce, is modernist. In an essay entitled 'Past and Present', Jones addresses himself to this question, pointing out that the content of an artist's work is less important in determining its quality of '"now-ness"' (139) than the 'form' or shape he gives it and the use he puts it to. Jones goes on to say that in our present culture 'a metamorphosis has occurred affecting the liaisons with our past' (139), and rendering the artist 'willy-nilly, un-integrated with the present civilizational phase' (139). This problem, Jones claims, is his 'abiding dilemma' in the 'whole of The Anathemata' (139), and the point is not merely that he believes, in the language of Maritain and de la Taille, in Neo-Mediaeval notions of a 'real presence', and 'participation' of signs in what they represent, but that he acknowledges, and cares about, the fact that he lives in a society where the sense of such a relationship has all but disintegrated. Although he talks of a 'Break' which occurred in the minds of his contemporaries in the 1920s and 1930s (A., 15), this, for Jones, involved essentially the acknowledgement of a historical fracture between mediaeval culture which believed valid signs expressed transcendental truth,[29] and modern society which is dominated by technological, and therefore utilitarian, values. An impersonal, functionally sophisticated society ignores its rooted and particular cultural traditions, and Jones's central diagnosis of the challenge posed for art today is founded on this insight into how technological advances enabled by the rise of science have driven apart art and religion. The theme resounds through his writings: utilitarian concern for technology, he says, is alien to church and tradition (*E.A.*, 101); the tempo of change in modern industrial society presents insuperable difficulties when it comes to finding valid signs (*A.*, 15); utility and technics have banished the fays (*E.A.*, 100); the new technology of warfare has divorced us from our creaturely instincts (*In P.*, xiv); the uncontaminated but wholly utilitarian beauty of technology is dehumanising (*E.A.*, 181), and so on.[30] Here is a characteristic passage:

Today we live in a world where the symbolic life (the life of the true cultures, of 'institutional' religion, and of *all artists*, in the last resort — however much we may disavow the association) is progressively eliminated — the technician is master. In a manner of speaking the priest and the artist are already in the catacombs, but *separate* catacombs — for the technician divides to rule. No integrated, widespread, religious art, properly so-called, can be looked for outside. enormous changes in the character and orientation and nature of our civilization, and this is beyond our horizon — however much such vistas may occupy our speculative thoughts. All will at least admit that civilization has many somersaults to turn before a corporate will can again project itself materially in such forms as, to choose very casually, the *Dies Irae*, the Prefaces, the Christ of the central tympanum at Vezelay, the Avignon *Pieta* — or whatever you like from a thousand and one years of integrated marvel (*E.A.*, 103).

When he makes statements like this, Jones also is aware of his predicament as an author who has received much of value from science and its practical applications. Archaeology, geology, and navigation provide fit language for poetry, and are lovingly dwelt upon throughout *The Anathemata*. But Jones is comfortable with such language only when its particular, humanising applications are clear. His painting of 'Hague's Press', though described as 'accurate'[31] by René Hague is rather a portrait of the owner than a depiction of the machine. Jones's main misgivings concern the contrary emphasis whereby technology tends to transform man and reduce his craft to assembly-line labour. And in this context we find a final application of the cross, for it is a sign of the self-consciousness which, as distinct from his mediaeval forebears, especially afflicts the modern artist with knowledge of his separateness in a world dominated by technology. Here we can juxtapose Jones's maxim that the artist must be dead to himself as he works with his sense that the artist must be acutely aware of the peculiar nature of his own experience. The ensuing tension (that modern, unmediaeval idea) is a necessary element in the creative enterprise itself, and the way for Jones to have art rediscover the quality he admires of unself-conscious integration with the culture at large, therefore lies through his work's prior acknowledgement of the separations between art, theology and science, which have occurred since the Middle Ages. Only by facing this split and recording its results upon his own sensibility can his poetry avoid escapism. Thus *The Anathemata* is burdened with its author's sense of the particular, fragmented elements of tradition in his own inheritance, and we may feel that the poetry carries a weight of self-consciousness threatening to replace the desired sense of significant interlace, personally perceived but traditionally derived, with something closer to idiosyncrasy forced into shape by a quasi-association of image, sound-pattern, and dubious etymology. It is both too difficult and too easy: in the particularity and tentativeness there is something opaque, which perhaps finds for itself a too quick justification in the arbitrary belief that the cross, historically unique and divinely revealed, objectively justifies such indirection. John Holloway complains of 'something at once willed and wrenched', of too much 'erudition and super-position' organised by immense elaboration, an 'array of not-plannedness', and a lapse from the public aim of the poem (to show a people itself from the roots) to the private and subjective. Jones's admirers can controvert this with predictable kinds of argument, but there are passages where even an admirer can appreciate the feelings upon which Holloway's lack of sympathy is based.[32] All of which raises the question of how much Jones's poetry may suffer because it works so directly through traditional religious beliefs in an age unattuned to receive these as a central assumption of epic poetry, so that he has to wrench them by a technique of concerted indirection, to render them acceptable. The obscurity itself, of which Holloway complains, is of course present in many great modernist works, whether by believers or not, but in view of Jones's poetic practice, his forthright commitment especially challenges us to ask again the question that came up in the comparison with Joyce. Does being a Roman Catholic make Jones a better or worse writer?

To help clarify the question it may be instructive to turn to a poet whose works are, like Jones's, distinguished though difficult in the modern manner, but who directly contradicts Jones's interpretation

of Christianity and the scientific revolution. Such a poet is William
Empson.

Empson's disparagement of Christianity is well known, and he
bases it firmly on a hatred of the cross.[33] Empson argues that great
steps forward were taken by civilisation in the years between 600–
500 BC, represented by Second Isaiah, Pythagoras, Buddha, and
Confucius (237). Christianity, however,

> is the only one which ratted on the progress, the only one which
> dragged back the Neolithic craving for human sacrifice into its
> basic structure. This is what is the matter with it; people recognised
> at once that the thrilling piece of religious engineering carried
> excessive strain at this crucial point. Public opinion would no
> longer allow regular performances of human sacrifice; the Roman
> officials, indeed, suspected that the early Christians were secretly
> doing what they were always talking about, and tried to catch
> them at it. They revived it only in the sense that they said nothing
> had ever been more important than doing one human sacrifice
> once for all, and nothing would ever be so important again as to
> excite oneself by representations of it (241–42).

'The symbol of the Religion of Love,' in short, 'is a torture' (251),
and the God who accepts, and apparently is pleased with, the sacrifice
of his son must be wicked. Only such a God could permit an
orthodox Hell where the damned endure eternal torments which,
authorities tell us, regale the blessed in heaven.

More important than the warped theology itself is its worst
practical consequence: persecution is an all too easy recourse, as
history shows, in a Christian society worshipping human sacrifice in
service of a tyrannical deity, and fearful of Hell (251 ff.). Empson
holds also that because such tendencies are built into its theology
Christianity will always be potentially corrupting (258), though a
check was put on its worst excesses at the period of the scientific
revolution, and especially by the development of a new secular and
sceptical philosophy. 'A decisive swing of public opinion against the
Christian use of torture heaved its way through Western Europe
from the sixteenth to the eighteenth centuries, so that Milton though
brave on the subject was by no means alone there' (253). Empson cites
Voltaire and Gibbon, and looks to the Victorian Buckle's *History of
Civilization* (1857–61) to demonstrate the importance of scepticism
in breaking the hold of vindictive religious authority. In a brilliant

essay on Donne, he goes on to make clear the tie-up between science and the cross in the important changes which occurred to effect such a liberation of the human spirit.

The key idea in 'Donne the Spaceman'[34] is that Donne's knowledge of Bruno, Galileo, and the new astronomical theory of a plurality of worlds allowed him obliquely to attack in his love lyrics the Christian doctrine of hell. By raising the question of redemption in other inhabited planets, the new speculation prompted tolerance in interpreting how we should love the inhabitants of this one. Although Donne continued a Christian and therefore worshipped the cross, science modified his attitude: 'He says that he could not be robbed of the Cross, because the loss of it (or, presumably, never to have been allowed to hear of it, like the Red Indians or the inhabitants of other planets) would itself be another cross. The cross indeed is inherent in the geometry of the universe, and this is bound to make it seem independent of a particular event on earth.'[35]

Empson argues the same point concisely in a review of a book on the Romantics. Science, he says, was 'naturally your main authority about the cosmos once you had rejected the Church,' which meant rejecting as wicked the 'God who could be bought off by the crucifixion'.[36] It follows that the major Christian authors whom Empson esteems are judged good despite their acceptance of Christ's passion. He admires their implied resistance to orthodoxy, and their attainment to an attitude wherein, as he says of *Tom Jones*, 'the secret is humanist, liberal, materialist, recommending happiness on earth and so forth'.[37]

Empson as historian therefore welcomes the rise of materialism, and as a scholar he is learned also about modern science, which he reads with a positivist slant. While an undergraduate he had switched in midstream from mathematics to literature and was educated by I. A. Richards, whose own scientific bent had led him to try to put criticism on a scientific footing. Moreover, as Kathleen Raine tells us, 'behaviourism and Wittgenstein were already afoot in Cambridge,' and there was a distinct sense that 'The scientists of the Cavendish and those other laboratories . . . had set the problem poets must resolve as they could: to discover the qualitative implications of their new modelled universe'.[38] Science, it seems, was unavoidably part of the ambiance during Empson's undergraduate years, and as a mathematician he knew how to speak its kind of language. His poems show the result. We meditate paradoxes of plenum and vacuum,[39] the 'dark spaces between stars' (19) and the 'unvalanced self-enclosing air of

Heaven' (37). The physics of soap bubbles can pose a love problem (13), and of wave motion the paradox of decision (23). Exact explanation ('A delta is a mathematical expression for the area of a triangle, here zero' [112]) can help us towards the precise sense of a line, though technical language also shades provocatively towards the personal, or evokes a whole sense of the mathematician's peculiar, modern, vacant universe: 'It is this deep blankness is the real thing strange' (81). As Kathleen Raine points out, the poems are full of 'surface tensions, the behaviour of reflections, galaxies, photons, chemical transmutations; and . . . man's predicament in our brave new universe'.

The contrast with David Jones could not be clearer. Empson the anti-Christian abhors the cross, welcomes scientific scepticism and material progress, and uses complex allusions to modern physics and mathematics as a major device in his verse. He and Jones clearly believe utterly different things, and yet, as soon as we begin to look even at their opinions on language, this convenient distinctiveness begins to blur. Jones insists on the importance of the 'contactual', the sense element in words which keeps us humble and respectful of our limits. We cannot say much about higher realities, and should not venture beyond our orbit. Empson, on the other hand, encountering a thorough-going positivism like Ayer's, balks at it. He objects to the attempt in *The Foundations of Empirical Knowledge* to reduce all we know to sense data, because it shows 'a desire to push out of sight the immense queerness necessary in a universe before we can get any knowledge at all.'[40] Empson respects the surprising strangeness of the fact that we *do* know, and he has a kind of reverence for the mystery. Replying to a charge of blasphemy against God the creator, he protests: 'I did not say he was bad because he created the world, and I think that idea a disgusting one. It is petulant snootiness to say "the world is not good enough for me"; the world is glorious beyond all telling, and far too good for any of us.'[41]

I should turn now to a poem.

Arachne

Twixt devil and deep sea, man hacks his caves;
Birth, death; one, many; what is true, and seems;
Earth's vast hot iron, cold space's empty waves:

King spider, walks the velvet roof of streams:
Must bird and fish, must god and beast avoid:
Dance, like nine angels, on pin-point extremes.

His gleaming bubble between void and void,
Tribe-membrane, that by mutual tension stands,
Earth's surface film, is at a breath destroyed.

Bubbles gleam brightest with least depth of lands
But two is least can with full tension strain,
Two molecules; one, and the film disbands.

We two suffice. But oh beware, whose vain
Hydroptic soap my meagre water saves.
Male spiders must not be too early slain.

This needs some working out, but (as with Jones) a story comes clear if we attend to it.[42] The opening stanza imagines prehistoric man making a home between the terrors of forest and sea. His position between opposites, each destructive, causes the primal fear which remains part of human make-up, reflected in philosophic and scientific language of later, more sophisticated times. Man therefore is like a spider, presumably a water-walking variety,[43] assaulted by terrors from above and below. He is vulnerable in his body (the fear is cthonic, coming from under like a fish rising to eat the insect), and also in his guilty conscience, awaiting the swoop from above (the spider-eating bird). Angelic dexterity, however, graces his bestial gait because he is such a paradoxical mixture of spirit and animal.

The spider's world is then a bubble, and human society exists in the surface tension, the paradoxes of consciousness which go to make up the human world, 'Earth's surface film'. Man's bubble is glorious just because it is thin: as some plants do best in shallow soil, so the 'superficial' animal, man, is most colourful when deep enough best to refract light. This occurs at two molecules thick, which is also just enough to keep the bubble up, thus bringing us back to the opposites which sustain the contradiction of human nature from the beginning.

Now the poem turns on us, because it is not just abstract, but a love poem, and the male speaker declares himself: 'We two suffice'. But, we discover, he fears the woman, and although he (the meagre water) needs her (the hydroptic soap) he is terrified because female spiders (like Arachne) are monsters of pride and may reject him, and also because they eat up the males. Molecules and spiders coalesce in this brilliant last stanza because a soap molecule is bigger than one of water, just as the female spider is bigger (so able to overpower) the male. Yet if he does not accept her (and face his fear) his warning to her (not to be proud, and accept him) will be of no avail and there will be no bubble.

The poem is impacted, but logically precise. Its point is that man lives in the midst of contradictions, and to relax the tension is to make him less than human. A note to *Bacchus* clearly applies also to *Arachne*: 'The notion is that life involves maintaining oneself between contradictions that can't be solved by analysis; e.g., those of philosophy, which apply to all creatures, and the religious one about man being both animal and divine.' To love one another properly, we must accept the limitations implied in this situation, not refusing life by thinking we know too much (pride), or by fleeing the problem and thereby denigrating reason (fear). 'Full tension' alone suffices, but Empson is wise enough to know that just stating such a position denies it by making it absolute, therefore pre-empting fullness. His poem overcomes this by combining a sense of reason's sinuous toughness courageously getting hold of the predicament, with reason's vulnerability, 'at a breath destroyed'. The seemingly hard analytic schemes of the first twelve lines are, as we see, the tender young man bracing himself against his fear of sex, and we could admire his courage and resource, except that reason does not prevent him turning on the girl at the end, 'boy being too rude to girl,'[44] as Empson says in a note. Fear, which the boy wants to get rid of, drives him through reason to the pride he accuses the girl of having. He needs instead courage and generosity to avoid both deadly extremes, and the poem itself shows these qualities because it sees the problem all round, while participating, compassionately, in its tensions.

I am not saying Empson's poem is exactly like David Jones; only that it is not so different as their beliefs, and that these two as poets are in some ways surprisingly alike. A similar sense of the limits of human knowledge and of the contradictions in which we dwell, a similar daunting exercise of reason to express, finally, how vulnerable we are, and a similar generous, tolerant attitude to the world characterise *The Anathemata*. Moreover, throughout Empson, other favourite Jones motifs help to embody a kindred sense of man's predicament. For instance, Empson's constant delight in spheres (the curvature of space, of the earth, bubbles, and so on) combines with repeated allusions to tunnellings, blind ends, and uncertain voyages, recalling Jones's similar combination of tangled pathways and circles to suggest the same contrast between man's vision of perfection and his restricted scope. Both authors also are deliberately emblematic, and conscious of the special linguistic problems faced by poetry in the twentieth century. Empson defends the difficult techniques of modernism along lines very similar to *Epoch and Artist*, even wondering if, in the 'new great machine or mass societies . . . there is the same room for the artist' (111) as in an earlier Christian society at war with worldliness.[45]

Admittedly, there is no mistaking Empson's idiom, and a 'styptic' quality (Christopher Ricks's term) which we would not confuse with Jones at all. *This Last Pain* offers a vision of man as 'A painted, small, transparent slide' (32), which can be hand-coloured at leisure (a variation on the bubble), and concludes:

> Imagine, then, by miracle, with me,
> (Ambiguous gifts, as what gods give must be)
> What could not possibly be there
> And learn a style from a despair.   (33)

Such despair might at first strike us as a poet's self-indulgence, except that the speaker argues that it has saved him from a degrading belief in hell, and so we must strive to acquire it, with this very quality of self-deprecatory irony, as a style. But the verse is contemptuous, not merely agnostic, about the real self-indulgence of 'large dreams' (32) of heaven and hell. Just so, Empson's description of marigolds as 'plump spaced-out saints, in their gross prime, at prayer' (39) is humorous, but sardonic because the line describes less the flowers than it mocks a pious delusion that blossoming saints are somehow not self-motivated or this-worldly.

Still, my main point is that when we look at their poems, even acknowledging the contribution of personal idiom, the importance of the authors' beliefs dwindles before their compassionate sense of the perplexity of man striving to know. Jones of course would say this is what the cross really stands for, while Empson would object that Jones, like Donne, universalises the cross (seeing it as a principle of nature, symbol for paradox, and so on), and that Jones thereby distorts the orthodox doctrine to make it yield poetry. In so far as Empson would approve of *The Anathemata*, it would seem no ordinary Christian testament.

Jones we imagine would reply that it is Empson who misunderstands the doctrine, because the cross, as de la Taille argues, repudiates human sacrifice while making us see that suffering and humility remain the human lot. Moreover, since all signs participate in this supreme sign, so all the tensions and paradoxes in Empson intimate the cross, truly understood. Empson himself may hint at such a possible undermeaning when he writes, 'I, a twister, love what I abhor' (64).

Empson, however, has long been wise to this kind of ploy, and would think it a cheap trick, typical of neo-Christians trying to find their creed in all kinds of anti-Christian literature.[46] Rosemond Tuve, he suspects, has even tried it on him: she 'seemed disposed to treat me as a pagan stumbling towards the light. Clearer now about what the light illuminates, I am keen to stumble away from it.'[47] Hugh Kenner, Empson points out, is notable for perpetrating such a reading on Joyce, but since Joyce too is plainly anti-Christian, the argument is merely obtuse.[48]

And so it could go on, but it is convenient to conclude with Joyce. When both contestants, with weighty reason, claim such an authority for themselves, it is not easy to take sides, and, in one sense, the challenge of belief remains before us, starker than ever. Faced with it, Jesus had advised, sensibly, that 'ye shall know them by their fruits'. Applying his words, we can perhaps conclude that a poet's plain credo does not tell the whole story about his work's fruitfulness. The question of what an author believes cannot be irrelevant, but it seems that poetry rounds out belief, embodying it in a personal idiom and rendering it humane and generous in unexpected ways. Consequently, if literature can make one's choice of explicit beliefs more problematic, it can also, in another sense, make it less important. The main thing is, that faced with the large questions about a modern crisis in Western culture, David Jones did not gloss them over because of belief, but in facing them out with intellectual integrity and artistic grace his poetry achieves its several qualities of distinction. It has humility, breadth of vision and tolerance to balance commitment, a combination of craftsmanship, learning, and a striking range of language. Most important, there is the irreducibly poetic achievement of true rhythm fitting the sense; of a voice, fully personal but expressing exactly its public meaning in its peculiar idiom. 'For men,' as Jones says, 'can but proceed from what they know, nor is it for/the mind of this flesh to practice poiesis *ex nihilo*' (79). Material signs, the hallmarks of human enterprise, are worked and fashioned and laid aside to reveal a glimpse of the 'home shore/home light' (181).

5 Belief in Fantasy: J. R. R. Tolkien's *Lord of the Rings*

I. LEWIS CARROLL AND MOTHER GOOSE

The rise of fantasy as a kind of fiction supposedly for children but taken seriously by adults, is comparatively recent.[1] A key figure in its history is Lewis Carroll, whose uniqueness lies partly in the fact that he wrote for children out of fun, and without moralising. But Carroll's peculiar genius has also been acknowledged in the twentieth century by a range of figures about whom Charles Dodgson could have felt only misgivings. He is praised in the first surrealist manifesto of 1924, admired and imitated by Joyce and by such diverse figures as Wittgenstein, André Breton, Vladimir Nabokov and Antonin Artaud.[2]

As these men saw, although Carroll's writing opens up to children a new, amusingly irreverent world, it is far from escapist or trivial. Alice's dreams down the rabbit hole and behind the looking glass remain oddly wide-awake, and her problems are certainly real. They have to do with fears about losing her identity or her name, about the parts and size of her body, about extinction, the process of growing, arbitrary authority and conformity to laws which she wants to learn because they are adult secrets and rules of the game, but which turn out, somehow, to be less than fully human.[3] The way Carroll deals with such subjects dramatises in a highly original manner the quandary of the mind's attempting to make sense of the world. On these issues the *Alices* are reassuring because the heroine grows in the end to 'full size',[4] able to relegate to proper insignificance her childish fears: 'You're nothing but a pack of cards' (97). But also, as she awakens, dead leaves fall on her face, and the price of growing up, we conclude, is a new knowledge of mortality. In this complexity, we recognise true literature, and it emerges from a conjunction of themes which George MacDonald, one of the earliest masters of the genre, saw as peculiar to fantasy itself.[5]

Fantasy, MacDonald thought, takes its life from a sense of conflict between an actual world of adult responsibilities and an imaginary, dream-like one, to which we cannot altogether escape, except, perhaps, through death. In raising the problem of mortality through an opposition between real and imagined worlds, fantasy presents us with the problem of belief. 'We live by faith, and not by sight,' MacDonald says in his essay, 'The Imagination', and in a world where many things are not clear, imagination moves as 'the presence of the spirit of God,'[6] directing and enticing us to a vision of happiness beyond. But faith must not deny the world we live in, and 'What can be known must be known severely.'[7] Such knowledge — especially the unavoidable severity of suffering and death — is best mitigated by the solace imagination alone offers.

It is no great step from here for the Christian MacDonald to conclude that Christ's cross is the most important example of suffering which shows faith opening up to imagination the perspective of hope: 'Sorrow the Pledge of Joy'.[8] Also, because the cross puts so clearly the problem confronting acceptance of what imagination seeks to reveal, Christ's cry of abandonment is 'the deepest practical lesson the human heart has to learn.'[9] MacDonald consequently maintains that great art, and especially fantasy, shows us something of this lesson by re-enacting how man 'gazing about him in pain . . . suddenly beholds the material form of his immaterial condition.'[10] In our own lives we must strive to imitate the cross, but not, MacDonald insists, by relying on 'formula or creed';[11] rather by attempting, like Christ, to do God's will.

MacDonald's argument shows clearly how he looks to the cross and resurrection as the supreme factual instance of an experience which imagination recreates. But we must not impose our religious beliefs, and the point is ruined, MacDonald implies, as soon as fantasy becomes allegory, for then the pain is not actual, and the problem of faith is not presented directly to the reader. The cross, it seems, must remain implicit if fantasy is effectively to delineate a beauty beyond death. In that case, the status of the resultant work as specifically Christian of course becomes questionable.

I want to return to this central dilemma of fantasy and implicit belief especially in the work of J. R. R. Tolkien, a Roman Catholic whose theory of imagination is much influenced by MacDonald. But first, by looking further at Lewis Carroll, I want to ask how fantasy as a literary form deals with death and imagination, and then to suggest that its history, with respect to this preoccupation, has a specific connection with science. Carroll's writing comprises both concerns because his reception by the moderns opens up the historical issue, and his work also shows him acutely aware of human mortality.

When Alice awakens with a new knowledge of death, we see that although she has overcome her childish fears, she does not outgrow the physical anxieties on which they are based. These instead are deflected into the world of adult decorum, and in one sense the *Alices*, simply, are about the arbitrariness of adult logic in an environment where, inexplicably and often terrifyingly, we live knowing ourselves mortal. Therefore, what we take for civilised order is often the imposition of shared prejudice, the bizarreness of which is plain if we analyse its conventions imaginatively. The Gryphon and Mock Turtle we agree are absurdly composite beasts, but they are recognisable social types as well as fantastic inventions, and their effectiveness depends on our seeing both elements. The Gryphon is heraldic and noble; the Mock Turtle ungainly and, in the extreme, ignoble. High-minded social pretensions are 'mocked' truly enough by the nonsensical combination of turtle and calf, as also by the Gryphon's inability to reproduce in his own (ignoble) speech the high symbolism of his nature. Although the Mock Turtle has had an impressive education, the result is a babble of ludicrous puns upon which he erects the twin self-indulgences of rudeness ('Really you are so dull!' [75]) and sentimentality concerning his own last end ('Soooop of the e-e-evening, /Beautiful, beautiful soup!' [85]).

But although the episode parodies Victorian adults, Carroll does not discount their society, for the Mock Turtle and Gryphon also represent conditions to which Alice must adjust. She may not offend by raising the subject of death (she keeps checking herself from saying she has had fish for dinner), and yet must not be intimidated. Everywhere, instead, she measures the claims of passions ungovernable and rude (the Red Queen), against those of the disembodied symbol-making intellect (the White Queen),[12] and the ensuing conflict raises imponderable questions about language itself. Humpty Dumpty's disquisition on words, like the white sheep's myopic attention to the particular sense, opens out upon an entire panorama of riddles, puns and parodies. These give delight, but help also to show us, with Alice, something of the odd discontinuity between language and things. They pose, in so doing, the question of how, in this bizarre world, we are to commit ourselves, even to achieve normality.

For writers such as Joyce and Wittgenstein such verbal games help to confirm a favourite preoccupation with problems of relating fictive or philosophical symbols to the structure of the world. But, for Carroll, word games, and especially parody, are doubly useful because they are amusing, while allowing him also to mock at authoritative masquerades of conventional, 'improving' society. Consequently, the poems and rhymes and literary allusions with which the *Alices* abound are all parodies — except for nursery rhymes, which Carroll quotes direct. On one occasion he mocks at 'Rock-a-bye-baby' (197), but the rule stands that his literary sources except Mother Goose are all subjected to his special ironic treatment.

The reason for Carroll's singular omission is, we conjecture, less that he had some special opinion of Mother Goose, than that he did not *need* to parody it: in a way, it is already his own fictional world. Nursery rhymes are every bit as nonsensical as the *Alices*, and with the same spirit of fun; yet they are also full of adult concerns:[13]

> A penn'orth of bread to feed the Pope,
> A penn'orth of cheese to choke him
> A pint of beer to wash it down
> And a good old faggot to burn him.[14]

That is a blatant example, absent from most modern nurseries. Nevertheless, part of the charm of the better-known rhymes is that when they do have these kinds of origins, they disguise them while keeping the abrasive edge. Does 'the cat and the fiddle' refer to Catherine la Fidèle, and 'the dish and the spoon' to courtiers who had special assignments at royal banquests and, in a famous case during Elizabeth I's reign, eloped?[15] Certainly the odd narrative sense of the usual 'Rub a dub dub' starts to come clear when we look at an older version:

> Hey! rub a dub, ho! rub a dub, three maids in a tub
> And who do you think were there?
> The butcher, the baker, the candlestick-maker,
> And all of them gone to the fair.[16]

Respectable burghers should not patronise peep-shows.

Of course it is heavy-handed, even wrongheaded, to subject

nursery rhymes to this kind of torment, but it helps to show (and demonstrate the limitations of showing) that although they are especially for children, nursery rhymes are steeped in the world of adult concerns. They tell of all kinds of domestic strife, violence and prejudice. Many have political origins, and they allude constantly to problems of sex and death. As late as 1937 a Professor Allen Abbott wanted the lot reformed, and in 1952 Geoffrey Handley-Taylor analysed a selection, finding an impressive catalogue of human perversion and violence, from cannibalism and mutilation to blasphemy and 'scorning the blind'. On the other hand, Walter de la Mare, some of whose best talents were in writing for children, defended the world of Mother Goose for its wordcraft, vividness, and jewel-like poetic beauty. It is, he claimed, an ideal introduction to poetry.[17]

Nursery rhymes, we might conclude, are beloved of small children just on the edges of language themselves, for whom there is delight in the patterns of rhyme and joy in the fanciful extravagance. But also, however peculiarly present, there is a sense of the real world of everyday objects and everyday adults, even though this world does not make complete logical sense. We learn to be merry in the wilful realm of Peter Pumpkin Eater and Jack Sprat, Cock Robin, Tom who shoots the pig and the old man who gets flung down the stairs by his left leg for not attending to his prayers. Although it is futile to go about trying to 'interpret' such stuff, a feeling of the actual is so mixed in with flights of imagination as to bring these down to earth, containing them, as it were, within the frame of a tiny narrative plot, so that the mind is teased to read a story which it cannot fully grasp. They remain, in short, peculiarly free-standing structures, enacting the challenge which language itself poses to belief, and in so doing they achieve the same kind of effect as Lewis Carroll's *Alices*, which is why he has no need to parody them.

Still, there is a difference between Mother Goose and the *Alices*, for the nursery rhymes have an unself-conscious, traditional component, whereas Carroll presents us with a continuous, deliberately crafted narrative structure in prose. The *Alices*, we might say, are Mother Goose remade in the mode of realistic fiction, and here Carroll directs us to a key technique of fantasy for children, a form which attained maturity in the late nineteenth century partly as a result of his example.

II. THE CONTEXT IN HISTORY

It seems that the society which produced throughout Europe the literature of folk tales, nursery rhymes, and ballads, was strangely (to us) unaware of differences we assume to exist between the child's world and that of adults. In his classical study,[18] Philippe Ariès argues that during the Middle Ages there was no concept corresponding to our modern idea of childhood.[19] The infant became all at once a young adult, exposed to the rigours of a grown-up world and to an educational system that had no idea, in practice or theory, of developmental psychology. The adults, on their part, joined readily in games and pastimes which have now become the preserve of children: for instance, playing with dolls or hoops, or celebrating Twelfth Night and dancing round maypoles.[20] In such a situation, folk-tales and ballads must have addressed audiences of children and adults together,[21] and, certainly, there is sufficient insight and structural skill in these folk arts to render them a repository of wisdom for all the ages and conditions of men.

In the Renaissance this began to change. As oral tradition surrendered increasingly to printing, folk-tales, especially in the seventeenth century, became the sophisticated property of court audiences, and were made 'literate' by the skills of such as Perrault and Mme d'Aulnoy.[22] Although their original complexity was often retained, the tales nevertheless became something different, for they were now a vehicle of social satire. Meanwhile, Europe was discovering childhood. From the sixteenth century, educational practice began to discriminate among the capacities of children, and to care for their needs in graded classes.[23] In the visual arts, family portraits showed a new interest in younger members, whose dress increasingly came also to mark their distinctive place in society.[24] In the seventeenth century, Henry Vaughan and Thomas Traherne produced a new kind of poetry celebrating the child's unspoiled vision, while John Locke composed his landmark manual *On Education* (1693), recommending an approach based on humane principles of mutual respect between adult and child. Much indebted to Locke,[25] John Newbery at the 'Bible and Sun' manufactured his famous series of titles for young readers.

Newbery's gaily designed and whimsical books were in some ways ahead of their time. Locke had distrusted the fictive imagination, and, although he respected children, felt they would be better kept away from imaginative literature. In the eighteenth century, children's books by and large confirmed Locke's prejudice, and although children were a good deal catered to in literature during this century, the edification was largely in prose, and was certainly moral.[26] Writers such as Anna Laetitia Barbauld and Hannah More exerted widespread influence, and Lady Eleanor Fenn caught their spirit in making clear that her fairy stories were really fables: that is, 'showing them [children] what may happen to them if they do not act as they ought to do.'[27]

Against this, Charles Lamb reacted vigorously, complaining that 'Mrs. Barbauld's stuff'[28] had driven out the happy books of John Newbery, and it remained for the Romantic movement to reverse the predominant eighteenth-century emphasis. If the child was in a sense father of the man, in being cut off from his childhood experience, the man had cut himself off from his own roots in nature.

While the chief Romantics made of their visionary attitude to childhood a philosophic statement expressed in language of revolutionary fervour, the later nineteenth-century by and large tempered the fervour and often tainted the vision with sentimentality. But a number of important enterprises had been set off by the new movement, for the sense of a child's visionary wisdom came to include not only the early years of the individual man, but of the culture itself. A consequent re-appreciation of fairy tales and ballads affected the mainstream of nineteenth-century literature, and re-installed the realm of faerie and folk wisdom in the nursery. From the Brothers Grimm to Hans Anderson and Andrew Lang we watch an attempt to recapture the richness of medieval European traditions, and, under the watchful eye of nineteenth-century sophistication both in scholarship and narrative skill, to make these once more widely available and respected forms of literature.[29] The extraordinary richness of children's books in the late nineteenth and early twentieth centuries lies in the fact that they combine a romantic insight into the importance of children's sensibilities, with a high moral purpose backed by the skills of scholarship and the techniques of narrative prose.[30]

One result was fantasy, a new genre which used narrative conventions to re-make the world of fairy stories by way of realistic fiction.[31] In so doing, fantasy provokes, deliberately, the question of belief as George MacDonald says, for it comes alive in that hesitation we feel in deciding clearly between reality and imagination.[32] The main difference between this and the traditional tale is that fantasy, by self-consciously using literary forms, *thematises the relationship itself of language to reality*. Lewis Carroll's *Alices* are key examples. Like the best fantasy, they show an actual, 'prosaic' social world confronted by a heightened, interior world of imagination, both complementing and challenging it. A further example is the *Jungle Books* of Rudyard Kipling.[33]

III. RUDYARD KIPLING: MOWGLI'S CHOICE OF WORLDS

Kipling's main focus is on Mowgli, the child who is lost and raised by wolves. But the Mowgli sequence is interspersed with stories on other subjects, partly to suggest that the 'law' the boy discovers is not confined to this particular jungle. Yet, although each Mowgli story is complete in itself and separated from the others by interspersed materials, his adventures form a sequence. Together, they make up a larger account of the boy's development towards the adult world. Civilisation is his birthright, but he must leave his friends and protectors in the jungle, together with their thrilling, unself-conscious, perilous existence, in order to realise it. The language of nature, we find, and the language of humans are tragically divorced, and, for Mowgli, growth also involves loss.

To create a sense of the larger narrative while presenting it thus discontinuously, Kipling is careful to establish links between his episodes. He often begins a new story with a recapitulation ('You will remember that Mowgli spent a great part of his life . . .'),[34] or indicates how a tale fits with the earlier sequence ('It was after the letting in of the Jungle that the pleasantest part of Mowgli's life began' [II, 159]). There are also hints that the stories chronicle only some parts of a wider history, which is too complex to tell completely ('So you will never be told how the Mad Elephant of Mandla . . .' [II, 159]), and which reaches beyond the compass of Mowgli's jungle existence ('years afterward he became a man and married. But that is a story for grown-ups' [I, 79]). The conventions of short story and narrative help to create a sense of verisimilitude; of a world of events faithfully recorded, though passing beyond the story's frame.

But the adventures also take place in an enchanted realm which is at once a child's play-world of imagination and a world of archetypal strangeness and fabulous power,[35] both of which resist the conventions of narrative realism. This is why the stories hint only discontinuously at narrative: in Mowgli's world reality is not differentiated into imaginative and actual, noumenous and socially conventional. Mowgli does not even speak human language, but converses with the beasts in their own fashion. He does not think with his head, but viscerally, by his instincts ('I have another thought in my stomach' [II, 64]). He experiences fire as a 'red flower' (II, 49), and money as 'The stuff that passes from hand to hand and never grows warmer' (II, 60).

On this kind of material, the lyrical range of Kipling's style, embellished with quaint, exotic artifice, provides a strangeness at once fresh and heightened towards the poetic. His writing evokes the preconceptual, fearless and wild world which Mowgli enjoys, but which cannot be described by the conventions of prose realism alone. Kipling therefore intersperses his narrative with songs and poems, for refrain and incantation suggest a rhythm of primary life enfolding self-conscious human thought.

This technique of mixing his genres in puzzling, often provocative ways enables Kipling to create the sense, comparable to the effects we find in Carroll, of exploring the limits of language for conveying the unself-conscious quality of Mowgli's innocent childhood. When the wolf pack howls to confuse the vain hunter, Buldeo, it does so in verse, and we are told, 'This is a rough rendering of the song, but you must imagine what it sounds like when it breaks the afternoon hush of the Jungle.' And then, 'no translation can give the effect of it' (II, 55–56). The problem of language therefore becomes the key to Mowgli's encounter with adults. 'What is the good of a man,' he said to himself at last, 'if he does not understand man's talk? Now I am as silly and dumb as a man would be with us in the Jungle. I must learn their talk' (I, 62).

As his name implies, Mowgli, the frog, is amphibious, and Kipling's achievement is to make us feel this predicament, which is also that of the child poised on the edge of words. Likewise, the stories themselves are poised, elegantly and strangely, between the songs and poems and the archaic lyrical speech of the boy to the animals ('but, oh, they have handled ye grievously, my Brothers! Ye bleed' [I, 51]), and the claim of man's language upon him ('I know not what I know! I would not go; but I am drawn by both feet' [II, 209]). To heighten the contrast, Kipling turns to mythology as well as verse. The elephant Hathai recounts, within a narrative frame which describes the jungle in severe drought, the myth of creation and fall among animals. He tells how the once golden tiger was marked with the killer's stripe because he ruined paradise by his hunting. In so doing he introduced to the animals a hairless creature going upon its hinder legs, the harbinger of fear: man (II, 15).

Of course the myth does not pertain just to animals; it is the story of Eden and Cain the first murderer and the fall from innocence which accounts for everyone's suffering in the world. We are meant to appreciate, in this similarity and overlap with the human realm, that men share nature with animals, and the story's form suggests such a meaning through the myth which contrasts but nonetheless fits into the framework of narrative prose. Here, again like Carroll, Kipling deliberately uses the conventions of realism to capture the effects of an older, dream-like mode of imagination. But Mowgli must awaken (as perhaps literature itself does) from the poetic but uncritical redolences of myth to a world marked by increasing analytic intricacy and the pursuit of objectivity: a world where nature is manipulated by the imposed categories of abstract thought, and wherein the problem of belief becomes explicit. In the *Jungle Books*, such awakening is a key for understanding the child's development, and how, proportionately to his self-consciousness, he is afflicted by awareness of separation and of his own mortality.

The King's Ankus opens with Mowgli reclining in the coils of the great python, Kaa, like a 'living arm-chair' (II, 107). The boy declares that life is better in the jungle, and denounces the ways of the 'Man-Pack' (109). But when Kaa tells of a ruined city with hidden treasure guarded by a cobra, Mowgli becomes restless and wants to see it, puzzled by his own desire, which he knows must have something to do with his humanity: 'I now remember that I was once a man' (111). The boy and giant snake make the journey together, and the cobra at first admits them entrance, but once Mowgli is inside and has chosen the ornate elephant goad, or ankus, the guardian breaks his truce. Mowgli manages to pin him with the ankus, but discovers that the cobra's poison has dried up on account of old age. The snake then furiously warns the boy about the treasure:

See, then, that the thing does not kill thee at last. It is Death! Remember, it is Death! There is enough in that thing to kill the men of all my city (117).

Mowgli takes the ankus nonetheless, but when he learns from Kaa that it is used to prod elephants, and the sharp jewelled point to wound their heads, he throws it away. A series of men who find it are killed, and Mowgli, puzzled and upset by the trail of murders, returns the ankus to the cobra, advising that a new, young snake come and help to keep it. When the guardian asks how Mowgli survived death, the boy can only admit, 'I do not know' (125).

The story is powerful and ambivalent. If Mowgli survives death because he is protected by innocence and incomprehension of human greed as well as by his obedience to the primal law against cruelty which prompts him to throw the ankus away, his innocence remains dangerous because he still releases the ankus into the world, and is to some degree instrumental in causing the series of deaths that follow. The prelapsarian bliss suggested by the boy at his ease within the coils of the giant uroboric snake is thus offset by his limited wisdom in denouncing men, for, an incomplete man himself, he is unable to forsee the results of his actions. Unfallen, he is unable to understand the meaning of death, and so to assume a fully human responsibility. Whereas the reader sees immediately the symbolic transference of the dried-up cobra's poison to the ankus, which physically resembles the snake, Mowgli does not. To the reader, but not to Mowgli, the story becomes a parable connecting the fall of man to an egocentric lust for forbidden treasure, which brings to birth the consciousness and fear of death. But Mowgli does not see these connections, and at the end knows less than the reader about why he has escaped.

In the subsequent story, *Red Dog*, Mowgli does, however, come to know death in a new way. When the boy first faces the red dog pack, he is wildly indifferent to physical danger ('here Mowgli wriggled with sheer joy – "it will be good hunting. Few of us will see another moon"' [II, 166]). He is not much changed here from the Mowgli of *The King's Ankus*, and still has no human fear of death. This could be admirable, except that there is a disturbing sense of savage incompleteness, and the remainder of the story confirms our misgivings, for it is a barbarous tale of slaughter and brutal heroism. The wild dogs are defeated, but as Akela, the old wolf-pack leader under whose protection Mowgli was adopted as a child, lies dying of his wounds, he reminds Mowgli of his human nature. The boy denies it, but Akela persists: 'Go back before thou art driven' (182).

The story is bitter, but Kipling's touch is perfect. The beginning of the series is recalled in Akela's death, which also intimates the boy's passing childhood. The barbarous action, albeit heroic, is in the end unsatisfying, but Mowgli transcends it because he is at last saddened by Akela's death. Although the boy's resourcefulness saves the pack, by relying on this very quality he is preparing to drive himself out, and the story is a kind of convulsion: a triumphant but bitter birth-pang of human self-consciousness, resourceful beyond the animal in defeating the red dogs, and saddened beyond the animal by Akela's suffering.

In *Spring Running* the boy at last renounces his life immersed in the language of instinct: 'my stomach is heavy in me,' he tells Bagheera (II, 192), but the animals, oldest friends and dearest to him, all agree he must go. Unhappiness covers him as water covers a log (196), and he hides for a time in a swamp. But the emergence into the world of full human consciousness is inevitable, and there is no turning back. ' "Having cast the skin," said Kaa, " we may not creep into it afresh. It is the Law" ' (209). In the village Mowgli meets his waiting family. A young girl, surprised by him, catches her breath in a moment of alarm and wonder.

The *Jungle Books* are masterpieces of fantasy, and present us with a fusion of effects that the form demands. On the one hand is the spontaneous, dreaming and interior world of visionary imagin-ation,[36] caught in the language of poetry and myth and the exotic description of jungle adventure; on the other, the conventions of realistic narrative fiction, suggesting an actual waking world to which the visionary psyche must adapt. As Rosemary Sutcliff says, Mowgli is faced with an 'unbearable choice to be made between world and world,'[37] and the mythopoeic sense of wonder cast against narrative technique raises, as Chesterton remarks of the *Just So Stories*, the deep question of relating 'knowledge and science':[38] this is to say, reality perceived respectively by the wondering imagination, and by objectifying reason, the 'habitual outlook' of positivism, as Harvey Darton says, which prevailed when Kipling wrote.[39]

Yet the process of Mowgli's growing up is also that of all children challenged by the puzzling impositions of human discourse upon complex living nature. The expression of this process recapturing an earlier literary mode of imagination by means of a later, more self-conscious one, is, once again, the central technique which gives us that remarkable flowering of fantasy in children's books during the reigns of Victoria and Edward VII. The genre, at its height in this period, depends upon, because it reacts against, the description of reality assumed by a positivist, empirical attitude to corporeal nature as pre-eminently describable in objective terms. Such an attitude informs (without of course determining the literary achievement of) realistic narrative prose itself. But fantasy confronts this universe with another, equally compelling reality of imagination, calling into question the primacy of the empirical view. In so doing, it grounds itself on our desire to avoid the inevitable end of all ordinary, observed, material things in the world: death and decay. The hesitation we feel, as we read a work of fantasy, about what is really real, presents us, therefore, with the challenge of belief in relation to language itself, and does so in an acute form because a modern self-consciousness nurtured on empirical 'realism' sees itself with special clarity as an ego set over against the world of objects. In such isolation it becomes all the more aware of how the problem of suffering can hinder commitment.

Belief, we could say, remains the major explicit concern of fantasy, and mortality its major implicit theme. Indeed, for J. R. R. Tolkien, the Christian gospels, because they centrally raise the problem of belief, are fairy stories of the highest order.[40] Moreover, Tolkien acknowledges himself preoccupied throughout his imaginative writing with death,[41] so that the conjunction of his writing and his Christianity comes to focus, as it does with George MacDonald, on the challenge posed to faith by Christ's cross.

IV. TOLKIEN: ARCHETYPE AND ARTIFACT

Faerie is for Tolkien a realm of enchantment where we discover the power of language for combining the elements of 'primary' creation to make a 'secondary' world of imagination. To enquire about the origins of faerie is therefore to ask about the origins of language (17), and, clearly, we must take seriously the enchanting, subcreative power of the human mind to make as it is made, for through it man explores some of the primal desires of his own nature (13). Fantasy, in short, is for Tolkien a human right, and only by unhappy misunderstanding were fairy stories dismissed, during the Renaissance (6), as unworthy of adult attention, and then relegated to the nursery.

This unfortunate process was accelerated by the advent of industrialism, and the advances of technology in his own century occasioned in Tolkien a resigned pessimism, for he saw the mechanisation of human society as directly opposed to the literary values he cherished.[42] These, even though founded in imagination, Tolkien vigorously maintains are not escapist (60), because the power of subcreation lies to a large degree in the sense of an actual world that it communicates. Faerie is not just dreamland; dreams are subjective imaginings, while in faerie we meet the primal human desire for 'realization, independent of the conceiving mind, of imagined wonder' (14). We want the deepest desires of our nature to be true, and the power of faerie lies in showing us that they are.

Tolkien here resorts to a neologism, 'Eucatastrophe,' to describe the happy reversal or turn of events which breaks through the tragic frame of suffering in a sucessful fairy story to reveal, in a moment of poignant joy, that the reader's profoundest wish really is for the end not to be in misery and defeat. He gives an example:

> Seven long years I served for thee,
> The glassy hill I clamb for thee,
> The bluidy shirt I wrang for thee,
> And wilt thou not wauken and turn to me?
>
> He heard and turned to her (70).

The verse is from 'The Black Bull of Norroway', but the 'turn' is in prose, and the contrast effects formally the breaking of the frame which the theory describes. Once more, Tolkien demonstrates the recurrent technique whereby fantasy mixes genres to represent thematically how the folk imagination operates. Our belief is challenged through the confrontation of two realms of experience; the actual-physical, to which belong suffering and death (the eucharist dependent on actual crucifixion), and the imaginary, which transcends these by pointing to another order, founded on desire (the eucharist as communion of saints).

In a much more worldly and pragmatic assessment of how fairy tales address our desires, the Freudian child psychologist Bruno Bettelheim alludes often to Tolkien's theory. *The Uses of Enchantment*[43] (the title itself recalls Tolkien) admires the literary structure and Freudian orthodoxy of some of the world's best-known fairy tales as bringing to bear a profound wisdom upon the minds of children faced with problems of growing up into a world of adult values. Sex, death, sibling rivalries, and the achievement of independence from family and parents in order to make one's way in the world, are some of the themes closest to the heart of this kind of literature. Of course the Freudian imbroglios were not explicitly understood by the original compliers, but are expressed nonetheless with a consistency and moving power which shows how imagination can often render effectively truths that the analytic mind may not fully grasp.[44]

Whereas Tolkien talks of Eucatastrophe to describe this reassuring function of imagination, Bettelheim argues (more empirically-minded but in the same spirit) that the happy turn is an encouragement to a child because it suggests that solutions to problems of adjustment in the adult world are emergent in the course of nature itself. Developing this point of view, Bettelheim laments the lack of appreciation of faerie in our own day, and, again like Tolkien, points to the period of the scientific revolution as a prime cause of modern disenchantment. He even suggests that 'What seems desirable for the individual is to repeat in his life span the process involved historically in the genesis of scientific thought.'[45] In other words, the emergence of a modern post-scientific and critical consciousness from an older mode of apprehension more fully steeped in imagination, requires a self-conscious recapitulation in the growth of each of us to adulthood. Bettelheim does not say how this is accomplished, but one means of expressing the same intuition is through the self-conscious re-capitulation of the development of literature itself in the practice of fantasy exemplified in Carroll and Kipling. The rise of scientific method and empirical philosophy is therefore important not only for explaining the rise of fantasy in historical terms, but for understanding the kinds of questions the genre poses to people growing up in a scientific age.

Both Bettelheim and Tolkien agree, then, that faerie is dreamlike, but not to be confused with dreams; that in it we explore the deep desires of the human heart, and are made conscious of the shaping power of imagination for structuring our lives. The appropriateness of a psychological approach to this kind of material lies in the fact, as Bettelheim says, that 'childhood is the time to learn bridging the immense gap between inner experiences and the real world',[46] and psychology is particularly concerned with such adjustments, especially when they go wrong. Not surprisingly, Kipling's *Jungle Books* were favourite reading of Freud's.[47]

Yet the modern psychologist who has most to say on the psychological implications of faerie is not Freud, but Jung, and there are marked affinities between his attempt to structure the interior, dreaming and imagining world through his theory of archetypes, and the practice of fantasy as a means of making conscious the recurrent human desires. Certainly, as a literary critic, Jung is best when dealing with folk-tales, and in turning to him as a guide to Tolkien's main writing, *The Lord of the Rings*, we can assess something of the means by which Tolkien contrives to render, according to the notion of eucatastrophe, the perennial drama of the human psyche seeking to know itself in the world. But first, there is a further, general point about the connection between fantasy and psychology, which Bettelheim does not mention. Insofar as psychology is an objective science of man's imagination, it usurps fantasy which presents imagination as something which cannot be understood in objective terms.[48] To determine, therefore, what it is exactly that makes the *literature* in fantasy, a psychological perspective can be potentially instructive, because the critic can use it to isolate the artist's special contribution.

First, the reader of the essay on fairy stories cannot easily avoid the Jungian flavour of several of Tolkien's key ideas.[49] He describes faerie in relation to dream, stating that in both 'strange powers of the mind may be unlocked' (13). He talks of the encounter with 'certain primordial human desires' (13), and claims that the stories are 'plainly not primarily concerned with possibility, but with desirablity' (40). He talks of a 'Cauldron of Story' as old as the human mind, which waits 'for the great figures of Myth and History' (29) to enrich it. In the essay on *Beowulf* he appreciates the balance and 'opposition of ends and beginnings', the hero's progress from youth to old age, and the satisfaction that comes from perceiving the 'rising and setting'[50] of a life.

We can easily feel here a Jungian kind of attitude to dream and fantasy, with hints of a collective unconscious which contains archetypes stirred into activity by the artist, and it is interesting to follow such hints into *The Lord of the Rings*, where Tolkien's theory finds full embodiment as literature. The story is of course set in faerie, at a time near the beginnings of man's ascendency in the history of the world, and Middle-earth is often dreamlike: a world of shifting contours and magical transformations, of nightmarish fear and exquisite beauty. Helpful and treacherous animals work for the powers of good and evil, and landscapes are sentient embodiments of human fears and desires. It is a short step to the appearance of nature spirits, like Tom Bombadil, and, as we move closer to those who possess deeper wisdom and power, distinctions of time and space themselves begin to blur. Although directed by narrative art and a complex plot, the story moves easily through a world where forms and images blend and flow and interpenetrate, and where the eye of the beholder determines fear and terror, beauty and glory, all of which have the quality of 'interior space'[51] which Owen Barfield names as Jung's special province.

Certainly, for Jung fairy stories and dreams are characteristically inhabited by helpful and treacherous animals and monsters. Land-scapes, especially when they involve woods and mountains, are favourite representations of the unconscious,[52] and Jung also talks of a common figure, the 'vegetation numen',[53] king of the forest, who is associated with wood and water, like Tom Bombadil. We learn also how 'the concentration and tension of psychic forces have something about them which always looks like magic',[54] and in this context Jung stresses a 'contamination' of images, by which he means a tendency to overflowing contours – 'a melting down of images'.[55] This may look like distortion and can be terrifying, but can also be a process of assimilation and a source of beauty and inspiration. 'The melting process is therefore either something very bad or something highly desirable according to the standpoint of the observer.'[56]

Jung also points to certain characteristic formal elements in fairy stories, such as 'duality', 'the opposition of light and dark', and 'rotation (circle, sphere)',[57] but insists that they should not be considered apart from the psyche's complex flowing energy. Moral choices are not a matter of black or white; there is a 'bewildering play of antinomies'[58] which contributes to higher awareness. Good may be produced by evil, and possibly lead to it. This process, which Jung calls 'enantiodromia',[59] is also clearly at work in Tolkien: a broad opposition throughout *The Lord of the Rings* of light and dark, good and evil, becomes confused as we enter the minds of individuals in the actual process of finding their way. Though Gollum hates light and loves shade, Frodo's relation to Gollum is complex, and throughout the trilogy the minds of men are especially ambivalent.

That Jung and Tolkien isolate such similar general motifs is not in itself surprising, but in *The Lord of the Rings* the general sense of 'interior' drama corresponds also with particular fidelity to details of the psychic process which Jung calls 'individuation'. This is, basically, the 'realization of the whole man'[60] achieved in a balanced and fulfilled life when 'consciousness and the unconscious, are linked together in a living relation'.[61] The process involves a journey to the Self, which Jung describes as 'not only the centre' of a person's psyche but also 'the circumference which embraces both conscious and unconscious.'[62] Characteristically, the Self is represented in dreams and mythology as a mandala – a square within a circle, or circle within a square, or in figures which are spherical or contain the idea of quaternity,[63] representing wholeness.

Jung insists that individuation, or Selfhood, is not identical with ego-consciousness,[64] but, as the short-sighted ego responds to demands for inner growth, the way forward is indicated by representations of the archetypes, a series of primordial and recurring images in human experience which express the psyche's basic structure, and which become increasingly noumenous, impressive, and dangerous as they emerge from the deeper levels of the unconscious. First, and nearest to the surface, so that we can become aware of it by reflection, is the shadow. This is the 'personal unconscious', and is the 'easiest to experience'.[65] It represents the elements which a person represses as incompatible with his chosen ideal – 'for instance, inferior traits of character and other incompatible tendencies'.[66] But the shadow is ambiguous; although it contains morally reprehensible tendencies, it can also display good qualities, such as normal instincts which have been repressed but 'are needed by consciousness'.[67] In dreams, it is represented as a figure of the same sex as the dreamer, and, in accord with its ambiguous status, may be a threat which follows him, or a guide. It turns dangerous when ignored or misunderstood.[68]

Further from consciousness is the anima/animus archetype, which represents the feminine side of a man's unconscious, and the masculine side of a woman's, respectively. The anima (more important for Tolkien) is, like the shadow, ambivalent. She is both the nourishing and destructive mother:[69] the Muse who inspires man to create, and the Siren who lures him to death and destruction.[70] For Jung, 'the animus and the anima should function as a bridge, or a door, leading to the images of the collective unconscious'.[71]

Often presented with the anima as friend or protector is the hero, who characteristically appears in a dangerous situation or on a difficult quest, signifying 'the potential anticipation of an individuation process which is approaching wholeness'.[72] The hero may bear an aura of the supernatural, offsetting his vulnerability, another essential trait, for he is both semi-divine and child. 'This paradox . . . runs through his whole destiny like a red thread. He can cope with the greatest perils, yet, in the end, something quite insignificant is his undoing.'[73] His appearance is often accompanied by strange and noumenous events: 'dragons, helpful animals, and demons; also the Wise Old Man . . . all things which in no way touch the boundaries of everyday. The reason for this is that they have to do with the realization of a part of the personality which has not yet come into existence but is still in the process of becoming.'[74]

More profound than the hero is the Old Wise Man, a helpful figure who, 'when the hero is in a hopeless and desperate situation . . . can extricate him.'[75] He is the magician, the Guru, a personification of wisdom. He seems not to be bound by time, and is endowed with magical power. Also, 'apart from his cleverness, wisdom, and insight, the old man' is 'notable for his moral qualities'.[76] But he, like the other archetypes, is also ambivalent,[77] and in him the enantiodromia of good and evil can appear most paradoxically.

In *The Lord of the Rings* the central quest involving a ring, symbol of binding and wholeness which must be preserved from the powers of darkness and evil by the powers of light and goodness, can indicate a typical journey towards individuation. It promises a 'true conjunctio' but involves the threat of dissolution. The ringbearer, Frodo, is at first childlike, and must endure the terrors of monsters, dragons, and the underworld. Aragorn, his companion, is, by contrast, of strange and royal origins, protector of a noble lineage, and a semidivine figure with the magic power of healing. Together, Frodo and Aragorn represent different aspects of the hero – Frodo his childlikeness, Aragorn his nobility and power, and each supports and learns from the other. But the hobbit, as we shall see, receives foremost attention, and the story is in a special sense his. As it proceeds, Frodo puts off more and more the childlike ways of the Shire and assumes the lineaments of heroism, acquiring, at the end, a noumenous quality. Also, as his understanding deepens, Frodo moves through a series of encounters with the archetypes, charted by the book's main action. He meets the shadow (Gollum), anima (Galadriel) and Old Wise Man (Gandalf). Each has a good and bad side, the good leading to understanding and fellowship, the bad to death, isolation, and loss of identity or Self. So Galadriel is opposed by Shelob, the heroes by the Ringwraiths, and Gandalf by the evil magician Saruman. Gollum is, by nature, ambivalent, for he is the shadow, or personal unconscious, and we will deal with him first.

At the beginning, Frodo is innocent of the world, and his naïveté is a danger to him. Certainly, he does not realise he has a shadow, or that he is being pursued by Gollum. But he comes to feel a vague discomfort, which increases as the story develops. As the fellowship sets out for Lothlorien, Frodo feels 'he had heard something, or thought he had. As soon as the shadows had fallen about them and the road behind was dim, he had heard again the quick patter of feet'.[78] The others do not notice. Soon after, Frodo is startled by 'a shadowy figure', which 'slipped round the trunk of the tree and vanished' (I, 360). Frodo alone sees Gollum, who moves in darkness for fear of the light.

Gollum is of the same race and sex as Frodo, which, for a shadow figure, is appropriate. He is a hobbit, fallen into the power of the ring and debased to a froglike, underground creature of primitive cunning and instinct. He is certainly a threat, but one which Frodo must learn to acknowledge as representing a potential evil in his own being. To ignore the shadow is to risk inflation of the ego,[79] and the relationship between Frodo and the repulsive Gollum must become one of mutual acknowledgment, even if disapproved by others. Sam, to his own consternation, sees the peculiar link between the two: they 'were in some way akin and not alien: they could reach one another's minds' (II, 225). So Frodo insists on unbinding Gollum and trusting his promise, and the shadow becomes a guide, though without ceasing to be dangerous. He leads Frodo first to Shelob's lair, but also saves him at the last moment from an inflation of pride which would mean the destruction of the quest: 'But for him, Sam, I could not have destroyed the Ring. . . . So let us forgive him!' (III, 225).

Frodo has confronted Gollum before the party arrives at Lothlorien, but only after the encounter with Galadriel does he learn how to bind and release the shadow. The meeting with Galadriel is an overwhelming experience for the entire company, and although she deals more with Frodo than with the others, she is not related to him in such a particular way as Gollum. Her significance is less in terms of a personal than a collective unconscious and she represents anima, a figure which, Jung says, is often 'fairy like' or 'Elfin'.[80]

Galadriel is, of course, an Elf, and she is also a bridge to the deeper elements of the psyche, revealing hidden contents in the souls of the company. 'None save Legolas and Aragorn could long endure her glance' (I, 372) as she shows to each the dangers of the quest and the personal weakness each brings to it. In her mirror she shows to Frodo 'parts of a great history in which he had become involved' (I, 379), and he responds with awe and terror. The noumenous power of anima almost overwhelms him, so that he even offers her the ring. Galadriel replies in words which indicate the dangers of fixation, and warns of the anima's destructive aspect:

> You will give me the Ring freely! In place of the Dark Lord you will set up a Queen. And I shall not be dark, but beautiful and terrible as the Morning and the Night. . . . All shall love me and despair! (I, 381).

Instead, Frodo must use Galadriel's knowledge and wisdom to

further the quest: she is a bridge to the darkness of Mordor, to which the hero still has to travel. But the hobbit now carries with him the influence of the anima's fairy-like, timeless, and magically radiant beauty, and it serves to protect him. She gives him also a phial of light to bear into the darkness. It not only shows the way, but helps him against the Ringwraiths, and enables him to face Shelob.

If Galadriel is beneficent, Shelob the spiderwoman is the destructive anima who often poisons to kill. Gollum talks of a mysterious 'she' who may help him win back the ring: 'all living things were her food, and her vomit darkness' (II, 332). But as Frodo meets her, he holds up the light: ' "Galadriel!" he called, and gathering his courage he lifted up the Phial once more' (II, 330). Galadriel's light and Shelob's darkness, the principles of life and death, of nourishment and destruction, contest for Frodo who must meet them both – the anima in her two aspects.

Other anima figures appear throughout *The Lord of the Rings*, and mainly we think of Arwen, another Elf, whose 'loveliness in living thing Frodo had never seen before nor imagined in his mind' (I, 239). She is destined to marry Aragorn, and their union represents the 'syzygy',[81] or ideal bond in which, says Jung, anima and animus 'form a divine pair.'[82]

Less fortunate than Arwen is Eowen, whose love for Aragorn cannot be reciprocated, with the result that she falls victim to her own animus. When Aragorn leaves her, as he must, Eowen goes in disguise as the warrior Dernhelm who 'desired to have nothing, unless a brave death in battle' (III, 242). In Jungian terms, she is possessed by the negative animus, often represented as a death-demon,[83] which drives her towards suicide. Such possession often results, says Jung, in 'a transformation of personality' which 'gives prominence to those traits which are characteristic of the opposite sex'.[84] Only through the love of Faramir does Eowen change – 'or else at last she understood it. And suddenly her winter passed, and the sun shone on her' (III, 243).

The heroic figures of the trilogy are Aragorn and Frodo. Aragorn is a king in exile, preserver of a noble lineage, who passes through the paths of the dead, fights a crucial turn in the epic battle, and proclaims a new dispensation. The hero, as Jung says, is a 'greater man . . . semi-divine by nature', who meets 'dangerous adventures and ordeals',[85] and encounters the Old Wise Man. But Aragorn's semi-divine quality is not immediately obvious, for he appears first as the ranger Strider, suspected by the party and by us. Only when we pass more deeply into the quest do we learn of his noble lineage, of his destiny and his power of healing. He grows in our minds in stature as he looks into the magic palantir, passes through the paths of the dead, and is received, finally, as king. Aragorn is thus the traditional quest hero, but we observe him, primarily, from the outside.

Frodo, though his birth is peculiar among hobbits, is not a born hero like Aragorn, and we observe him more from within, often sharing his point of view. As the story opens, we find in Frodo a child's vulnerability, which, according to Jung, often compensates the hero's powers. But Frodo gradually develops away from his early naïveté; from the diffident questioning of why he was chosen, and his callow thoughts of destroying the ring with a hammer (I, 70). Growth into higher consciousness, we discover with him, is painful. Yet, as he carries the burden his power increases, and as he passes through the dark experiences which lead to the Council of Elrond, the noumenous aura and magic of the hero archetype adhere increasingly to him. He finds he can see more clearly in the dark. In Galadriel's mirror he sees the depths of the history in which he is involved, and becomes the bearer of magic light into perilous realms. Slowly he acquires wisdom and nobility comparable to Aragorn's so that, as we accompany Frodo's development and participate in it, we come to understand Aragorn himself more fully. And as the tale ends, Frodo has achieved a heroic stature verging on otherworldliness.

As each archetype has a negative aspect, so the hero, says Jung, is especially threatened by dissolution 'under the impact of the collective forces of the psyche'. The characteristic challenge is from 'the old, evil power of darkness'[86] which threatens to overwhelm the self-identity the hero strives to bring about. The power of Sauron the Dark Lord is exactly such an old and evil force, and in *The Lord of the Rings* his representatives, the negative counterparts of the heroes, are the Black Riders. Their menace balances perfectly the power that emanates from Aragorn, while their own dissolution in Sauron's old and evil darkness, representing the loss of Self, is indicated by the fact that the riders have no faces.

As the heroes resist losing their identity they grow towards wisdom, represented by the Old Wise Man, who appears in the trilogy primarily as Gandalf. More mysterious than the heroes, Gandalf's part in the quest is often beyond the story's reach, and his knowledge remains unfathomable. When we first meet him, he seems more a clown than a powerful magician, but seeing wisdom as foolishness is the traditional error of fools, and, in this case, reflects the naïveté of the comfortable hobbits. Gandalf's 'fame in the Shire was due mainly to his skill with fires, smokes, and lights. . . . To them he was just one of the "attractions" at the Party' (I, 33). But Gandalf, like Aragorn, grows in stature as we learn more about him. He is continually ahead of the quest, exercising a strange, quasi-providential control. He reproves Frodo for many mistakes and seems to know the whole story in detail, even though it happened in his absence. 'You seem to know a great deal already' (I, 231), says Frodo. We do not question Gandalf's understanding, but know that its source is beyond our ken.

According to Jung, the Old Wise Man appears especially when the hero is in trouble ('In a situation where insight, understanding, good advice, determination, planning, etc., are needed but cannot be mustered on one's own resources'[87]), and often he adopts 'the guise of a magician'.[88] He is, essentially, a spirit archetype,[89] and therefore is sometimes represented by a ' "real" spirit, namely, the ghost of one dead'.[90] Tolkien, interestingly, once described Gandalf as 'an angel',[91] and we are to believe that he really died in the struggle with Balrog, reappearing as Gandalf the White, an embodied spirit. Also, as Jung points out, the Old Wise Man gives to the hero 'the necessary magical talisman',[92] which, in Gandalf's case, is the ring itself.

The Old Man, however, has a wicked aspect too. Just as Galadriel has Shelob, and the heroes their Ringwraiths, so Gandalf has the magician Saruman. They meet on equal ground, and between them the great struggle for self or dissolution of self is once again fought: 'Like, and yet unlike' (II, 183), says Gimli as he observes the two at Isengard. Their contest is based on a symbolism of light: Saruman is at first White, and Gandalf, the lesser magician, is grey. But as Gandalf becomes white Saruman falls to the powers of darkness and his robes become multi-coloured, 'woven of all colours, and if he moved they shimmered and changed hue so that the eye was bewildered' (I, 272). Saruman's multi-colours, like the facelessness of the riders, suggests a dissolution of identity. White is whole; fragmented, it is also dissipated.

The final, most elusive, archetype is that of the Self. Tolkien's trilogy as a work of art reconciling a variety of psychological types is its most satisfactory representation. But the character who comes closest to attaining wholeness is Sam Gamgee. He has become, at the end, Samwise, but is less removed from us than Frodo or the other main characters. As he leaves, Frodo says to Sam: 'You will have to be one and whole, for many years. You have so much to enjoy and to be, and to do' (III, 309). The commendation of Sam's maturity and the directive to return to the ordinary world is a directive also to the reader: ripeness is all. But such wisdom as Sam achieves is not easily come by, as the story indicates. The shire is not a haven, and the tale insists that there are no havens in a world where evil is a reality.

The correspondence, in all this, between *The Lord of the Rings* and the Jungian classification reflects equally creditably on Tolkien the teller of tales, that he intuits the interior structure of the psyche so well, and Jung, who analyses with such penetration the images of poetry. But it also raises more clearly the question about analysis as an objectification of a quality (imagination) the function of which is to *resist* analysis. If Tolkien's book opens up in such a satisfactory way to the archetypes, why do we need to read it?

One answer is in terms of what Tolkien sees as fantasy's implicit Christian theme. The sense of pain and separation which is one side of eucatastrophe (Christ's death) must be realised vividly because, without it, the other, joyful side (resurrection) cannot appear convincing. But now the problem restates itself, for theology is more analysis, another kind of imposition on imagination, which in this case threatens to reduce the story to Christian allegory. Tolkien is well known for his dislike of allegory,[93] but he admits that his entire tale is about death, its inevitability and the sense of it as an 'unjustifiable violation'. 'You may agree with those words or not, but those are the keyspring of *The Lord of the Rings*.'[94] The actuality of suffering in a real world is, indeed, something that faerie cannot ignore without becoming escapist, and the theory of eucatastrophe is as close as Tolkien can come to explaining the analogy between gospel history and fairy story, while still maintaining that in fantasy the Christian element must be implicit. Of all the myths which man has created to explain his suffering condition, Tolkien argues, one is different because it was a historical fact. The Christian story 'entered History and the primary world', and in it the 'desire and aspiration of sub-creation has been raised to the fulfilment of Creation. The Birth of Christ is the eucatastrophe of Man's history. The Resurrection is the eucatastrophe of the story of the Incarnation' (71−72). Just as resurrection breaks the frame of the story of Christ's suffering and death, so the end of a good fairy story has the sudden effect of miraculous grace, giving a 'fleeting glimpse of Joy' (68). Clearly, if this conviction is to become more than theory, Tolkien must realise in his own tale that irreducible sense of a primary world where the suffering actuality of human nature is found,[95] which helps to explain the inordinate and painstaking creation for Middle-earth of an elaborately detailed history with a set of languages, traditions, legends, myths, annals, as well as a precisely described geography. The combination of Tolkien's academic perfectionism with his love for invented languages (which had engaged him since childhood)[96] helps to create the book's extraordinary effect of having recorded some actual, past civilisation. Only with such a real sense of time and place can Providence be made so believably obscure, and Frodo declare, in a manner that convinces us, 'I am tired, weary, I haven't a hope left' (III, 195). Only, that is, in terms of a real, physical cross, and with it the sense of total abandonment, can the resurrection, the joy at the end of the tale, show to man the persistence and profundity of his desires, and transform the dream-scape of archetypes into an experience of a real world.

Yet there is a difference between Tolkien's use of fiction and that of Kipling and Lewis Carroll, for whom the actual world, on which their narratives impinge, is recognisably the society of their own time. Disraeli, Darwin, and a parade of Victorian stereotypes remind us, in the *Alices*, of where we really are, while Mowgli has to assess the relative merits of British and native justice, and come to terms with living in a real native village, among cattle herders and hunters and cultivators of the land. But Tolkien's hobbits and his entire 'historical' world remain a fantasy, and their author execrates every attempt at allegory connecting them with social history. Only the most extraordinary care could go the long way round, and make all this seem real, not bogus: only something approaching dementia, we might add, could make a man *want* it to seem real, and to pursue his task so tirelessly. And at this point the critics divide. The defenders claim a work of genius (*The National Review* names *The Lord of the Rings* the best book of the century, though allowing, inscrutably, *Ulysses* to be the greatest),[97] while the detractors, beginning with Edmund Wilson,[98] say that it is an escapist fake.

The debate begins to have a familiar ring: is this bogus or genuine art, is it eccentric or touched with genius, is it escapist from actual concerns of the twentieth century or a triumph of individual invention in a time given over increasingly to shoddy values, are the handbooks and readers' guides which the literary industry has created (as it has for so many 'difficult' modern works) evidence of esoteric wantonness, or keys unlocking the author's achievement in depth? It all sounds like the critical debate on modernism itself. And here a final point can bring us back to the *Alices*, for Tolkien, like Carroll, was fascinated by that modern preoccupation with the sheer process of language in structuring, and in a sense creating, reality. 'He had been inside language', C. S. Lewis once said, and that is why his writing, even on academic subjects, was always lively.[99]

Tolkien himself talked repeatedly about language in a manner suggesting its autonomy as a symbol-structure, entailing the complete universe of its implicates. As a child he had invented private languages, and he tended to do so backwards, on historical principles, thus in a sense finding out what was involved in the meaning of his invented words, rather than being content just to invent more of them, forwards as it were, as he required.[100] Rather, he was concerned with the logic of his invention, and his attitude carried over also into his early experiments with poetry. On taking up some verses to develop them into a story, he was asked by his friend G. B. Smith what the verses were really about. 'I don't know,' Tolkien replied, 'I'll try to find out.'[101] It seems that language implies its own story, and is not subject to the free-inventiveness of the author. Language is autonomous, and it is for us to discover the consistency and meaning which lie within it, so that the problem of escapism in *The Lord of the Rings* becomes, in the end, one with the problem of language and its relation to reality.[102] Michael Holquist, writing on Lewis Carroll's modernist qualities, could be writing also of Tolkien, attempting 'to insure through the structure of his work that the work could be perceived only as what it was, and not some other thing; the attempt to create an immaculate fiction, a fiction that resists the attempts of readers, and especially those readers who write criticism, to turn it into an allegory, a system equatable with already existing systems in the non-fictive world.'[103]

Tolkien, however, would disagree on one point, for in the *Essay on Fairy Stories* he accuses Lewis Carroll of avoiding the real issue by having his stories occur as dreams (14). Carroll, in short, does not go far enough, whereas Tolkien, in attempting so self-consciously to recapture by means of a realistic narrative the very quality of faerie, has indeed gone the whole way: in his work, *realistic narrative itself is held up for our inspection as a literary genre*. It too is a kind of imagination, and when we see this we can see how fantasy in *The Lord of the Rings* has been pushed to its logical limits, beyond Kipling and beyond Carroll too, finally presenting itself to itself as a peculiar combination of literary conventions.

Tolkien's enterprise reaches a bizarre but uncannily fitting conclusion with the *Silmarillion*,[104] which provides not only a mine of legend and a creation myth upon which the annals of Middle-earth and the saga of *The Lord of the Rings* are based, but an actual scholar (Christopher Tolkien), who turns up to edit the documents from their incomplete manuscript sources. Because the *Silmarillion* is his earliest work, and was left incomplete, to be printed in a modern 'scholarly' edition, Tolkien creates, inadvertently, the pattern itself of the historical development of myth into folk-tale, novel and finally fantasy, a genre which is, in turn, partly a result of scholarly appreciation (with editions) of folk literature. The process of recapitulation is complete, and, in Tolkien, itself appears as a fiction. Within it, we experience the 'interior psychodrama' of the archetypes and the 'objective' world of the history, which Tolkien presents alike as imaginary structures. In the interplay between them we watch the process of the heart's desires in conflict with the inevitable historical fact of suffering and death (the implicit Christian theme of fantasy is the cross), and we can apply as we may the resultant literature to the world in which we live, according to whether or not we deem it credible (the obvious theme of fantasy is belief).

To summarise: I have shown that the challenge offered to belief by human mortality is a central concern in modern fantasy, and that the genre itself can be described in terms of a relationship between history and the rise of science. Besides being a reaction to positivism, fantasy reminds us how the growing psyche is challenged by the world to act imaginatively, and Bettelheim claims that traditional fairy tales are an important encouragement to psychological maturity in a scientific age.

By analysing *The Lord of the Rings* according to the system of a major psychologist, we see how firm (at least according to this psychologist's terms) is Tolkien's sense of the structure of interior life. Yet Tolkien takes his place in the history of fantasy not just because of this, but by recreating the world of faerie through realistic narrative, and then pushing fantasy's typical concern with language and belief towards an unprecedented limit of ingenuity. Fantasy's central challenge becomes real, not allegorical, only if the story hits us with the force of actual history. Only after feeling the weight of an impediment can we be gratified by release.

But for Tolkien at this point, the quandary I raised with George MacDonald returns in force. If fantasy is not allegorical, its author's Christian beliefs must be implicit, and we then ask how we can call them Christian at all. On this question, Tolkien offers his theory of eucatastrophe, explaining that faerie operates in the same way as the death and resurrection of Christ, which is a true story. Yet this argument only serves to show in what a curious way Tolkien's fantasy flirts with Christian ontology. The story of Christ's death is significant because it happened: a man died, a fact on which Christianity places immense theological weight. No Christian, certainly, would be content to say that the crucifixion, though not factually true, is imaginatively true. Isn't it then worrying that Middle-earth and the rest are just a story?

Here, Tolkien's special ingenuity suggests that the fictional world itself constitutes, with its special autonomy, a part of the fabric of reality, and therefore can capture, by way of true analogy, the experience of death and resurrection. But the problem, despite Tolkien's subtlety, will not be shaken off. In so far as the fictional world is autonomous, it can say nothing about *us*, unless we think all events are imaginative. And in so far as it says something about *us*, it is representative, not autonomous and thus not part of the fabric of fact.

It is interesting that many great writers of the golden age of children's fantasy were Christian. They seem to realise in common the potency of the genre for expressing the psychological importance of belief, especially in a materialist age given to scepticism and disposed to dampen optimistic faith that all manner of things will be well. But these writers seem also to discover the importance, in such matters, of writing, like Lewis Carroll, without moralising. Though Christian, their belief remains secretly within their stories, showing itself most clearly in a quality of wondering acceptance that pain mingles strangely with joy, which is, at least, a predisposition to religious belief.

6 Belief in Thinking: Owen Barfield and Michael Polanyi

Owen Barfield is a literary critic in the Romantic tradition, who looks to the history of science, especially to the crucial period of the seventeenth century, for clarification of the relationship between poetry and religious belief in his own time. Michael Polanyi is a scientist who looks to the language of religious faith to help illuminate the function of science in an open society, which he sees beginning in the seventeenth century and which he wishes to defend in the twentieth. The theories of both men meet and overlap on the questions of imagination and the place of art in society. Polanyi contends that appreciating the structure of a work of art can help us to acknowledge the importance of similar principles in procedures of scientific investigation. Barfield sees the poem as a structure wherein forgotten original meanings are made conscious by the yoking of incompatibles as metaphor, and argues that the nature of metaphor in modern literature is deeply influenced by the scientific revolution. From divergent starting points in fields in which they are distinguished, both men find themselves concerned with science in relation to religious belief, and both find in the activity of imagination the paradox of faith within which man as scientist and artist is constrained to operate.

I. OWEN BARFIELD

A recent critical assessment[1] of Barfield claims that when the literary history of our time is written, he will be mentioned as a matter of course. The main reason offered is that Barfield brings up to date a romantic tradition which had lost respectability in the early years of this century, and establishes it on a sound epistemological footing. From his first book, *Poetic Diction* (1928), Barfield's preoccupation has been the generally Romantic, more specifically Coleridgean, notion that the human mind does not merely look upon the world, but constructs it in perceiving it.[2] To interpret this idea, Barfield looks also to the anthroposophical writings of Rudolf Steiner,[3] whose early interest in Goethe had helped Barfield to find an alternative to the positivistic bias of modern science, and encouraged him to pursue this problem in context of Romanticism.[4] Steiner's 'occult' side, however, has left Barfield open to a charge of uncritical enthusiasm for arcane speculation, to which Barfield replies that Romanticism without the development Steiner brings to it is puerile.[5] With Steiner, Romanticism comes of age and his key contribution is to appreciate the favourite Romantic idea that mind participates in what it knows, and then to show this discovery as a key step in the evolution of consciousness.

Assuming the main anthroposophical teaching about a historical development of the human mind, and developing this by way of Coleridge, Barfield holds that it is necessary for our moral and spiritual welfare to understand that there is an interior aspect to evolution. Such understanding has been obscured in the twentieth century by a materialist view of the world, and especially by the widespread acceptance of a Darwinian model of mind emergent from inanimate nature. To develop this argument, Barfield draws heavily on etymology,[6] maintaining, for instance, that primitive people were not simply mistaken in attributing animistic power to objects which they could name but only explain naïvely or superstitiously. The study of language reveals rather that the holophrase[7] precedes the single name for a single object, just as mythology shows us a universe of multiple meanings interpenetrating. Early men experienced this 'original participation'[8] (the sense, that is, of spirit moving in the world and in the heavens as well as inside individuals) to a degree more pronounced than is the case today. Men, it appears, were once conscious in a different way than we are now,[9] and Barfield sees two periods before the Romantics as being especially significant in charting the evolution of the modern mind.[10]

First, Christianity introduced an original insight by way of incarnation, and, as a result, human consciousness was made so decisively aware of itself as to be able to pursue the return to at-one-ment wherein man had, at first, dwelt unself-consciously.[11] With Christ, a new value is placed on the human personality as a particular, self-aware, responsible being.[12]

The second period occurred with the scientific revolution of the sixteenth and seventeenth centuries.[13] The new science is, in a way, itself a consequence of Christianity, because the world of inanimate, quantifiable objects depends on man's self-awareness set over against extended substance.[14] But the Cartesian and Empiricist split between subject and object presupposed also a modern isolation of the ego,[15] now driven in upon itself by the widespread notion that the outside world, to be known truly, must be known impersonally and in an explicit manner. Barfield argues, to the contrary, that things in our experience are shaped by our minds,[16] and he sees the Romantics' contribution mainly in their repudiation of a positivist idolatry of objects. The imagination, they were able to show, is active in perception itself. Yet the great Romantics were without a sense of where such a demonstration should lead them; that is, towards a situation where man could, self-consciously and systematically, use his imagination to re-invest with meaning the world which a sceptical self-consciousness and scientific positivism had drained of significance other than the measurable.[17] Barfield points out that modern physics, in dealing with micro-particles, reveals more and more clearly that the roots of matter are unrepresentable,[18] and so the most recent development of science itself challenges the arbitrariness of the Cartesian co-ordinates upon which the history of physics since Descartes depended. Radically new ways of conceiving the structure of matter seem inevitable,[19] and Barfield anticipates a reunion of science and religion brought about by a progress towards convergence through separation. Such a reunion will be founded, moreover, on a mutual appreciation among scientists and men of religion of the transformative power of imagination in human thought and perception.

As is the case with any worthwhile idealism, it is diminished by summary. For Barfield this is especially so because the transformative power of imagination would be demonstrated best by the author actually using it. At this point, therefore, we can turn towards some assessment of Barfield's own gifts as a writer, and also to his sensitivity to poetry, which plays an important part in his work.

Barfield thinks, first of all, that although imagination has always been at work in literature, it is a comparatively recent development to understand *how* it has been at work, and the special achievement of Romanticism was to pioneer such an understanding. Coleridge's main insight on this question is expressed in a metaphor itself deriving from science, whereby he represents the mind as a polar structure, able to fuse together in a new meaning things which are divided, as was the world itself, according to Descartes, into extended and thinking substances. Taking up this idea, Barfield goes on to point out that polarity is not a logical concept, and must itself be grasped by imagination:

> Where logical opposites are contradictory, polar opposites are generative of each other — and together generative of a new product. . . . We can and must distinguish, but there is no possibility of *dividing* them. . . . The point is, has the imagination grasped it? For nothing else can do so. At this point the reader must be called on, not to think about imagination, but to use it. Indeed we shall see that the apprehension of polarity is itself *the basic act of imagination.*[20]

The circle is neatly closed. Polarity is basic to the act of imagination by which polarity is to be grasped, and by this device the entire gamut of human experience can be soon wonderfully collapsed. 'The ontological status of imagination turns on the relation between the mind of man and his environment; particularly on the relation between mind on the one hand and nature on the other.'[21] Imagination therefore is the activity which transmutes the dichotomy itself between subject and object: only by knowing 'that' imaginatively can I know myself, and it is absurd to claim that mind emerged (as Darwin says) from a world of inanimate objects, because objects are but one element in a bi-polar structure involving subjects. Imagination, which unites them, bespeaks rather an anterior spiritual reality, out of which our awareness of the autonomy of extramental things has developed to a degree equivalent to our self-consciousness. Only by an idolatrous mistaking of the material for the 'real' have we lost sight of this rootedness of things in the originally given meaning in which we, and the world before us, subsist.

However, because the polarity at the heart of perception is reproduced in the relation between images and structure in poetry, the experience of imagination in literature can become a guide to misdirected theories of perception. The poem, typically, shows us a passionate utterance quenched in an adapted form or frame, while the reader, a transcendent third, contains this polarity while participating in it.[22] This is explained in *Poetic Diction*, Barfield's first book, which, as he says himself, determined the future direction of his studies,

leading him through Coleridge and Steiner to a fuller exploration of
how man becomes aware of himself in history.

II. THE QUALITY OF IDEALISM

Barfield's interest in poetry is convenient because it justifies in
advance an approach which sympathetic critics of idealistic philosophy are often forced to adopt, and which involves defending an
author in the name of imaginative coherence, despite logical
deficiencies or empirical thinness. Certainly, Barfield's writing is
strongest when he attends, imaginatively, to metaphoric effects of
compound verbal structures, and *Poetic Diction* relies heavily on its
author's literary sensitivity. The extended discussion of 'ruin', for
example, evokes older meanings of the word, and is itself an
attractive, graceful exposition, with a certain literary resonance: 'Like
sleeping beauties, they lie there prone and rigid in the walls of Castle
Logic, waiting only for the kiss of Metaphor to awaken them to fresh
life.'[23] The discussion characteristically combines scholarly acuteness
with romantic plangency, while staying close to the wellsprings of
literature, and citing examples throughout from major poets.

Effective in the same way is the discussion of mediaeval experience
and language ('A farm cart would do for Elijah's fiery chariot on its
way up to heaven'),[24] or of the pidgin English for steamboat ('thlee-
piecee bamboo, two-piecee puff-puff, walk-along-inside, no-can-
see').[25] Statements of fact are constantly enlivened by surprising or
challenging insight, whether on the significance of the Photian heresy
in *Unancestral Voice*,[26] or the confusion of 'equality' with 'uniformity',[27] or in the image of an angel in a lounge suit as a way of
distinguishing mediaeval conventions from our own.[28] Here is a
passage on the soul in modern times:

> For the soul is the Cinderella of twentieth-century civilisation. She
> lives on sentiment: of which we are mortally afraid, preferring to
> rush out of it either to the physical extreme of violence or of
> appetite on the one side, or on the other to a rarefied and contentless
> spirituality; or perhaps to try both in turn, like Aldous Huxley.[29]

The diagnosis is provocatively tacked down at both ends: first by the
fairy story, which sets our minds in pursuit of analogies, and then by
the reference to Huxley, hardly a Cinderella, whose cerebral urbanity

offsets the suggestion of the merely fanciful with which the passage opened. Everywhere we encounter aphorism and provocative phrasing: ('interior is anterior'; 'residue of unresolved positivism'; 'I am all those wherein I am contained'; 'Nature unperceived is the unconscious').[30]

The literary quality of Barfield's writing, in short, is the life-blood of his theory. If the skeleton of his thought consists of abstractions, he presents some attractive flesh, if only to ask: What do you think supports such a wonderful body? Plato had discovered this technique for all his tribe: the validity of his intuitions depends on him proving them on the pulses, by the clash and interaction of dialogue, the dramatic display of personality, and the play of living imperfections upon the underlying ideology. The speculative mind in full flight, it seems, has to discover itself trammelled by the jesses and blinkers of ordinary experience. And this is as should be. Man is not a rational animal: his glory as well as his imperfection is to be *rationis capax*.

One consequence is that an approach to human thinking such as Barfield's is not to be taken as mainly logical. Indeed, on its own terms you cannot prove such a speculative system wrong. If you find fault, say, with the notion of etheric bodies, you will be told that the term 'etheric body' is just a metaphor, or representation, and you don't yet see what it really means. If you take any point of the argument too literally, that proves the idealist's case that you are spiritually obtuse. If you do not, you can understand it in terms of . . . What? By degrees you may be taken, as Barfield intends that you should, through an imagined past when human consciousness was different from the present, to an even mistier condition when there was consciousness but no material objects as we know them today, until you arrive at the unimaginable condition, the entirely meaningful ground, as it were, of all subsequent meanings.[31] You are faced with a version of the ontological argument: the human mind is aware of its limitations in having to struggle after the meaning of things, but it can conceive a condition, at least in negative terms, free of this limitation, and prior to our fall into individual personalities.[32] This condition, because it suggests a universe immersed in whole meaning, must exist, because meaning and existence are assumed identical.

Barfield, moreover, tries to root this kind of argument in history, and appeals to etymology to show that human consciousness was indeed different in past times. This, of course, has the immediate effect of making the material world itself different in past times, threatening even to dissolve it. And so we are back with the mind itself, and its proof of the Absolute deduced from the processes of its own operation. Against this, Kant long ago levelled his guns, and although Barfield's study of etymology can be fascinating, it ultimately involves metaphysical assumptions unnecessary to his examination of the materials he discusses.[33] These assumptions, besides, soon involve us in imponderables; clearly we would need to be rid of the human-mind-as-it-is-today in order to appreciate the human-mind-as-it-was. Yet neither Barfield nor we can be rid of the human mind as it is today, and to replace it with an account of the imagined object appearing to the human-mind-as-it-was would leave us still explicating a doubly determinate structure without justifying the conclusion that one meaningful cosmos is anterior to our struggle for meaning and significance.

The problem lies not only in Barfield's conception of the past, but the future too: his idea of final participation is stirring, but imprecise. We are told that it will involve us using our imaginations systematically,[34] but not what this means in terms of day to day living. In a recent interview Barfield has this to say:

You can only *envisage* that [final participation] in terms of rather crude imagery. I tend to think of it as something like this: if you take a circle or a sphere you can have that sphere colored in all shades of color and all degrees of shading of a particular color. In the physical world as we know it, you can't have them all together, because one color washes out another one. But it isn't so very difficult to imagine that all the colorings of the whole sphere could coexist at the same time, in which case each one would in a sense be the whole, but would also be itself. Something in that way. Of course it's a crude picture, but it's the only way I can envisage final participation in a form that is expressible in words.[35]

It is not just a matter of the image being 'crude': it embodies no particular sense, and is a failure of imagination to appear convincingly.

But we should not ignore Barfield for such reasons any more than we ignore Plato because of our doubts about the Ideas or the Demiurge. Plato's most famous pupil had the right attitude. The master's idea of Absolute Justice is good, elevating and noble, but what use is it in the market place? Indeed, Plato himself had fought hard with problems of reconciling the high ideal with the just man's persecution and suffering, and it was not for Aristotle alone to ask the question of how to bring abstractions down to the complex, unlovely facts. Precisely because Barfield appreciates such claims of contingency upon his idealism, he is more readable for most people than his mentor, Rudolf Steiner. This is partly a matter of style; two books[36] even take the form of Socratic debates, and the discretion of indirection is, in literary terms, the better part of Barfield's success in plying his theories upon us. Certainly, the continuing struggle to engage the viewpoints of a number of opposing persuasions and to keep up to date with the philosophy of science, historiography, theology and particle physics, lend an energy to his writings, for which the Platonic dialogue is a natural vehicle.

Still, the attempt to establish individual characters among the speakers in *Worlds Apart* (Ranger's youthful impetuosity, Brodie's methodical thoughtfulness) does not really affect the outcome of the argument. Whereas in Dostoevski, for example, we are continually aware of the recalcitrant, living complexity of human personalities trying to mould themselves in the form of ideas they find appealing, in Barfield it is the ideas which are recalcitrant and complex, and the characters (for the most part appealing) are easily manipulated to fit the turns of argument. People conform to their semi-allegorical names: Ranger is a rocket researcher, Burrows a depth-psychologist, and, thriving at the centre, is Burgeon, while Dunn, a logical positivist, has a 'large car' with a 'shabby body and perfectly tuned engine'.[37] Whimsy notwithstanding, the idealist's rarefied atmosphere diminishes the vigour of the various human types gasping to breathe it, and the results show stylistically.

Yet there is density in Barfield's thought, and a passion for ideas, which make his dialogues good reading. Take the passage on the feeling of heaviness in the limbs with which we awaken after deep sleep:

. . . he slowly came to realize, as he had never quite succeeded in doing before, the identity between precisely this heaviness and the recreation which was sleep. The hugeness of the one was the hugeness of the other caught, as it were, in the act; so that during the day that was coming the intolerable might of its oppressive mass would be the effortless ease with which his will would again inform those inert limbs, or with which (as long as they were passive) his mind would exploit their passivity for its own vigilance. There was, after all, no more mysterious transformation than this nightly one of the fagged and jaded into the active and energetic. How could one ever hope to understand the transformation of matter into energy, of the heaviness of matter into the weightlessness of energy, without seeking also to penetrate this? For this *was* the transformation of matter into energy; only it was the inside of it. [38]

The firmness with which the common physiological experience, rooted deeply in instinct, combines with Burgeon's abstract pre-occupation with matter and energy, gives the passage complexity and novelty, and on this sort of subject Barfield is at his best.

III. THE CROSS AS POLARITY

I have drawn attention to literary effects in *Unancestral Voice* and *Worlds Apart* not just to complain about weaknesses, but to point out problems inherent in bringing Barfield's kind of idealism down to earth. This leads now to the figure of the cross, because Barfield's concern for incarnation and polarity suggests that such a symbol would be especially useful to him.

Throughout his career, Barfield has been preoccupied with unity achieved from the strife of opposites. Tension, he says, is 'an essential feature of polarity',[39] and at the 'highest level', this principle leads to trinitarianism: 'The Father, from his unity, projects the Son, the Logos, and then ultimately there's a unity on another plane, another level, the Holy Spirit'.[40] The concept is examined exhaustively in *What Coleridge Thought*, where we find that 'the polarity, God–Man is the basis of all polarity, in nature and elsewhere'.[41] Life, we are told in *Romanticism Comes of Age*, 'consists in the strife of opposites', and there is a cross-shaped figure to illustrate this.[42] The 'very heart' of Steiner's teaching about the self-conscious re-ascent of man to God is that it 'was made possible by the Incarnation and Death of the Divine Man (whom he also called "The Representative of Humanity") in Palestine 2,000 years ago'.[43] Christ, we learn in *Unancestral Voice*, is the 'archetype of all transformations', in which the 'death of the old' is born 'into the life of the new form', and the process of 'self-transformation through death and rebirth' is basic to our becoming individual men.[44] In a letter, Barfield makes clear how he regards the cross as an archetypal symbol of these kinds of tension, and how they symbolise man in the world:

As I see it, it is impossible to separate the idea of the true nature of human being from the symbol of the cross. This was so long before Christianity, that is the Crucifixion, *embodied* the symbol as history. Plato in the *Timaeus* speaks of the soul of the world being stretched upon the body of the world in the form of a cross. Again, as the essential sign of *space*, it symbolises the whole of phenomenal existence.

I think it has long been felt, in the East as well as in the West, that, within the plane of spatial manifestation (on which imagery depends for its existence) vertical direction symbolises the Man–God relation and horizontal direction the Man–Man relation, and clearly the two meet in the intersection of the arms of the cross. Both relations are, to my feeling, best understood as polarities, and the two polarities intersect at their point of maximum 'tension', that is, midway between their extremities. Psychologically and theologically one would say – all too glibly: Maximum love of one another is reached at the same point or in the same 'moment' as maximum love of God.[45]

In view of this, it is of some interest that in his main books Barfield avoids analysis of the crucifixion as an historical event involving physical suffering. Although he insists on the singular importance of history for a proper understanding of man's evolution and place in the world, he looks to the Incarnation rather than the cross to develop this theme. The cross, important as it is, is mainly a symbol of transformation occurring 'at the turning-point of time, by that central death and rebirth which was the transformation of transformations'.[46] As Coleridge has it, the crucifixion and resurrection were 'the epiphanies, the sacramental acts and *phaenomena* of the *Deus Patiens*, the visible words of the invisible Word'.[47] The symbolic function, not the suffering of the just man, attracts Barfield's attention, and his enthusiasm for René Guénon's *Symbolism of the Cross*, which is concerned totally with metaphysics, makes this emphasis clear.[48]

In *Saving the Appearances*, however, there is a passage which seems to break the rule. Barfield analyses the crucifixion in terms of a human failure among the Jews to realise that God was immanent as well as transcendent, and among the Graeco-Romans to hold together their 'representational consciousness' with the Jewish teaching on idolatry. By a rejection of idolatry that at the same time permitted the images to enliven the heart, a smooth absorption of the significance of

Christ's incarnation could have been effected. Because it failed, the crucifixion instead took place.[49]

Here indeed we begin to see the problem of the cross in terms of the suffering just man. But this aspect of the event remains undeveloped, and the cross instead comes to represent the kind of problem consequent on a misunderstanding. There is, after all, no spilt blood to think about. In an essay entitled 'The Light of the World', where we do find blood, this is how Barfield describes it:

> What sort of experience shall we have? We shall have read Rudolf Steiner's description, in the Cassel lectures on the Gospel of St. John, of how, when the blood flowed from the cross on Golgotha, it was much more than a merely physical event. How there was then a change in the aura of the Earth itself, so that, from being a mere planet, a mere receiver of light from the sun, it began itself to emit light.[50]

The physical is acknowledged but immediately deflected so that we contemplate the earth's aura. The emphasis is repeated in an essay on 'The Fall in Man and Nature',[51] where the fall has to do with the emergence of human self-consciousness, and the feeling that the ego is separated from the world of nature. But Barfield avoids entirely the problem of pain, traditionally a consequence also of the fall, and the omission is equivalent to the lack of attention to suffering, contingency, and fully-rendered character in the Socratic dialogues.

On Barfield's cross, therefore, is no real suffering or abandonment. He admits these occurred, certainly, but does not realise them when he writes. The argument that the crucifixion should not, if properly understood historically, be conceived as two things (a spiritual symbol and a factual execution) but as one symbolic event, is compelling, but insufficient to conjure away the hanging up of a man with nails, any more than the theory of evolution of consciousness conjures away the existence of hard rocks and bright flowers because mind-as-it-is-today was not observing them yesterday. It may be indeed that the sense of enormity in the crucifixion *was* mitigated for some observers who appreciated, in faith, the fuller symbolic dimension, though the record tells us that even the disciples, who had been given enough hints about what to expect, fled away. But to go a step further and suggest that the Man hanged felt the horror less because he did not separate history and symbol would be to coddle us, and not to enliven our imaginations with a truer sense of the world.

Idealism, it seems, must validate itself in the thick intensities of the merely contingent, where we cannot readily assume the precedence of act over potency, essence over existence. Barfield remains best when he stays close to poetry, his first love, for he has an acute sense of how imagination works in complex verbal structures expressing particular experiences. Similarly, his wide learning, abundant insight and capacity to evoke the poetic qualities of past civilisations are continually exciting, and his theory takes on an imaginative quality of its own. At one point, Burgeon's *alter ego*, Burden, protests: 'What is all the excitement about? You know perfectly well it is simply the old Neo-platonism turning up again. It's *always* turning up in one place or another. In different disguises.'[52] This is both the strength and the weakness of the kind of thought Burgeon pursues. Human beings experience intuitions of value and enduring beauty, and these form part of the meaning of life. Barfield first found such ideals imaginatively expressed in poetry, and he then set out to try to identify the structure of poetry with the structure of life itself.

IV. MICHAEL POLANYI

Michael Polanyi (1891–1976) is a challenging thinker, who demonstrates also the kind of sophistication a trained scientist can bring to the aesthetic questions this book raises. I do not suggest that somehow Polanyi is a spokesman for modern philosophy of science, though he does represent the kind of interest in history and methodology through which science increasingly promotes *rapprochement* with the humanities.

By contrast with Barfield, who began with poetry and developed towards an interest in science, Polanyi began with science, and ended writing about the artistic imagination. If Barfield's problem has been to render his intuitions concrete, Polanyi's is to render his scientific experience into theory, and his main solution is to say that before the complexity of knowing things in themselves, no theory is adequate. Polanyi's thought is, in a way, a theory about the limitations of theory for knowing how to deal with facts, and his reason for inventing it is to correct all the other theories which have caused trouble through people believing they could produce impossible results. Here Polanyi especially points to the sceptical and empirical approach to knowledge by Descartes and his followers, and to ideologies which developed from it, for instance the French Revolution and Marxism.[53]

Polanyi's thought has the advantage of being rooted in rich practical experience. He began his career as a physician, and after the First World War worked as a chemist in Berlin, where he associated with such as Irwin Schroedinger, Max Planck and Albert Einstein. When the Nazis came to power, he left Germany to take a chair in Chemistry at the University of Manchester, later changing the focus of his academic interest, and becoming professor of social studies. This new interest was prompted by the fact that after the Second World War Polanyi had become concerned about the future of science in a society increasingly given over to ideology and planned economies.[54] The central malaise of the twentieth century, particularly made manifest in the violence of two recent wars and a revolution in Russia, he came to attribute to a combination of unrealistic hopes in ideological modes of thought, and an intense critical scepticism engendered by the founders of empiricism.[55] An immediate effect of the critical philosophy of Locke and his Enlightenment disciples, Polanyi thought, was to separate the concerns of religious faith from those of secular society, and in so doing to weaken the prestige of traditional ecclesiastical authority. At the same time, the Englightenment placed a high value on toleration, and on the ideal of a humane, secular culture. Social reform on a wide scale during the following two hundred years was therefore largely an outcome of the combined advantages of technical progress and anti-authoritarian philosophies.

Yet the reforms also required ideals to motivate them, even though the secular impulse encouraged a disregard for the traditional aspirations of a millenium and a half of Christian practice. Men of the Middle Ages had been inspired with high ideals (for example the City of God), but were assured also of failing to realise them on earth because of Original Sin. The new movement contrived to keep, in secular form, the old desire for moral perfection in a heavenly city, and combined it with a secular pursuit of material progress and widespread scepticism about man's fallen nature.

Such an unstable mixture of moral passion and scepticism in European history led eventually to disastrous vicious circles which Polanyi calls 'moral inversion'. A man, for instance, who desires physical well-being for his fellows soon encounters the recalcitrance of society, and then confirms the purity of his moral passion by denouncing complacency and hypocrisy in those who have compromised with the imperfections of society by accepting its traditional values. One way to preserve integrity is therefore to react violently against morality in its traditional forms. Nihilism is one result, and with it comes a kind of ruthless immorality, a pitiless machinery of violence which paradoxically becomes the vindication of moral honesty and of an ideal material progress.

Polanyi applies his idea of 'moral inversion' to the main events of recent European history, and, with various degrees of elaboration and subtlety, to many of its principal thinkers and writers. But the argument is not merely academic; Polanyi believes that moral passions need to be guided by the kinds of skilled knowledge slowly and painstakingly developed by civilisation, and this goes for science as well as government. Modern science is the fruit of an enormously complex development beginning at the Renaissance and, in those countries where it manages to thrive, its traditions have been handed on by the skills of teachers and through the processes of accreditation which in turn afford opportunities for research whereby science sustains itself. [56] However, by introducing the concept of methodical doubt, science also has done much to undercut the respect accorded both to tradition and authority, and this is especially the case in a period of political turmoil such as the twentieth century, when zeal for reform, itself nurtured in the climate of sceptical secularism, is likely to dictate the ends to which science should be directed. But to attempt detailed scientific planning is to ignore all that history shows about the development of scientific method: that it is a skilled kind of knowledge learned by apprenticeship within an immensely rich and complex tradition, making progress by tentative gropings forward, whereby new discoveries are assimilated by the scrutiny and skilled assessment of experts. The process is open-ended, and its future results are unpredictable. [57] For that very reason, it seems to offer an opportunity to morally concerned politicians who see loose rather than open ends, and who then plan to tie these up, harnessing science for social reform.

During the Second World War the British Association for the Advancement of Science itself founded a division to recommend planned research, and Polanyi opposed it. [58] His concern continued after the war, and, by way of the Lysenko affair, came to involve his critique of Marxism, which he saw as a major manifestation of moral inversion. To bring off his defence of science in such circumstances, Polanyi was forced increasingly to argue his case in epistemological terms: only if we can describe the structure of the human mind in the act of knowing, can we prescribe how it best operates in making scientific discoveries.

Polanyi's epistemology and his social theory therefore develop together, and in epistemology his major insight has to do with the dynamics of what he calls the 'tacit dimension'. This corresponds to his analysis of the non-explicit aspirations which influence social progress, and constitute the sense of tradition in a culture. Basically, it implies that we always 'know more than we can tell'. For example, in ordinary experience 'We know a person's face, and can recognise it among a thousand, indeed among a million. Yet we usually cannot tell how we recognise a face we know'.[59] This is because we 'attend, from a large number of clues most of which we cannot identify, to the physiognomy which they indicate'.[60] The focus of our attention (the physiognomy) is thus the meaning of the clues which make up the coherent shape, but we are only subsidiarily aware of the clues as we attend to the face we know. If we focused on the clues themselves we would lose sight of the face, just as we can lose the meaning of a word by attending focally to the syllables as mere sounds, or as a piano player will freeze if he focuses on his fingers instead of the music.[61]

After analysing numerous such examples, Polanyi concludes that because of the bodily rootedness of human reason, and the dependency of language on powers of sensitivity and attention present in animals, we cannot make articulate the ultimate framework of what we know. Rather, we are committed to it 'passionately and far beyond our comprehension', for we 'live in it as in the garment of our own skin',[62] and cannot divest ourselves of this responsibility by setting up objective criteria of verifiability. Consequently, even at the heart of science, the art of knowing (or skill, connoisseurship) remains unspecifiable.

The principles of tacit knowledge apply also to art, and on this subject Polanyi resorts to a further distinction between 'self-centered integrations' and 'self-giving integrations' to explain some relative differences within the same general structure between scientific and artistic endeavours.

The main point about self-centred integrations is that the focus of attention is more important than the subsidiary clues, and this is the case with most 'scientific' knowing, and with our knowledge of 'objects'. But in self-giving integrations the subsidiary clues are more important, so that we are forced to participate in the integration more fully. In short, the 'participation of the knower in his object deepens with the complexity of the object'. On the one hand, those integrations which are 'mainly cognitive or mainly practical' are 'essentially tacit', and we can see the epistemological foundations for this in the theory already outlined: we are interested, for practical purposes, in knowing the face or naming the object, and not in *how* we do these things by attending from subsidiaries. On the other hand, 'we know such matters as moral principles by being altogether immersed in them',[63] and a key (though extreme) example of a self-giving integration of the type which includes poetry, morality and religion, is the symbol of a national flag and our manner of reacting to it. If our reaction to a flag on a solemn occasion is to be meaningful, we must 'surrender entirely to it', so that 'this otherwise meaningless piece of cloth becomes then a moving spectacle.'[64] 'In this case we ourselves with all our pale memories enter into an integration,'[65] and we let the flag symbolise all the subsidiaries which constitute what we feel about fatherland, home, sacrifice, and other things pertaining to our sense of the patriotic. Each man's experiences here will be different, and each will feel intensely and privately in his own way before his flag (if he gives himself up to it), for each has his own experience of sacrifice, fatherland and so on.

We are now in a position to discuss poems, for a poem, we learn, is neither simply denotative nor simply like a flag, and in discussing the integration effected by metaphor, Polanyi claims that both the subsidiary and the focal elements are of equivalent interest: 'a metaphor combines these two structures by bringing an interesting matter subsidiarily to bear on another interesting subject'.[66] The poem, like the flag, is a focus for personal emotions and memories which we are not accustomed to evoke, but the poem also gives to these some explicit focus and form which claims to be meaningful. But, unlike the flag, a poem can be analysed and critically assessed, and engages us also with some statement about things we all know, or have experienced as matters of significant human interest. The subjects of poems may, indeed, be clichés, but the poem then claims that the *meaning* of these clichés *is in* the emotions we are now invited to re-experience in reading the poem, and so the cliché is enlivened. The poem therefore tells us something about language (our abstract words focus subsidiary experiences which are the meaning of the words, and from which concepts emerge), and about the shape of our past lives (the poems give shape to the chaos of our memories and experiences, thus enabling us to participate and to 'dwell in' the poem).

The notion of self-giving integrations has an interesting application also to formal structures in art, and especially painting. Taking as an example the perspectival illusion of continuity between the pilasters supporting a vault and the columns painted on the vault by the Renaissance artist Andrea Pozzo, Polanyi argues that our sense of distortion is very strong if we view the vault from anywhere except the centre of the aisle. However, if we view a conventional painting from the side, our sense of distortion is not nearly so acute. This, says Polanyi, is because we have a subsidiary awareness of the frame and of the flat surface of a painting, and we accept this formal convention even though it is incompatible with the depth suggested by the painting's central representation. The Pozzo picture, on the other hand, is deceptive because its columns appear to be a real continuation of the church's architecture, and so 'the Pozzo painting is subject to distortion, because its perspective is not counteracted by an awareness of the ground on which it is painted'.[67] In other words, a key integration necessary for painting, as for all art, is interfered with in the Pozzo example, for we must be aware that the work of art assumes a subsidiary framework which embraces the incompatible idea represented: 'Art appears to consist, for painting as for drama, in representing a subject within an artificial framework that contradicts its representative aspects, and I think we find the same structure in all representative arts'.[68] In poetry, for instance, meter, rhyme, and metaphor become 'fixtures of the poetic frame' which 'function as subsidiaries', and 'together with such content of the poem as can be put into prose, form the meaning of the poem'. Polanyi concludes that the 'power and beauty of the poem' lies 'in a subsidiary framework embracing a simple idea'.[69] The poem, like the painting, is an integration of contradictory elements: a rigid metrical frame with a passionate, necessarily evanescent assertion, and the incompatible elements within metaphor itself. Polanyi describes the result as 'transnatural' because it provides something not found in nature or practical affairs, but creates meaning in which we dwell.[70]

V. THE QUALITY OF EMPIRICISM

Polanyi's analysis of poetry reaches back into his diagnosis of the origins of science. Like Barfield, Polanyi believes that poetry is not separate from our universe of values in science and in morality and religion, and so it is of interest to notice the kind of weakness Barfield perceives in Polanyi's thought. This has to do with a Cartesianism so deeply assumed that it deceives even the liberal philosopher who wishes to denounce dualism in all its forms. Polanyi continually assumes that we 'dwell in' our bodies,[71] and this, says Barfield, implies an independence of thought and object persistently reasserting itself in Polanyi's language despite his theory. Certainly Polanyi does indulge what Barfield considers the cardinal error of thinking about the universe as 'inanimate matter' from which human life has evolved, without considering what function the evolution of consciousness may have for our understanding of what 'inanimate matter' is. Barfield's thought on this question itself confounds us in problems beyond logic, and, consequently, I have no qualms in following Polanyi when he talks about the practical skills of riding a bicycle or reading x-ray photographs, claiming that we extend our physical bodies out to contain these objects as tools, learning to use them as extensions of ourselves. But Barfield will not be so easily shaken off, for we do not need to swallow his whole metaphysical theory to acknowledge that Polanyi's language often assumes, as Barfield says, a suppressed dualism.

For instance, Polanyi says of his paper 'On Body and Mind', that it offers 'a unified view of consciousness' which 'includes the body-mind relation in its entirety'. Yet he talks about using things outside of ourselves 'in the way we use our body',[72] and the problem is reproduced also in Polanyi's attitude to the personal, which, he claims, transcends both subjective and objective, and is the hallmark of human nature.[73] Personal choices, we learn, result in a set of self-set standards by means of which we explore the world. But these personal choices are not, it appears, subjective, for Polanyi allows criteria independent of our beliefs, against which we can test ourselves. In the tension between subjective and objective, that hazardous realm between body and mind where these are described as distinct yet known to be one, Polanyi locates what he asks us to recognise as the person, but without speculating on what kind of agency enables us to transcend the dichotomy.

Barfield, in a way, had begun at this point by calling upon imagination, and asking us to acknowledge the action of the mysterious third force which reconciles the polar opposites from which understanding is wrought. But Polanyi's descriptions of human learning are both more existential and more doggedly practical than Barfield's. The problem of imagination is not central to

Polanyi's main work at all, and when he does begin to show an interest in it, he describes it as functionally as he can: 'I call all thoughts of things that are not present, or not yet present — or perhaps never to be present — acts of the imagination. When I intend to lift my arm, this intention is an act of my imagination. In this case imagination is not visual but muscular. . . .'[74] *Personal Knowledge* is in many respects a brilliant and thorough-going book, but it has remarkably little to say on this subject, and only late in Polanyi's career does the question begin to become urgent. It is as if the unlived life of his own theory had begun to catch up with it, and in a series of papers and lectures written towards the end of his life he explores the creative imagination in myth, ritual, poetry and modern art.[75] Here we first find the distinction between self-giving and self-centred integrations.

Polanyi's attempt to extend the theory of tacit knowing into the sphere of aesthetics has the effect of immediately bringing to the surface those assumptions hidden by his earlier pragmatic agnosticism. For instance, he now repeatedly describes imagination as a 'power', and within five lines we hear of 'wider powers of meaningful integration', a 'whole range of dynamic powers in art', a 'mental power which can establish a meaning'.[76] We can understand, it seems, the structure of the integrations Polanyi describes if we first of all grant that there is a power which enables them. The occult qualities which empiricism fought hard to banish as underminers of sound method, we now find returning through a back door. Unless, that is, the seat of these powers is itself explained. And occasionally Polanyi does venture upon the fringes of territory Barfield has marked for his own. Indeed, the only place Polanyi ever quotes Barfield is in these late essays,[77] where he flirts also with the problem of polarity ('Opposites may conflict, but on a deeper level they are one'),[78] and where we find an occasional sense of Barfieldian mystery about the nature of matter ('A belief in the gradual emergence of man from an inanimate universe reveals to us that the dead matter of our origins was fraught with meaning far beyond all that we are presently able to see in it').[79] But Polanyi stops short of Barfield's conclusions: the *rapprochement* is tentative, and Polanyi distrusts the other man's metaphysics. Speculation on the spiritual, it seems, even to the end, is no business for the scientifically practised mind.

In these late essays, however, Polanyi also develops an insight to modernism that Barfield does not have. Here we should look again at the notion of 'transnatural integrations', describing the interaction between a poem and its structure, a painting and its frame, a drama and stage conventions, and assuring us that we are not watching either an illusion or real life:

> The mechanisms that serve to arouse us from our private concerns and to open our minds to follow a work of art are artificial products: their power to arouse and isolate our minds lies in their artificiality, which sharply clashes with our day-to-day experience. [80]

Polanyi, in this vein, insists everywhere that 'the artist's interpretation of experience must differ sharply from our usual perceptions', [81] and his point is that art is different from life. Admittedly, art, like science and morality, has a bearing on everyday things, without which there would be none of these sciences at all. A symbol, for instance, has to be 'akin to the matter that it embodies', [82] and, conversely, our appreciation of art can help us to give form to the muddled contents of our personal lives. We 'make it our own and clarify our lives by it. Art moves us, therefore, through influencing the lived quality of our very existence. In other words, without art our existence would mean much less to us,' [83] and, like myth and ritual, it invites our submission to the order it presents. Also, like science, it seeks to discover the hidden pattern which becomes part of the universe of self-set standards by which we attempt to deal with the world. [84]

Still, we must acknowledge that art has a 'comprehensive context', [85] whereas life does not, and from this point of view Polanyi approaches the question of modernism, joining the ranks of the neologisers on this subject by coining the term 'Visionary Art' [86] to describe the artistic revolution which took place at the beginning of this century. He looks to Baudelaire, Rimbaud, Mallarmé, Eliot, Pound and the surrealists for examples, and claims they are inheritors of the problems of moral inversion with which European civilisation has been burdened since the scientific revolution. But instead of ignoring the chaos into which the universe of traditional values has fallen, the painters and poets looked to imagination to shore up the ruins against decay:

> Because painters and poets condemned the world as absurd, they represented it as a heap of fragments. But because they were artists, their vision brought this supposedly dead pile to life in their works of art! These artists thus preserved the honor of their nihilistic

protest by cutting the world to pieces; but they inadvertently triumphed over this destruction of meaning in our social life by evoking in this rubbish meaningful images never witnessed before. This triumph at once crowned the artists as creators of meaningful visions and succeeded in allowing them, in their own minds, to leave the 'pile' there as an expression of protest against the chaotic conditions of the age.[87]

In a way, by contributing to the destruction of coherence, modernism itself may be accused of nurturing nihilism, but Polanyi claims the artistic achievement justifies the risk: 'On balance, therefore, it would seem to have achieved more meaning, in spite of itself, than it has destroyed'.[88]

Polanyi's view of modernism is plainly at one with the sense, shared by critics and aestheticians alike since the late nineteenth century, that art is not essentially representative. 'Since a purely visionary poem says nothing that can be expressed in a prose statement, the problem of mimesis cannot arise',[89] and much modern art, consequently, calls attention to the redeeming fact itself of the imagination's capacity to fuse incompatibles together:

. . . only modern art has made it clear that what art does is to create facts of our imagination. It is these facts of our imagination, presented to us by our artists, that form part of the thought that makes up our culture.[90]

By thus claiming that art is at one with the whole range of the human sciences, and that these in unison attempt to widen the range of our self-set standards, Polanyi insists ultimately on the differences between art and the meaning of things in themselves. The contribution of modernism is to call attention to this very difference, and therein lies its genius. Barfield, whose interest in the Romantics encouraged him to stress the continuity between art and life, as he did between consciousness and existence, has little sympathy with such a view. In *Saving the Appearances* he complains of the 'riot of private and personal symbolisms'[91] that characterises modern art, and welcomes attacks on it, such as Graham Hough's *Image and Meaning*.[92]

Despite such differences, however, Barfield and Polanyi conspicuously agree in their central analyses of metaphor and the complex integrations through which the imagination declares itself, demanding the personal participation of the knower in the known. Both analyse the importance of Christianity to the history of science, and agree upon the importance of the scientific revolution to modern consciousness. As with Barfield, the peculiar cast of Polanyi's attitude to these questions is expressed in his treatment of the cross.

VI. THE CROSS AS COMMITMENT

Polanyi's repeated teaching that we can never make articulate the premises of our knowledge, and that in every act of knowing we are committed beyond our understanding, leads him to affirm repeatedly the Augustinian maxim, *nisi credideritis non intelligitis*; unless you believe you will not understand. [93] Just as we do not know clearly our intellectual roots, so we do not know where our discoveries will lead us, or what fruit they will bear. Instead, we 'dwell in' the articulate framework we inherit from our culture, using it to move our knowledge forward to more adequate conceptions of that reality with which we make contact by way of our theories. [94] Indwelling is a prior condition of breaking out, and in our lives as thinking human beings, continual restlessness calls in question whatever satisfactions we achieve.

The main point about '*nisi credideritis*', therefore, is that it enables us to acknowledge the tension and uncertainty inherent in our human manner of being in the world, and for Polanyi the key insight of Christianity is that it 'sedulously fosters, and in a sense permanently satisfies, man's craving for mental dissatisfaction by offering him the comfort of a crucified God'. [95] The cross represents the conditions of knowledge itself, for the cross is fraught with anguish and inherent dubiety [96] while it calls upon faith and directs us towards an 'unthinkable consummation', [97] assuming at the same time the burden of our past imperfections. The cross, moreover, teaches that it is 'the Christian's duty to believe in this epochal event and to be totally absorbed by its implications. Faith, faith that mocks reason, faith that scornfully declares itself to be mere foolishness in the face of Greek rationalism – this is what Paul enjoined on his audiences'. [98] Polanyi concludes, provocatively, that the Pauline scheme of faith, works and grace, based on the cross, is the 'only adequate conception of scientific discovery', [99] and he would have us acknowledge the symbol as effective because we can make it stand for such a complex range of modern, sophisticated knowledge.

But on the cross as a 'given' symbol, divinely revealed, Polanyi has little to say, as he has on the spiritual nature of the 'powers' of human imagination. His view of art, as of human experience in general, is rather that our statements are concretions out of a world of flux, that man is being-in-a-world,[100] and condemned to doubt, always in process towards truth which he can never make finally explicit. Human culture, like modern visionary art, shores up the fragments, and man's rootedness in potential thought is the central fact of his nature. Unlike Barfield, Polanyi feels the primacy of potency to act. We are left, admittedly, open to acknowledge a higher meaning for religious symbols, but the risks in affirming these are our own, and the cross remains the sign of our suffering incompleteness in all things.

VII. CONCLUSION

Barfield and Polanyi both approach the problem of a dissociation in sensibility occasioned by the rise of science during the seventeenth century, and each takes one of the two broad routes open to philosophy on such a question: Barfield's bias is rationalist, and Polanyi's empirical. Barfield, so to speak, works down, whereas Polanyi works up, so that the challenge in the first case is to have language concretise the author's intuitions of transcendence, and in the second to open up the technical discussion to mystery broached by the theory. If the rationalist needs to express convincingly a sense of the anomalous contingencies of human existence, the empiricist needs to dream of higher things, and it seems that in the history of Western culture during the last three hundred years a universe of discourse permitting a seamless continuity between these realms of human experience has been increasingly hard to find. Traditionally, their mediation had been by way of what St Augustine called 'spiritual vision', indicating that effect of language by which we appreciate most clearly the mind's capacity to experience the concretised universal, the particularised general. In short, Augustine propounded a theory of imagination in which images are the dynamic centre of human language, and his insight remains valid, for without it we court either an excess of rationalism (ignoring the recalcitrance of things) or of empiricism (leading to an idolatry of things). Still, the practising scientist and the Neo-Platonist aesthetician start, as we expect, from the bias determined by the universe of discourse with which each is familiar. With Barfield and Polanyi, such starting points are, in a way, polar opposites, but it is a measure of their understanding of human experience in language that their theories should overlap on the question of imagination, and on the structure of art as a paradigm for the dynamic, incarnate centre of human knowledge.

7 Conclusion: Typology and a Critic's Choice

During the seventeenth century empirical science helped to discredit the literary imagination as a mediator between nature and God. The mediaeval sense of correspondence between meaning and appearance yielded to scepticism about what human perception could truthfully tell of the world. A fifth-columnist had lain within the human mind all along, and the new thinkers subjected perception itself to more careful scrutiny than it had ever received before. Locke's *Essay Concerning Human Understanding*, the work most representative of the new movement, is the first full length philosophical study in Europe devoted entirely to epistemology.

Although questions raised about imagination by science do not determine literary achievement, they do offer for literature a new kind of concern about its own relationship to the world, and we can best appreciate this if we grasp the critical questions at their inception, in a historical context. The six authors chosen for this study would sympathise, in a broad way, with such an approach. All of them look to the rise of science for better understanding of challenges they face as writers in the twentieth century, intrigued by problems of belief in a world where things seem to have lost the autonomy words have gained. Because their literature is haunted by an awareness of itself as a mimesis not of the world according to God's plan, but of *the condition of humans using words*, it feels directly its separateness from theology and science. However tentatively and with whatever implicit humility they approach their subject matter, the theologian and scientist state general truths. Theology attempts to order our aspirations in terms of values which we desire as ultimate; science to conceive general laws describing order in nature.[1] Men, meanwhile, continue to face things and each other in concrete relationships which language should not betray. The poet makes this clear, demanding, from scientist and theologian alike, the humiliation of the abstract.[2]

This problem of contingency in conflict with ideals introduces the cross, again a common concern of the six subjects of this study. Through the cross they address specifically the problem of faith in a world which, in becoming highly self-conscious, lost its traditional sense of the continuity between imagination, divine Idea and material substance. One conclusion on what our authors make of such a predicament can be put simply: in so far as their literature deals with theology, its special area is faith, and the poet as theologian leaves us with the sign of the cross.

If this seems a curiously mediaeval statement, we should recall that mediaeval man had no aesthetic theory separate from theology and natural philosophy. The cross for him was a divinely-revealed sign of God in man, of incompleteness of faith, and of human nature in space and time. A man not fully stretched out upon it was not fully human, his discourse not fully rhetorical. The difference between such an assumed continuity and the modern experience of a divorce between the disciplines is, for the theologically-minded poet today, that the sign of the cross as we have discussed it can stand autonomously for the artifact itself, uncertainly poised between the world of nature and the realm of Ideas.

At this point the problem arises of whether or not such a general diagnosis can contain sufficiently the variousness of artistic achievement. Is there a way to hold my point that poetry resists generalisation in order to restore a kind of agnostic complexity to concrete experience, without confounding the argument in simple-minded relativism, untrue certainly to the practice of the opinionated writers discussed in these pages?

To begin, we might point out that each of our authors displays some distinctive, prejudiced attitude, and occupies a position based on and calling for 'opinions'. Yet the discourse of each is only successfully literary in so far as it develops the complementary and opposed elements of experience which show the shortcomings of his characteristic belief, or, let us say, starting point in which opinion is rooted. We must begin somewhere; we have to be arbitrary in order to mean, and thereby take the risk of making our wrongheadedness plain. About these starting points, moreover, we cannot say much in advance. They are the result of temperament, education, and the variety of circumstances of one's being in the world. But if they are indefinite, they must not be trivial, for then the attitude they represent will not support the insight they must bear if the resultant work is to have range and depth.

Considered in this light, our authors hold a range of commitments forcefully declared, yet also enriched and transformed by the impingements upon their claims of the realms of experience they seem initially to discount. Their characteristic positions we can represent by the figure of the cross itself, if we imagine three intersecting straight lines which give the symbol in its three dimensional form. We can now consider the main oppositions as extremities on each of three separate axes.

Aldous Huxley tells us that *Grey Eminence* is an experiment occasioned by his desire to compensate for the inadequacies of traditional literature (time-bound to images and preoccupied with suffering) in expressing the ultimate importance of mystical insight. Unitive experience is the true end of human nature, and Western man especially is distracted from it by his preoccupation with history and with a literature engrossed by suffering and by its own structures.

Yet Huxley, the philosopher of mysticism who advocates transcendence, himself remains fascinated by the problem of man's cruelty to man, and *Grey Eminence* diagnoses the destructiveness of modern technological civilisation which has culminated in the catastrophe of two world wars. Fr Joseph is a vividly imagined creation, and Huxley's literary gifts evoke, in order to analyse, the quality of one man's devotion to the sensible image of the cross as a symbol of where Western religion took a decisively wrong turn. However tendentious the analysis, the imaginative vividness and drama of the literary portrait are compelling.

In *Island*, another experiment in form, the same opposition between mystic and artist continues. The most moving quality of the book is the confrontation between the author's intuitions of eternity and acknowledgement of the 'essential horror', the irreducible fact of suffering in the world. Throughout Huxley's later career, with which I have been mainly concerned, the rationalist and mystic who deplored the image of the cross also submitted to the truth about experience which it implies. The fullness of his humanity is evident in the very failure of his mysticism to stand as disembodied theory, free from the unlovely facts of experience and the compassion bred of familiarity with ordinary human imperfection.

Huxley's opposite is Owen Barfield. Both share an explicit concern for mysticism, and focus their main attention on the manifestation of eternity in time. Barfield has described his life's work as being 'to express mystical truth in intelligible thoughts rather than in symbol, as far as that can be done'.[3] Yet Barfield also criticises Huxley's spirituality as rarefied and contentless, and unlike Huxley, sees history as far from an impediment to vision. Rather, it is a principal means towards vision, and the careful study of history reveals the pseudo-absolutes which men have erected as idols, distracting themselves from God. History for Barfield therefore frees man from the bondage to which Huxley thinks it confines him, and also, Barfield believes, the cruciform tensions of polar opposition are the modality itself of human knowledge, retained in some manner at higher levels of being. Consequently, our characteristic manner of thought is imaginative, and Barfield does not approve, as Huxley does, a desire for unitive experience which regards imagination (like history) merely as an impediment. But Barfield lacks Huxley's imaginative gifts with language and there is nothing in his work comparable to the portrait of Father Joseph. Although Barfield reaches towards the complexity of literature when he needs to prove his theory on our pulses, his achievement in this respect is not especially distinguished.

For different reasons, Huxley and Barfield experience the challenge of rendering sensible on the plane of everyday activity their insights into transcendent reality. They stand at opposite ends of a vertical axis, so to speak, as wisdom-figures whose contribution reminds us that man is, at the centre of his being, metaphysical. Their opposition consists mainly in the fact that Barfield's wisdom depends on memory, or history, which Huxley eschews in the name of unmediated religious insight. Yet to render their theories convincing, each reaches towards the other's special contribution, Huxley embracing the paradox of the cross, and Barfield attempting to bring to his philosophy the vitality of artistic creation.

In contrast to Huxley and Barfield, the four remaining authors find their starting points on a horizontal plane representing the realm of human affairs in space and time, rather than on a vertical where man addresses eternal truth. So conceived, their prejudices stand opposed not only to each other, but to the challenge of the vertical axis, to which each tries also to establish some relation.

Michael Polanyi's career shows him to be a man of great intellectual resourcefulness and drawn to practical problems. His examination of religious belief, developing the Augustinian maxim on faith and understanding, is conducted mainly to illuminate the practice of science in modern society. Applying his experience also to the history of science, Polanyi warns about the moral risks run by a civilisation which ignores customs and institutions which have guaranteed its stability in the past. Man, he claims, cannot make clear the principles by which he knows, for the bodily roots of knowledge are irreducibly complex. As a being in the world, none of us can analyse objectively that of which he is constituted, and human learning is attended by a dubiety inherent in the conditions of knowledge itself. A sign of this is the religious symbol of the cross.

About our ultimate beliefs, properly the sphere of religious commitment, Polanyi has little to say as distinct from his analysis of how the structure of religious commitment remains one with the structure of other branches of human thought. Yet as his career advanced, Polanyi became increasingly concerned with the reality of spirit, and although never venturing into the occult, his late lectures on imagination lead him to appreciate how art, literature and myth display in action the 'powers' for which his earlier theory did not account.

Opposite to Polanyi is Tolkien. Both have in common that their beliefs remain implicit in their work, but Tolkien's main achievement is artistic, not philosophical. His aim is to render the enduring desires of the human heart concrete by way of imagination and through the medium of fantasy, a 'subcreation' which, according to the theory of eucatastrophe, somehow expresses the author's belief but does not draw its terms from his religious commitment.

Our approach to Tolkien reveals a marked coincidence in tone, spirit and structure between *The Lord of the Rings* and the main ideas of analytic psychology, and reflects a sophisticated intuitive understanding of the cartography of the inner life (to the extent that we agree, that is, that Jung's classification is reliable). Tolkien's literary skills, however, distinguish his writing from the analogues in Jungian thought, and his narrative gift creates his distinctive sense of historical actuality. The central themes of *The Lord of the Rings* remain death and belief, and, within these, the problem itself of the mind's adjustment to reality in an increasingly disenchanted post-Renaissance world where faerie has been relegated increasingly to the nursery and man has lost contact with his deep desires and the magic of language alike. In Tolkien's fantasy, the process itself of this disenchantment from the development of myth to legend to Romance and realistic fiction is recapitulated and held up for our examination.

The romantic spirit of *The Lord of the Rings* stands clearly in contrast to Polanyi's pragmatism, and yet we can see how both authors encounter a similar problem concerning the literary relevance of religious belief which remains implicit in their work. In Tolkien's fantasy the specific Christian component is elusive, and Polanyi's insistence on the tacit commitment implied in all knowledge forces him to a position wherein the presuppositions of knowledge endlessly precede its conceptualisation. For Polanyi, it would seem that no man could vouch for the rationality or veracity of his own views unless, *per fidem*, such pre-conscious knowing-how is in a manner infallible. And yet, in the very act of broaching such quandaries, Polanyi and Tolkien also achieve singular insight into man's immersion in a world of potential meaning within which he struggles to define himself, discovering significance.

This leaves the final pair, David Jones and Robert Graves. They differ from Polanyi and Tolkien in that their beliefs are explicit, and from Barfield and Huxley in that their starting points remain on the horizontal plane, and neither is primarily a mystic. They resemble each other in that they share a strong sense of actual place and of the importance of local cult, while their main differences lie in the attitudes they assume towards these common concerns.

Jones's orthodox Catholicism commits him to the traditions of Latin European civilisation, the continuity of which he sees disturbed by the rise of 'technics'. For Jones, the most significant act in history is the crucifixion; it affirms the nature of man as sign-maker, and shows also how art is religious. Specifically, Jones combines orthodox Catholic sacramentalism with modernist practice by adapting to the uses of poetry the theories of Jacques Maritain's *Art and Scholasticism* and Maurice de la Taille's treatise on the relationship between the Last Supper and Calvary in the Roman Catholic mass. The sign of the cross becomes increasingly Jones's preoccupation as he explores how it symbolises the nature of poetry itself as a sign, and he interprets the poet's craft as an act of oblation rooted in a concrete historical experience of immolation.

But Jones's orthodoxy is not glib, and everywhere he acknowledges the difficulty of interpreting traditional religious values in a modern world of industrial utilitarianism which has forced the artist away from the centre and self-consciously onto the perimeter of society. The sense of this difficulty encourages a humble and tolerant attitude towards the sign-making of men from all ages and civilisations, extending alike to pagan witches of Celtic Britain and ancient goddesses of the world before Christ.

Graves, in contrast to Jones, argues for an equally explicit, if perverse, orthodoxy which starts by putting the ancient female deities at the centre. In their name, Graves execrates Christian dogmatism, for he sees it as promoting the 'prosaic' in a modern world dominated by a technology which divorces man from poetry and consequently from his roots in nature. The besetting sin of 'Apollonian' Christian civilisation, Graves claims, is the assumption that human reason is autonomous, and such arrogance is inevitably crucified by the more ancient power of the female, the muse to whom poetry is dedicated.

From the *White Goddess* we can see that Graves's position has much in common with the mythography of pre-Puritan Europe, and readings of *Wife to Mr Milton* and *King Jesus* show the importance of the cross to his historical theory. But the irony of Graves's position is that his own extraordinary 'Apollonian' scholarly equipment is necessary to make clear his anti-Apollonian argument, and in this tension lies the most engaging energy of his work.

Like Jones, Graves remains dedicated to poetry as the most fully human expression of man's uncertainty in the world, but, in relation to Jones, Graves stands also as a kind of shadow figure. Whereas Jones's personal life, for instance, is private and barely revealed in his writing (even in controversy his opinions are without personal animus), Graves is deliberately a *bête noire*, publicising his personal idiosyncrasy, and in controversy he is openly aggressive.[4] Jones we might say is the poet of man's uncertainty supported by a tradition of respected standards and the time-honoured symbols of religion, while Graves is the poet of man's uncertainty despite these conventions. His stubbornness, defiance, and comedy have their uses as an antidote to unreflective smugness about civilised values, a corrective likewise prompted, however, from another direction by Jones's humility, humour and tenderness.

The foregoing sets of paired oppositions are of course not exhaustive, and the very neatness forces even more urgently the question of what kind of general conclusion I now hope to establish. Faced with this kind of typology and the reasoning that has led to it, it seems we can take one of two fairly obvious directions: first, to develop the argument into a theory of psychological types; second, to make some kind of statement of belief about the cross as a religious symbol. But in the first case, we venture into the domain of science, and in the second, of theology. Criticism refuses both, and comes to rest instead by making, from the critic's choice, some statement of interest about relationships between literature and other kinds of learning and experience. As with the authors themselves, the critic's starting point remains arbitrary to some degree, though it may not be trivial.[5] Consequently, my subjects are determined first by the fact that they are distinguished in their own right, and then because on each I believe I have something new to say. Also, they conform to a set of criteria having to do with epistemological problems occasioned by the rise of science and given paradigmatic modern form during the seventeenth century, and with the symbol of the cross. My choice clearly has a pattern behind it, and the issue therefore remains whether or not the discussion justifies seeking such a pattern out, by providing through particular cases a broader sense of the vitality of literature and the range of human temperament and kinds of experience it can express, as well as some account of its relations to other branches of learning. Criticism which attempts in some such manner to balance argument and insight, strives also to open up according to its merits, both as an act of expression and one of assessment, upon that plenitude of being which words reveal.

Notes

CHAPTER 1

1. See Christopher Hibbert, *Charles I* (London: Weidenfeld and Nicolson, 1968), p. 136.
2. See 'An Epitaph upon King Charles' by J. H. (possibly John Hewett), in *Eikon Basilike. The Portraiture of His Sacred Majesty in His Solitudes and Sufferings*, ed. Philip A. Knachel (New York: Cornell University Press, 1966), p. 195.
3. Thus Cromwell told his commissioners. See Maurice Ashley, *Oliver Cromwell, The Conservative Dictator* (London: Jonathan Cape, 1937), p. 154.
4. Andrew Marvell, 'An Horatian Ode upon Cromwell's Return from Ireland', ed. H. M. Margoliouth, *The Poems and Letters of Andrew Marvell*, 2 vols. (Oxford: at the Clarendon Press, 1952), I, 88–89.
5. See St Augustine, *Confessions*, XIII, 10, trans. E. B. Pusey (London: Everyman, 1907), p. 315. The well-known accounts of C. S. Lewis, *The Discarded Image* (Cambridge: University Press, 1964); E. M. W. Tillyard, *The Elizabethan World Picture* (London: Chatto and Windus, 1943); A. O. Lovejoy, *The Great Chain of Being* (Cambridge, Mass.: Harvard University Press, 1936), remain excellent introductions to the theory of inclusive and hierarchical structures underlying the mediaeval view of the world.
6. See Ernst H. Kantorowicz, *The King's Two Bodies. A Study in Medieval Political Theory* (Princeton: Princeton University Press, 1952), for a full account of mediaeval kingship and the social complexities attendant upon it. C. S. Lewis, *English Literature in the Sixteenth Century, Excluding Drama* (Oxford: Clarendon Press, 1954), pp. 46 ff., gives a good brief account of the emergence of absolutism, and of the main differences between the Tudor and mediaeval views of kingship.
7. *Eikon Basilike*, pp. 78, 49, 26, 128.
8. Ibid., p. 46.
9. *The Rebel*, trans. Anthony Bower (Middlesex: Peregrine Books, 1951), p. 90.
10. Ibid., p. 112. Camus talks here of 'vertical' transcendence contrasted with an emphasis on the end of history. In 'Thought at the Meridian' (pp. 243 ff.) he suggests that man dwells in a crux, between the intersecting lines of a 'philosophy of eternity' (251) and the facts of history.
11. See Paolo Rossi, *Francis Bacon. From Magic to Science*, trans. Sacha Rabinovitch (Chicago: University of Chicago Press, 1968), esp. pp. 1–36.
12. See Patrick Grant, *Images and Ideas in Literature of the English Renaissance*, chapter I.
13. Ibid., passim.
14. For a sense of how these developments affected the philosophy of science, theology and literature respectively, see Richard A. Watson, *The Downfall of*

Cartesianism 1673–1712: A Study of Epistemological Issues in Late 17th Century Cartesianism (The Hague: Martinus Nijhoff, 1966), pp. 1–12; James P. Mackey, *The Problems of Religious Faith* (Chicago: Franciscan Herald Press, 1972), pp. 153 ff.; A. D. Nuttall, *A Common Sky. Philosophy and the Literary Imagination* (London: Chatto and Windus for Sussex University Press, 1974), pp. 13 ff.

15. See *De gen. ad litt.* for the fullest account of Augustine's main divisions. Also, see Vernon T. Burke, *Augustine's View of Reality* (Villanova, Pa.: Villanova University Press, 1964), pp. 7 ff.; Ronald H. Nash, *The Light of the Mind: St. Augustine's Theory of Knowledge* (Lexington: The University of Kentucky Press, 1969), pp. 1 ff., et passim.

16. For Augustine's Theory of Rhetoric, see especially *De doctrina Christiana*, also Marcia L. Colish, *The Mirror of Language: A Study of the Mediaeval Theory of Knowledge* (New Haven and London: Yale University Press, 1968), pp. 19 ff.; J. A. Mazzeo, *Renaissance and Seventeenth Century Studies* (New York: Columbia University Press; London: Routledge and Kegan Paul, 1964), ch. I, 'St. Augustine's Rhetoric of Silence: Truth vs. Eloquence and Things vs. Signs', pp. 1–28.

17. See *Letter 140* for Augustine's association between the cross and faith, and *Letter 147* for an allegorical interpretation of the 'arms' of the cross as comprising the 'whole action' of a Christian.

18. See *The Mind's Road to God*, VII, 2–3, 5, trans. George Boas (New York: Bobbs Merrill, 1953), pp. 43–45.

19. *The Hours of the Divine Office* (Collegeville, Minn.: 1963), Vol. III, p. 1534.

20. Horton Davies, *Worship and Theology in England: From Cranmer to Hooker* (Princeton: Princeton University Press, 1970), p. 354.

21. *The Works of George Herbert*, ed. F. E. Hutchinson (Oxford: at the Clarendon Press, 1967, first published 1941), p. 40.

22. 'Jordon I', ed. Hutchinson, *Works*, p. 57.

23. See Keith Thomas, *Religion and the Decline of Magic: Studies in Popular Beliefs in Sixteenth and Seventeenth Century England* (London: Wiedenfeld and Nicolson, 1971), for an exhaustive account of the complexities of Puritan reform.

24. See William G. Madsen, *From Shadowy Types to Truth. Studies in Milton's Symbolism* (New Haven and London: Yale University Press, 1968), on how Puritans preferred literature to the graphic arts.

25. David Morton, *A Sociology of English Religion* (London: SCM Press, 1966), p. 88, claims that hymns became the central item in British religion. In the following account I am indebted to Lionel Adey, whose article 'Great Aunt Tilly's Beautiful 'ymns: A Victorian Sub-culture', *Wascana Review* (Spring, 1977), pp. 21–43, makes the contrast between Venantius Fortunatus and English hymns of the eighteenth and nineteenth centuries.

26. *Interpretations of Poetry and Religion* (New York: Harper Torchbooks, 1957), pp. 93–94.

27. Owen Barfield describes this error as 'logomorphism'. See *Poetic Diction: A Study in Meaning* (London: Faber and Faber, 1962, first edition, 1928), p. 90. On the same point, C. S. Lewis, 'Is Theology Poetry'. in *They Asked for a Paper* (London: Geoffrey Bles, 1962), p. 160: 'It is very probable that most (almost certainly not all) of the first generation of Christians never thought of their faith without anthropomorphic imagery: and that they were not explicitly conscious, as a modern would be, that it *was* mere imagery.'

28. Jurgen Moltmann, *The Crucified God. The Cross of Christ as the Foundation and*

Criticism of Christian Theology, trans. R. A. Wilson and John Bowden (Munich: Christian Kaiser Verlag, 2nd ed., 1973, first British ed., London: SCM Press, 1974), p. 92.

29. Ibid., pp. 7 ff.; 72; 221 ff.

30. Once there is a split between event and significance, Moltmann's approach, which begins by facing the hard fact of the execution, represents one of the two main ways of engaging the problem. The other is to treat the cross as metaphysical, as does René Guénon, *Le Symbolisme de la Croix* (Paris: Les Editions Vega, Deuxième Édition, 1950). In so far as Guénon's account is psychologically suggestive it still leaves us with the task of accepting the cross as a fact: the '*application contingente*' (p. 14) with which Moltmann begins, and which causes him to demand that the cross be stripped of the (symbolic) rose (pp. 35−36).

31. *Dynamics of Faith* (New York: Harper Torchbooks, 1958), pp. 97, 42 ff.

32. Ibid., p. 97.

33. *The Crucified God*, p. 278.

34. Anne Sexton, 'For God While Sleeping', *All My Pretty Ones* (Boston: Houghton Mifflin Co., 1962), p. 24.

35. 'Religion and the Visual Arts' (1955). Unpublished paper for the Theological Discussion Group, Washington.

36. The modernist preoccupation with 'tension', the patterned energies of 'vortex', and so on, is relevant here. Allen Upward, who influenced Pound, in *The New Word* (Fourteenth Head), has a fascinating passage: 'The cross is the Sign of Matter, and as such it reminds us of the nature of Matter. Not only is it a rude picture of a knot . . . but it shows us how the knot is made. It is by two lines of string meeting cross-wise. Thus it reminds us that two Ways of Strength must meet cross-wise to become entangled.' Compare Hugh Kenner, *The Pound Era*, 'Knot and Vortex' (London: Faber and Faber, 1972), pp. 145 ff., where the knot is also described in terms of crossed strings making a 'self-interfering pattern' which Kenner then calls 'a whole time's way of thinking' (147).

37. 'The Metaphysical Poets', p. 289.

38. See Gabriel Josipovici, *The World and the Book. A Study of Modern Fiction* (St Albans: Paladin Books, 1973). Josipovici's main point on modern art calling attention to itself, has, in a sense, been argued from the beginnings of a critical tradition on this subject in Edmund Wilson's *Axel's Castle. A Study in the Imaginative Literature of 1870−1930* (New York, London: Charles Scribner's Sons, 1936), pp. 275 ff. All depends on whether or not we see modernism as wantonly obscure and escapist, as does Graham Hough, *Image and Experience. Studies in a Literary Revolution* (London: Gerald Duckworth and Co., Ltd., 1960), or attempting to meet the demands of an unprecedentedly difficult civilisational phase, as does Hugh Kenner, *The Pound Era*.

39. On this paradox in Locke, and its effects on the literary imagination, see A. D. Nuttall, *A Common Sky*, esp. p. 28 ff.

40. As modern philosophers of science have acknowledged the paradox of Lockean empiricism by realising the importance of intuition and imagination for the scientist, so the theologians have insisted that men are 'metaphysical animals' (Illtyd Trethowan, *Mysticism and Theology: An Essay in Christian Metaphysics* [London: Geoffrey Chapman, 1975], p. 79). By this we may mean no more than the fact that one is forced to admit to one's knowledge while realising that there are areas into which that knowledge could extend. The range of my conception can thus

embrace the imagined limits of the universe itself. The mystery, as Maritain says, lies in what we do not know.

CHAPTER 2

1. Sybille Bedford, *Aldous Huxley: A Biography* (London: Chatto and Windus, 2 vols., 1973–74), II, 53. See also I, 152: Huxley's dissatisfaction with his writing began with *Those Barren Leaves* (1925). T. S. Eliot talks of Huxley's 'variety of fiction', indicating his unconventional talents, and goes on to say that Huxley's place in English literature is assured. See Keith M. May, *Aldous Huxley* (London: Elek Books, 1972), p. 9.

2. Bedford, *Biography*, II, 240.

3. *Themes and Variations* (London: Chatto and Windus, 1954, first published 1950), pp. 1–152.

4. *Letters of Aldous Huxley*, ed. Grover Smith (London: Chatto and Windus, 1969), p. 608n.

5. Bedford, *Biography*, II, 291.

6. *Grey Eminence. A Study in Religion and Politics* (London: Chatto and Windus, 1944, first published 1941). References are cited in the text.

7. *The Perennial Philosophy* (New York: Harper and Row, 1970, first published 1944), p. 190.

8. Ibid., p. 189.

9. *After Many a Summer Dies the Swan* (London: Chatto and Windus, The Vanguard Library, 1953), pp. 89, 86, 87.

10. See *The Perennial Philosophy*, pp. 216 ff., 263 ff., and 'Adonis and the Alphabet', in *Adonis and the Alphabet and Other Essays* (London: Chatto and Windus, 1975), pp. 187 ff.

11. See *The Perennial Philosophy*, pp. 134 and 194; *After Many a Summer*, p. 97; 'Adonis and the Alphabet', p. 186.

12. *After Many a Summer*, p. 179.

13. See Bedford, *Biography*, II, 70, on Huxley's declining interest in Proust; *Vulgarity in Literature* (London: Chatto and Windus, 1930), p. 9; 'Breugel', In *On Art and Artists*, ed. Morris Philipson (New York: Harper & Brothers, 1960), p. 204; 'Music at Night', *On Art and Artists*, p. 315.

14. 'Variations on a Philosopher', *Themes and Variations*, p. 100.

15. On art becoming idolatry, see *The Perennial Philosophy*, pp. 138–39. Huxley also thinks art can give a glimpse of a sublime order. See 'Music at Night', pp. 313–14. For Sebastian Barnack's remark, see *Time Must Have a Stop* (London: Chatto and Windus, 1971, first published 1945), p. 284.

16. *Ends and Means* (London: Chatto and Windus, 1948, first published 1937), p. 127.

17. *After Many a Summer*, p. 97, et passim.

18. For an account of the relationship, see Etienne Gilson, *La Liberté Chez Descartes et la Théologie* (Paris: Librarie Félix Alcan, 1913). See also L. J. Beck, *The Metaphysics of Descartes. A Study of the Meditations* (Oxford: The Clarendon Press, 1965) pp. 4–5, 212.

19. *Oeuvres complètes de Bérulle*, ed. J. P. Migne (Paris: 1866), col. 161.

20. For an account of the differences, see Henri Brémond, *Histoire Littéraire du*

Sentiment Religieux en France, Depuis la Fin des Guerres de Religion Jusqu'à nos Jours (Paris: Bloud et Gay, 1916), III, 111 ff., 137 ff.

21. There are many good accounts of Bérulle's life and works. See Henri Brémond, *Histoire*, III, 'l'École Française'; Paul Cochois, *Bérulle et l'École Française* (Paris: Editions du Seuil, 1963); M. Houssaye, *M. de Bérulle et les Carmélites de France, le Père de Bérulle et l'Oratoire, le Cardinal de Bérulle et le Cardinal de Richelieu*, 3 vols. (Paris: 1872–75); A. Molien, 'Bérulle', art., *Dictionaire de Spiritualité* (Paris: Gabriel Beauchesne, 1937–), vol. I, cols. 1531–1581.

22. See Cochois, *Bérulle*, p. 153: '*pas une page . . . qui ne cite le pseudo-Denys*'; Molien, 'Bérulle', col. 1544: '*l'atmosphère spirituelle que respirait Bérulle semble donc avoir été saturée d'influences venues des pays-bas.*'

23. See Jean Dagens, *Bérulle et les Origines de la Restauration Catholique (1576–1611)* (Paris: Desclée de Brouwer, 1952), pp. 150–65. Etta Gullick, 'The Life of Father Benet of Canfield', *Collectanea Franciscana* 42 (1972), p. 62.

24. See Gullick, *Life*, pp. 63 ff.

25. See *Grey Eminence*, pp. 32–37; A. Duval, *La vie admirable de la Bienheureuse Soeur Marie de l'Incarnation* (Paris: 1893; first published 1621), pp. 25–26.

26. See Anthony Levi, S. J., *French Moralists: The Theory of the Passions, 1585–1649* (Oxford: Clarendon Press, 1964), pp. 234 ff., 248.

27. Parts I and II are edited by D. M. Rogers, *English Recusant Literature 1558–1640*, vol. 40, *William Fitch, 'The Rule of Perfection' (1609), James Tyrie 'Refutation of John Knox' (1573)* (Yorkshire: Scolar Press, 1970). The following account refers to the Scolar Press edition, and page numbers are given in the text.

28. See Optat de Veghel, *Benoit de Canfield (1563–1610), sa vie, sa doctrine et son influence* (Rome: Institutum Historicum Ord. Fr. Min. Cap., 1949), pp. 328–44.

29. Huxley was aware of the depth of this paradox in language itself. See *The Perennial Philosophy*, p. 11; Bedford, *Biography*, II, 211.

30. Letter to Agnes E. Meyer, ed. Donald Watt, *Aldous Huxley. The Critical Heritage* (London: Routledge and Kegan Paul, 1975), pp. 345–46. See also E. M. Forster's complaint on Huxley's lack of warmth in a review of *The Devils of Loudun*, ed. Watt, *Critical Heritage*, p. 381, and John Wain's in 'Tracts Against Materialism: *After Many a Summer Dies the Swan* and *Brave New World*', ed. Robert E. Keuhn, *Aldous Huxley. A Collection of Essays* (New York: Prentice-Hall, 1974), pp. 26–29.

31. Huxley became increasingly perturbed by the problem of pain in his later works. See Joseph Bentley, 'The Later Novels of Huxley' in *Aldous Huxley*, ed. Keuhn, pp. 142–53. Philip Thody, *Aldous Huxley: A Biographical Introduction* (London: Studio Vista, 1973), pp. 62 ff.

32. *Island* (Middlesex: Penguin Books, 1964, first published, Chatto and Windus, 1962). Page numbers are cited in the text.

33. See Bedford, *Biography*, II, 330.

34. Review in *Partisan Review* (Summer, 1962), xxix, 472–73, ed. Watt, *Critical Heritage*, pp. 453–54.

35. Review in *Yale Review* (June, 1962), li, 630–32, ed. Watt, *Critical Heritage*, pp. 451–53.

36. *The Power and the Glory* (Middlesex: Penguin Books, 1962), pp. 8–9.

37. Cited in Bedford, *Biography*, I, 242.

38. See Bedford, *Biography*, II, 328.

39. Ibid., II, 322.

CHAPTER 3

1. *An Essay Toward the Theory of the Ideal or Intelligible World* (1704), II, 85 ff.

2. Burton Feldman and Robert D. Richardson, *The Rise of Modern Mythology: 1680−1860* (Bloomington and London: Indiana University Press, 1972).

3. See G. S. Kirk's assessment of Malinowski in *Myth: Its Meaning and Function in Ancient and Other Cultures* (Cambridge: Cambridge University Press; Berkeley and Los Angeles: University of California Press, 1970), pp. 19 ff. and 280 ff.

4. *The Classical Review*, 69 (1955), p. 208.

5. See *Handbook*, p. 10; *The Greek Myths* (Harmondsworth: Penguin Books, 1955, revised ed., 1960), I, 20−22. Hereafter referred to in the text as *G. M.* And see *Five Pens in Hand* (New York: Books for Libraries Press, 1958), pp. 67−69.

6. *The White Goddess: A Historical Grammar of Poetic Myth*, amended and enlarged edition (London: Faber and Faber, 1961), p. 389. Hereafter referred to in the text as *W.G.*

7. *Boccaccio on Poetry: Being the Preface and the Fourteenth and Fifteenth Books of Boccaccio's 'Genealogia Deorum Gentilium'*, trans. and ed. Charles G. Osgood (New York: Bobbs-Merrill, 1956), p. 39. The following account is annotated in the text from this edition.

8. Ibid., p. xvii.

9. Ibid., p. xxiv.

10. Ibid., p. xvi.

11. *Steps* (London: Cassell, 1951), p. 237.

12. 'The Second Fated', *Collected Poems, 1965* (London: Cassell, 1965), p. 249, warns us not to be too readily satisfied with views 'formed scientifically/From whatever was there before Time was.' *Poetic Unreason* (London: Cecil Parker, 1925), p. 156, suggests that history reflects the interpreter.

13. *An Essay on Man: An Introduction to a Philosophy of Human Culture* (Toronto, New York, London: Bantam Books, 1970), p. 84.

14. See John B. Vickery, *Robert Graves and the White Goddess* (Lincoln: University of Nebraska Press, 1972); Sydney Musgrove, *The Ancestry of the White Goddess* (University of Auckland, Bulletin No. 62, English Series No. 11, 1962). Admittedly, Graves is fond of scholars with peculiar theories.

15. *Collected Poems, 1965*, p. 170.

16. *Five Pens in Hand*, 'Don't Fidget, Young Man' (New York: Books for Libraries Press, 1958), p. 128.

17. 'These Be Your Gods, O Israel!', *The Crowning Privilege* (London: Cassell and Co., 1955), p. 135.

18. *Love Among the Haystacks and Other Stories* (Harmondsworth: Penguin Books, 1962), p. 125. Subsequent references are cited in the text.

19. See for instance John Bayley, *The Uses of Division, Unity and Disharmony in Literature* (London: Chatto and Windus, 1976), pp. 43 ff.

20. *D. H. Lawrence, Novelist* (New York: Knopf, 1956), p. 56.

21. For the influence of George Moore on D. H. Lawrence, see Leslie M. Thompson, 'The Christ Who Didn't Die: Analogues to D. H. Lawrence's *The Man Who Died*'; *D. H. Lawrence Review*, 8, 1 (Spring, 1975), 19−30.

22. 'Don't Fidget, Young Man,' p. 128.

23. See Lawrence on 'Christs in the Tirol', *Phoenix*, ed. Edward D. McDonald,

The Posthumous Papers of D. H. Lawrence (London: William Heinemann Ltd., 1936), pp. 82 ff., where the whittlers of crucifixes come to understand suffering and thereby relieve it. Also, Samuel A. Eisenstein, *Boarding the Ship of Death: D. H. Lawrence's Quester Heroes* (Le Hague, Paris: Mouton, 1974), pp. 126 ff., deals with *The Man Who Died* and the problem of suffering as a rite of passage.

24. *The Mabinogion: A New Translation*, 2 vols. (Oxford: Clarendon Press, 1929).

25. *Les Mabinogion, traduits en entier*, 2 tom. (1899), ed. M. H. Arbois de Jubainville, *Cours de littérature celtique* (Paris: 1899), tom. 3–4.

26. *Matho van Mathonwy. An Inquiry into the Origins and Development of the Fourth Book of the Mabinogi, with the Text and a Translation* (Cardiff: University of Wales Press Board, 1928).

27. See, for instance, *The Problem of the Picts*, ed. F. T. Wainwright, *Studies in History and Archaeology* (Edinburgh: Thomas Nelson and Sons, 1955), pp. 9 ff.

28. Pointed out in 'Through the Wild Centuries', review of the first edition, *TLS* (Feb. 5, 1949), p. 94.

29. Thomas F. O'Rahilly, *Early Irish History and Mythology* (Dublin: Institute for Advanced Studies, 1946), pp. 141 ff.; 194 ff.; 413; Myles Dillon and Nora Chadwick, *The Celtic Realms* (London: Weidenfeld and Nicolson, 1967), pp. 146 ff.

30. John Peradotto, *Classical Mythology: An Annotated Bibliographical Survey* (Urbana, Ill.: University of Illinois Press, 1973), p. 10.

31. *The Classical Review*, 69 (1955), p. 208.

32. 'To Juan at the Winter Solstice.', *Collected Poems, 1965* (London: Cassell, 1965), p. 177.

33. Douglas Day, *Swifter Than Reason. The Poetry and Cirticism of Robert Graves* (Chapel Hill: University of North Carolina Press, 1963), p. 173.

34. *Encounter* (Dec. 1964), p. 70.

35. 'What Has Gone Wrong?' in *Difficult Questions, Easy Answers* (London: Cassell, 1972), p. 117.

CHAPTER 4

1. *In Parenthesis* (London: Faber and Faber, 1937, 1963 ed.), p. viii.

2. René Hague's term. See *David Jones* (University of Wales Press, 1975), p. 28.

3. See Aneirin Talfan Davies, 'A Note on David Jones', *Agenda*, Vol. 5, Nos. 1–3 (Spring–Summer, 1967), pp. 172 ff.

4. *Ulysses* (New York: Vintage Books, 1966), p. 76.

5. See *Anathemata* (London: Faber and Faber, 1952, 3rd ed., 1972), p. 10; *Epoch and Artist* (London: Faber and Faber, 1959, 2nd ed., 1973), where the index has many references.

6. Recounted in Bedford, *Biography*, I, p. 216.

7. *Anathemata*, preface, p. 29. Hereafter, references to the *Anathemata* and *Epoch and Artist* are cited in the text by page number, the titles being indicated *A*. and *E.A.* respectively.

8. The following account is based on Etienne Gilson, *The Christian Philosophy of St Thomas Aquinas*, trans. L. K. Shook, C.S.B. (London: Victor Gollancz, Ltd., 1961). Page numbers are indicated in the text.

9. *David Jones*, p. 26.

10. Jacques Maritain, *Art and Scholastism, With Other Essays*, trans. J. F. Scanlan

(London: Sheed & Ward, 1930), pp. 24–25. Page numbers are cited in the text.

11. *David Jones*, p. 2.

12. Maurice de la Taille, S. J., *The Mystery of Faith and Human Opinion Contrasted and Defended* (London: Sheed and Ward, 1930). Page numbers to this edition are cited in the text. Jones cites the book in the 'Preface' to the *Anathemata* among his main authorities, with a note saying how he had first heard of de la Taille's ideas around 1930. The key phrase, 'He placed himself in the order of signs' appears in this edition on p. 212 (cf. *E.A.*, 179). And see *E.A.*, 163, note, for further explicit reference to de la Taille. René Hague, *A Commentary on the Anathemata of David Jones* (Wellingborough: Christopher Skelton, 1977), pp. 4, 34, 240, et passim, makes clear how important de la Taille was to Jones, and has said in conversation that Jones must have come across de la Taille's ideas 'well before 1930', suggesting 1920–21.

13. Letter, cited in Hague, *David Jones*, 56.

14. Ibid., pp. 39–40.

15. William T. Noon, S.J., *Poetry and Prayer* (New Brunswick, N.J.: Rutgers University Press, 1967), 241.

16. Jones is self-effacing with regard to his own learning. See for instance, *David Jones. Letters to Vernon Watkins*, ed. with notes by Ruth Pryor, foreword by Gwen Watkins (Cardiff: University of Wales Press, 1976), pp. 20, 61.

17. See St Augustine, *Enchiridion*, 1, 5; Letter 147, ch. 34–35, Letter 55, and my discussion in Ch. 1.

18. *Analecta Hymnica Medii Aevi*, ed. Guido M. Dreves, S.J., and Clemens Blume, S.J., 55 vols. (Leipzig: O. R. Reisland, 1886–1922), 8, 18, No. 11, St. 7 a–b. For a sense of the various iconographic traditions, see Gertrud Schiller, *Ikonographie der Christlichen Kunst* (Gutersloh: Gutersloher Verlagshaus Gerd Mohn, 1968), Band 2, 'Die Passion Jesu Christi'; Heransgegeben Van Engelbert Kirschbaum, S.J., et al., *Lexikon Der Christlichen Ikonographie* (Rome: Freiburg, Basel, Wien: Herder, 1968–70), 'Kreuzallegorie', cols. 569 ff.

19. See David Blamires, 'The Mediaeval Inspiration of David Jones', in *David Jones: Eight Essays on his Work as Writer and Artist*, ed. Roland Mathias (Llandysul, Dyfed: Gomer Press, 1976), pp. 73 ff.

20. See 'Vexilla Regis', painted in 1947; *The Sleeping Lord and Other Fragments* (London: Faber and Faber, 1974), p. 32; *E.A.*, 260 ff.

21. See David Blamires, *David Jones, Artist and Writer* (Manchester: Manchester University Press, 1971), p. 48.

22. *An Introduction to the Rime of the Ancient Mariner* (London: Clover Hill Editions, 1972), p. 31.

23. See also 'The Bride', 'Tristan ac Essyllt', 'The Victim', 'He Frees the Waters', for further examples of Jones's use of typology in the visual arts.

24. *In Parenthesis*, pp. 151 ff. Further references are cited in the text.

25. *The Sleeping Lord and Other Fragments*. References are cited in the text.

26. The two voyages could easily be mistaken for one. See Hague's note in *Commentary*, which cites Jones.

27. *Anathemata*, 65, note 2, suggests that all art participates '*directly* in the benefits of the passion', in the sense that the cross signifies all signs. See also, p. 165, note 2.

28. Hague, *Commentary*, identifies him as St Guthlac, 'feeling his way up the river Welland with sounding pole, to found the monastery of Crowland in the year 716.'

29. See David Blamires, 'The Mediaeval Inspiration of David Jones'.

30. Hague, *Commentary*, pp. 2, 18, 248, makes clear how profound was Jones's

concern for the ill-effects of technology. See also Colin Wilcockson, 'David Jones and "The Break" ', *Agenda*, 15, 2–3 (Summer–Autumn, 1977), p. 126: 'This Break to which he refers was occasioned primarily by the consequences of the industrial revolution. . . .'

31. In conversation.

32. John Holloway, *The Colours of Clarity. Essays on Contemporary Literature and Education* (London: Routledge and Kegan Paul, 1964), pp. 116–22.

33. The following account derives from *Milton's God* (London: Chatto and Windus, rev. ed., 1965), and page numbers are cited in the text. In particular, chapter 7, 'Christianity' (pp. 229–77), makes Empson's case against the Christian religion, a topic which has increasingly preoccupied him in his later career.

34. 'Donne the Spaceman', *The Kenyon Review*, Vol. 19, No. 3 (1957), pp. 337–99.

35. Ibid., pp. 379–80.

36. Review of *The Active Universe*, by H. W. Piper; *Critical Quarterly*, Vol. 5, No. 3 (1963), p. 267.

37. 'Tom Jones', *The Kenyon Review*, Vol. 20, No. 2 (1958), p. 221.

38. 'Extracts from Unpublished Memoirs', in *William Empson: The Man and His Work*, ed. Roma Gill (London: Routledge and Kegan Paul, 1974), pp. 13–14.

39. 'Plenum and Vacuum', *Collected Poems* (London: Chatto and Windus, 1977), p. 7. All references to the poems are to this edition, and page numbers are cited in the text.

40. *Horizon*, Vol. 3, No. 15 (1941), p. 223.

41. Letter, in *Critical Quarterly*, Vol. 6, No. 4 (Spring, 1964), p. 83.

42. Empson's notes in the *Collected Poems* are a help, and some further explanation was given in note form to Rintaro Fukuhara. See his 'Mr William Empson in Japan', in *William Empson*, ed. Gill, p. 24. See also Christopher Ricks's excellent discussion of 'Empson's Poetry' in *William Empson*, esp. pp. 195–97.

43. There is a case also for seeing a web here, a good image for the tensions man spins out of himself. 'Streams' then means streamers of filament.

44. Cited by Ricks, 'Empson's Poetry', p. 196.

45. Empson's 'Your Teeth are Ivory Towers' is a witty defence of obscurity in verse, and the note on p. 111 ends with the observation: 'I suppose the reason I tried to defend my clotted kind of poetry was that I felt it was going a bit too far.'

46. See especially 'Literary Criticism and the Christian Revival', *The Rationalist Annual* (1966), pp. 25–30.

47. Review of *George Herbert* by T. S. Eliot: *New Statesman* (Jan 4 1963), p. 18.

48. *Milton's God*, pp. 232 ff.

CHAPTER 5

1. See Tzvetan Todorov, *The Fantastic. A Structural Approach to a Literary Genre*, trans. Richard Howard (Cleveland and London: Case Western Reserve University Press, 1973), pp. 166 ff., for an account of this. The 'Golden Age' of children's fantasy is in the reigns of Victoria and Edward VII. See, for example, Roger Lancelyn Green, 'The Golden Age of Children's Books', in *Only Connect: Readings on Children's Literature*, ed. Sheila Egoff, G. T. Stubbs, L. F. Ashley (Toronto and New York: Oxford University Press, 1969), pp. 1–16.

2. See Michael Holquist, 'What is a Boojum? Nonsense and Modernism', *Yale French Studies*, XLIII (1969), pp. 145—64, reprinted in *Alice in Wonderland*, ed. Donald J. Gray (New York: A Norton Critical Edition, 1971), p. 404.

3. For a fascinating discussion of this, see William Empson, *Some Versions of Pastoral* (New York: New Directions, 1935), pp. 253—94. Reprinted in Gray, *Alice*, pp. 337—65.

4. *Alice's Adventures in Wonderland*, ed. Gray, p. 97. All references to this as well as *Through the Looking-Glass, and What Alice Found There* are to Gray's edition and are indicated in the text.

5. For an account of MacDonald's theory, and its German sources, see Frank Bergmann, 'The Roots of Tolkien's Tree: The Influence of George MacDonald and German Romanticism upon Tolkien's Essay "On Fairy Stories",' *Mosaic*, X, 2 (1977), pp. 5—14.

6. 'The Imagination: Its Functions and its Culture', *A Dish of Orts. Chiefly Papers on the Imagination and on Shakespeare* (London: Edwin Dalton, 1908), p. 28.

7. Ibid., p. 29.

8. Title of a sermon, in *The Hope of the Gospel* (London: Ward, Lock, Bowden and Co., 1892), pp. 97 ff.

9. *Creation in Christ*, ed. Rolland Hein (Wheaton, Ill.: Harold Shaw, 1976), p. 333.

10. 'The Imagination', p. 8.

11. Ibid., p. 36.

12. Lewis Carroll provides hints of these interpretations when he describes the Queen of Hearts and the Red Queen in terms of the passions, and the White Queen as physically helpless to the point of imbecility. See '*Alice* on Stage', ed. Gray, p. 283.

13. The reader addressed is also an adult. Robinson Duckworth, describing the genesis of *Alice*, says 'the story was actually composed and spoken *over my shoulder* for the benefit of Alice Liddell. . . .' See Gray, *Alice*, p. 272.

14. *The Annotated Mother Goose*, ed. William S. Baring-Gould and Ceil Baring-Gould (New York: Clarkson N. Potter, Inc., 1962), p. 15, n. 3. The rhyme appears in a book published in Britain and the United States in 1925.

15. Ibid., pp. 56—58.

16. Ibid., p. 106.

17. Ibid., pp. 20—21.

18. Philippe Ariès, *Centuries of Childhood* (Harmondsworth: Penguin Books, 1973; first published 1960).

19. Ibid., see especially ch. I, 'The Idea of Childhood', pp. 13 ff.

20. Ibid., pp. 60 ff.

21. As any history of children's literature will point out. See, for instance, Cornelia Meigs, Anne Thaxter Eaton, Elizabeth Nesbitt, Ruth Hill Viguers, *A Critical History of Children's Literature* (New York: The Macmillan Co., 1953), ch. I, 'The Deepest Roots', pp. 3 ff.

22. One thinks of Perrault's verse morals and sly jokes, for instance on the lizards (which don't appear in older versions of *Cinderella*), where he plays on the French saying, 'lazy as a lizard', to jibe at the servant class. See further, Marc Soriano, *Les Contes de Perrault* (Paris: Galliard, 1968). Mme. Villeneuve's elegant *Beauty and the Beast* clearly shows the new emphases.

23. Ariès, *Centuries of Childhood*, 'The Origins of the School Class', pp. 171 ff.

24. Ibid., 'Pictures of the Family', pp. 327 ff., and 'Children's Dress', pp. 48 ff.

25. The preface to the epoch-making *A Pretty Little Pocket Book* (1744), derives directly from Locke.

26. See Meigs, et al., *A Critical History*, 'The Age of Admonition', pp. 72 ff.

27. *Fables in Monosyllables* (1780–90), cited in Meigs, et al., *A Critical History*, p. 89.

28. See Meigs, et al., *A Critical History*, p. 76.

29. See Todorov, *The Fantastic*, p. 168, on fantasy as the bad conscience of a positivist era.

30. For a discussion of fantasy as a 'direct reversal of ground rules' assumed by a piece of writing, see Eric S. Rabkin, *The Fantastic in Literature* (New Jersey: Princeton University Press, 1976), esp. ch. I, 'The Fantastic and Fantasy', pp. 3–41. The above phrase is on p. 14. Rabkin considers, as does Todorov, *The Fantastic*, 163 ff., the fact that all narrative contains an element of the fantastic, which breaks the equilibrium of ordinary events to make a story. 'In more or less degree, a whole range of narratives uses the fantastic. At the far end of this range, we find Fantasy, the genre whose center and concern, whose primary enterprise, is to present and consider the fantastic.' *The Fantastic in Literature*, p. 41. See also C. S. Lewis, 'On Stories', in *Essays Presented to Charles Williams*, ed. C. S. Lewis (London: 1947, reprinted Grand Rapids, Mich.: 1966), p. 103, where Lewis argues that the 'series of events' in a story is really 'to catch something else'.

31. For a sense of how this line of argument can be extended into fantasy more exclusively for adults (for instance, the Gothic novel), see Rabkin, *The Fantastic in Literature*, 'The Fantastic and Genre Criticism', pp. 117 ff.; 'The Fantastic and Literary History', pp. 151 ff.

32. Todorov's main point. See *The Fantastic*, p. 31, et passim.

33. Kipling had read Lewis Carroll when young 'so completely that it was as much a part of him as the Bible or the Prayer Book.' See Shamsul Islam, *Kipling's 'Law'. A Study of his Philosophy of Life* (London: Macmillan, 1975), p. 122. On the theoretically vexing question of what *is* children's literature I am thinking mostly of authors who set out to address a juvenile audience. This does not preclude the author also addressing adults, as, for instance, Kipling, who claimed that sometimes the best way to get at the adults was by writing for children.

34. *The Second Jungle Book* (London: Pan Books, 1975), p. 3. Quotations from this and from *The Jungle Book* (London: Pan Books, 1975) are indicated in the text.

35. See J. M. S. Tompkins, *The Art of Rudyard Kipling* (London: Methuen, 1959), pp. 66 ff., on the interpenetration of these 'worlds'.

36. Fantasy can also be concerned with what we might call the supernatural in its relationship to everyday nature, but this soon raises the question of imagination.

37. 'Kipling for Children', *The Kipling Journal*, XXXII, 156 (Dec. 1965), 26.

38. Signed review of *Just So Stories*, the *Bookman*, XXIII (Nov., 1902), pp. 57–58, reprinted in *Kipling. The Critical Heritage*, ed. Roger Lancelyn Green (London: Routledge and Kegan Paul, 1971), p. 274.

39. F. J. Harvey Darton, *Children's Books in England: Five Centuries of Social Life* (Cambridge: Cambridge University Press, 1958), pp. 314–16.

40. See 'On Fairy Stories', *The Tolkien Reader* (New York: Ballantine Books, 1966), pp. 70 ff. Page numbers in the following account are cited in the text.

41. See Daniel Grotta-Kurska, *J. R. R. Tolkien, Architect of Middle Earth*, ed. Frank Wilson (Philadelphia: Running Press, 1976), p. 100.

42. On Tolkien's pessimism and dislike of machinery (including automobiles,

with which he had the misadventures of Mr Toad without the enthusiasm) see Humphrey Carpenter, *J. R. R. Tolkien, A Biography* (London: George Allen and Unwin, 1977), pp. 31, 136, 241, 163, 216, 222.

43. *The Uses of Enchantment. The Meaning and Importance of Fairy Tales* (New York: Alfred A. Knopf, 1976), pp. 60, 117–18, 143, 144.

44. From another direction, Bettelheim's point (also Tolkien's, in arguing that fantasy is a human right co-eval with language) is supported by Jean Piaget and Bärbel Inhelder, *Mental Imagery in the Child*, trans. P. A. Chilton (London: Routledge and Kegan Paul, 1971), pp. 351 ff., suggesting that the ability to anticipate by way of imagination is indispensable for a child's adjustment to reality. For a more sustained literary analysis than Bettelheim provides, but consistent with his views in a manner suggesting links with Tolkien's, see Max Lüthi, *Once Upon a Time. On the Nature of Fairy Tales*, trans. Lee Chadeayne and Paul Gottwald, with introduction and notes by Francis Lee Utley (New York: Frederick Ungar Publishing Co., 1970).

45. *The Uses Of Enchantment*, p. 51. For a recent, less sympathetic but critically astute reading of modern fantasy, which still places the origins of the genre in the scientific revolution, see C. N. Manlove, *Modern Fantasy. Five Studies* (Cambridge University Press, 1975), esp. pp. 259 ff.

46. Ibid., p. 66.

47. See John Bayley, *The Uses of Division* (London: Chatto and Windus, 1976), p. 51.

48. Freud's well-known point that his theories were unself-consciously present in earlier literature is relevant here. Bettelheim avoids the problem of his own Freudian theory causing disenchantment by addressing children's literature. Since the theory would mean nothing to children, literature remains a good way of getting it across. On the conflict between psychology and fantasy, see Todorov, *The Fantastic*, pp. 160 ff.

49. Many critics notice the point, though there is no systematic analysis. See J. S. Ryan, *Tolkien: Cult or Culture* (Armidale, New South Wales: University of New England, 1969), ch. X, 'Middle-Earth and the Archetypes', pp. 153–61.

50. '*Beowulf*: The Monsters and the Critics,' ed. Donald K. Fry, *The Beowulf Poet: A Collection of Critical Essays* (New Jersey: Prentice-Hall, 1968), p. 34.

51. *Romanticism Comes of Age* (Connecticut: Wesleyan University Press, 1967, first published 1944), p. 193.

52. 'The Phenomenology of the Spirit in Fairy Tales', ed. Sir Herbert Read, Michael Fordham, Gerhard Adler, trans. R. F. C. Hull, *The Collected Works of C. G. Jung*, vol. 9, pt. 1, pp. 231, 233, 235.

53. Ibid., p. 226.

54. Ibid., p., 219.

55. *Mysterium Conjunctionis, Works*, Vol. 14, p. 325.

56. Ibid.

57. 'On the Nature of the Psyche', *Works*, Vol. 8, p. 203.

58. 'The Spirit in Fairy Tales', *Works*, Vol. 9, pt. 1, p. 239.

59. Ibid., p. 215.

60. 'On the Nature of Dreams', *Works*, Vol. 8, p. 292.

61. Jolande Jacobi, *The Psychology of C. G. Jung* (London: Routledge and Kegan Paul, 1962), p. 102.

62. 'Psychology and Alchemy', *Works*, Vol. 12, p. 41.

63. 'Two Essays on Analytical Psychology,' *Works*, Vol. 7, p. 175.

64. 'On the Nature of the Psyche', *Works*, Vol. 8, p. 266.

65. *Aion*, ed. Violet S. de Laszlo, *Psyche and Symbol* (New York: Anchor, 1958), p. 6.

66. 'Conscious, Unconscious, and Individuation,' *Works*, Vol. 9, pt. 1, p. 285.

67. *Man and His Symbols*, ed. C. G. Jung (New York: Dell, 1968), p. 178.

68. Ibid., p. 182.

69. *Aion*, p. 11.

70. Ibid., p. 14. See also *Man and His Symbols*, pp. 188—89.

71. *Memories, Dreams, and Reflections*, trans. Richard and Clara Winston (New York: Vintage, 1965), p. 392.

72. 'The Psychology of the Child Archetype', *Works*, Vol. 9, pt. 1, p. 166.

73. Ibid., p. 167.

74. 'On the Nature of Dreams', *Works*, Vol. 8, p. 293.

75. *Works*, Vol. 9, pt. 1, pp. 217—18.

76. Ibid., p. 225.

77. Ibid., p. 227.

78. *The Lord of the Rings* (London: George Allen and Unwin, 1966), I, 351. All further references are cited in the text.

79. 'Psychology and Religion: West and East', *Works*, Vol. 11, p. 341.

80. See *Man and His Symbols*, p. 191; Jacobi; *The Psychology of C. G. Jung*, p. 117.

81. *Aion*, p. 9.

82. Ibid., p. 20.

83. *Man and His Symbols*, p. 202.

84. 'Concerning Rebirth', *Works*, Vol. 9, pt. 1, p. 124.

85. 'On the Nature of Dreams', *Works*, Vol. 8, p. 293.

86. 'Concerning Rebirth', *Works*, Vol. 9, pt. 1, pp. 146—47.

87. 'The Spirit in Fairy Tales', *Works*, Vol. 9, pt. 1, p. 216.

88. Ibid.

89. Ibid., p. 217.

90. Ibid., p. 215.

91. Edmund Fuller, 'The Lord of the Hobbits', ed. Neil D. Isaacs and Rose A. Zimbardo, *Tolkien and the Critics* (Notre Dame: University of Notre Dame Press, 1968), p. 35.

92. 'The Spirit in Fairy Tales', *Works*, Vol. 9, pt. 1, p. 220.

93. See the Preface to *The Lord of the Rings*. Carpenter records a series of remarks on allegory. See *Biography*, pp. 92, 189—90, 202—3, 243.

94. Cited in Daniel Grotta-Kurska, *J. R. R. Tolkien, Architect of Middle Earth*, ed. Frank Wilson (Philadelphia: Running Press, 1976), p. 100.

95. Tolkien was pessimistic, but not cynical. See Carpenter, *Biography*, p. 129, et passim. Tolkien wrote to his son Christopher: 'for wars are always lost, and The War always goes on; and it is no good growing faint.' Cited in *Biography*, p. 200. Tolkien had thought of a sequel to *The Lord of the Rings*, entitled *The New Shadow*. See *Biography*, p. 228.

96. On these points, see *Biography*, pp. 135, 138, 194—95, and 31 ff.

97. Guy Davenport, 'J. R. R. Tolkien, RIP', *National Review* (Sept. 28, 1973).

98. 'Oo, Those Awful Orcs!' *The Nation* (14 April, 1956), pp. 312—14.

99. Cited by Carpenter, *Biography*, p. 134.

100. See *Biography*, p. 37.

101. Ibid., p. 75.

102. Some interesting studies which examine in detail this general approach to language in *Lord of the Rings* are, Anthony J. Ugolnik, '*Wordhord Onleac*: The Mediaeval Sources of J. R. R. Tolkien's Linguistic Aesthetic', *Mosaic*, X, 2 (Winter, 1977), pp. 15–31; Elizabeth D. Kirk, ' "I Would Rather Have Written in Elvish": Language, Fiction and *The Lord of the Rings*,' *Novel* (Fall, 1971), pp. 5–18; J. S. Ryan, 'German Mythology Applied – The Extension of the Literary Folk Memory', *Folklore*, 77 (Spring, 1966), pp. 45–59.

103. 'What is a Boojum?', ed. Gray, pp. 404–05.

104. *The Silmarillion*, ed. Christopher Tolkien (London: George Allen and Unwin, 1977).

CHAPTER 6

1. R. J. Reilly, 'A Note on Barfield, Romanticism, and Time', in *Evolution of Consciousness. Studies in Polarity*, ed. Shirley Sugerman (Connecticut: Wesleyan University Press, 1976), p. 183.

2. See *What Coleridge Thought* (Connecticut: Wesleyan University Press, 1971).

3. See especially *Romanticism Comes of Age* (Connecticut: Wesleyan University Press, 1967; first published 1944), for a collection of essays written from an anthroposophical view-point.

4. See especially, Shirley Sugerman, 'A Conversation with Owen Barfield', in *Evolution of Consciousness*, p. 12.

5. See *Romanticism Comes of Age*, pp. 16 ff; and R. J. Reilly, *Romantic Religion* (Athens: University of Georgia Press, 1971), p. 16.

6. See especially, *History in English Words* (London: Faber and Faber, 1953). Also *Poetic Diction* (London: Faber and Faber, 1962, first published 1928), *Saving the Appearances: A Study in Idolatory* (London: Faber and Faber, New York: Harcourt, Brace and World, Inc., 1965), and *Speaker's Meaning* (Connecticut: Wesleyan University Press, 1970), all make use of the history of words.

7. See *Poetic Diction*, esp. chs. III and IV, pp. 60–89.

8. The phrase is distinguished from 'final participation', and the concept is analysed especially in *Saving the Appearances*, esp. pp. 28 ff.; 40 ff.; 133 ff.

9. See, for example, *Romanticism Comes of Age*, pp. 70, 184; *Unancestral Voice* (Connecticut: Wesleyan University Press, 1965), p. 14.

10. See 'Participation and Isolation, A Fresh Light on Present Discontents', in *The Rediscovery of Meaning and Other Essays* (Connecticut: Wesleyan University Press, 1977), p. 204: 'Another thing which these books of mine have in common is that their standpoint is always historical.'

11. See *Romanticism Comes of Age*, p. 231; 'Philology and the Incarnation', in *Rediscovery*, p. 234. Barfield's view of the process is summarised by Reilly, *Romantic Religion*, pp. 22 ff.

12. See *Romanticism Comes of Age*, p. 43, and 'The "Son of God" and the "Son of Man"', *Rediscovery*, pp. 249 ff.

13. Barfield insists everywhere on the crucial nature of the scientific revolution. See for instance, *Saving the Appearances*, 6, 8, 10, 11, 18, 20, 21, et passim; *Unancestral Voice*, 95, 109; 'Participation and Isolation', 7; *What Coleridge Thought*, 48;

Romanticism Comes of Age, 58, 59; *Speaker's Meaning*, 11; *The Case for Anthroposophy* (London: Rudolf Steiner Press, 1970), p. 7.

14. See *Unancestral Voice*, p. 40; 'Participation and Isolation', p. 9; *Saving the Appearances*, pp. 92 ff.

15. See 'Of the Consciousness Soul', *Romanticism Comes of Age*, pp. 84 ff.

16. See *What Coleridge Thought*, passim.

17. This is Barfield's 'final participation'. See *Saving the Appearances*, pp. 133 ff.; *Romanticism Comes of Age*, 60, 61; *Speaker's Meaning*, p. 114.

18. See *Unancestral Voice*, pp. 119 ff.; *Worlds Apart* (Connecticut: Wesleyan University Press, 1963), pp. 76 ff., et passim.

19. *Unancestral Voice*, p. 133.

20. *What Coleridge Thought*, p. 36.

21. Ibid., pp. 71–72.

22. Ibid., p. 70. Barfield says the poem is 'imagination appearing'.

23. *Poetic Diction*, p. 115.

24. *Saving the Appearances*, p. 73.

25. *Poetic Diction*, p. 49.

26. Pp. 101 ff.

27. 'Participation and Isolation', pp. 12 ff.

28. *Saving the Appearances*, p. 73.

29. *Romanticism Comes of Age*, p. 174.

30. *Unancestral Voice*, p. 16; Sugerman, 'A Conversation', p. 13; *Unancestral Voice*, p. 163; *Romanticism Comes of Age*, p. 211.

31. *Unancestral Voice*, pp. 14, 90; *Romanticism Comes of Age*, 70; *Speaker's Meaning*, pp. 93 ff.; *Saving the Appearances*, pp. 4, 7–8.

32. An interesting embodiment of this conception in literature is described by U. Milo Kaufmann, *Paradise in the Age of Milton*, English Literary Studies, No. 11 (1968), as '*Finitude manqué*'.

33. See John J. Mood, 'Poetic Languaging and Primal Thinking. A Study of Barfield, Wittgenstein, and Heidegger', *Encounter*, XXVI (1965), p. 426, accusing Barfield of making assumptions. There is a brief, energetic attack on Barfield in Nuttall, *A Common Sky*, p. 221.

34. *Saving the Appearances*, p. 137.

35. Sugerman, 'A Conversation', pp. 27–28.

36. *Worlds Apart*, and to a lesser degree, *Unancestral Voice*.

37. *Worlds Apart*, p. 62.

38. *Unancestral Voice*, p. 104.

39. Sugerman, 'A Conversation', p. 19.

40. Ibid., p. 20.

41. *What Coleridge Thought*, p. 113.

42. *Romanticism Comes of Age*, pp. 154, 156.

43. Ibid., p. 231.

44. *Unancestral Voice*, pp. 111, 158.

45. Letter, dated 7 June 1977.

46. *Unancestral Voice*, p. 163.

47. *What Coleridge Thought*, p. 156.

48. In a letter Barfield recommends this book as essential reading on the subject.

49. *Saving the Appearances*, p. 172.

50. Supplement to *Anthroposophical Movement* (Feb., 1974), p. 3.

51. *Romanticism Comes of Age*, pp. 205 ff.

52. *Unancestral Voice*, p. 23.

53. See *Personal Knowledge. Towards a Post-Critical Philosophy* (New York: Harper Torchbooks, 1964; first published 1958), pp. 269 ff.; and 'Beyond Nihilism' (1960), ed. Marjorie Grene, *Knowing and Being* (Chicago: University of Chicago Press, 1969), pp. 3–23. These themes recur throughout Polanyi's writings.

54. *Science, Faith and Society* (Chicago: University of Chicago Press, 1964), 'Background and Prospect', pp. 7–19. This new introduction gives an account of how the book came to be written in 1946.

55. The following account of scientific method and moral inversion summarises a theory which recurs throughout Polanyi's writings, for example: *Personal Knowledge*, 203–45; 'Beyond Nihilism', ed. Grene, pp. 3–28; *The Tacit Dimension* (New York: Anchor Books, 1966), pp. 55 ff.; *The Logic of Liberty* (Chicago: University of Chicago Press, 1951), pp. 8 ff., 93 ff. Good critical summaries can be found in Harry Prosch, 'Cooling the Modern Mind', *Skidmore College Bulletin* (1971), pp. 5 ff., and 'Polanyi's Ethics', *Ethics*, 82 (Jan. 1972), 91–113; 'Polanyi's Tacit Knowing in the "Classic" Philosophers', *Journal of the British Society for Phenomenology*, Vol. 4, No. 3 (Oct., 1973), pp. 201–16. For a full scale application of Polanyi to the history of philosophy, see Marjorie Grene, *The Knower and the Known* (Berkeley: The University of California Press, 1974).

56. See, for example, *The Logic of Liberty*, pp. 8–14; 53 ff.; *Science, Faith and Society*, pp. 24, 26, 74 ff.; *Meaning* (with Harry Prosch), (Chicago: University of Chicago Press, 1975), p. 145.

57. The open-endedness of scientific enquiry, and the unpredictability of the results of research are favourite themes. See for instance *Personal Knowledge*, p. 5, et passim; *The Tacit Dimension*, pp. 53 ff.

58. The story is summarised in Polanyi's new preface to *Science, Faith and Society* (1964), and the grounds of his opposition are stated in the book.

59. *The Tacit Dimension*, p. 4.

60. 'On Body and Mind', *The New Scholasticism*, 43 (1969), p. 199.

61. Ibid., p. 200.

62. *Personal Knowledge*, p. 64.

63. 'Meaning'. Unpublished lecture given at the University of Chicago, April, 1970, pp. 18, 4.

64. 'The Meaning of Paintings'. Unpublished lecture (1967), pp. 7–8. I acknowledge with thanks the generosity of Professor Harry Prosch in providing typescripts of Polanyi's lectures. These, in collaboration with Michael Polanyi, Professor Prosch has since edited in *Meaning*. I refer to the lecture drafts when the emphasis seems different from the edited version.

65. 'Meaning', p. 5.

66. 'The Meaning of Paintings', p. 14.

67. 'What is a Painting?', *The American Scholar*, 39 (Autumn, 1970), p. 656.

68. Ibid., p. 664. Polanyi does not mean that all painting must be representative, and he examines also the structure of non-representative paintings (e.g., p. 663).

69. Ibid., p. 664.

70. Ibid., p. 665.

71. See *What Coleridge Thought*, p. 247, n. 29. Barfield also has brief remarks on Polanyi in *The Case for Anthroposophy*, pp. 11–12, and *Rediscovery*, p. 181.

72. 'On Body and Mind', p. 199.

73. *Personal Knowledge*, pp. 300 ff.

74. 'The Creative Imagination', *Tri-Quarterly* (1966), p. 118.

75. Some of these were gathered and edited by Polanyi and Harry Prosch in *Meaning*.

76. 'The Meaning of Paintings', pp. 4–5.

77. *Meaning* cites only one reference in the index, but the lectures mention Barfield more frequently—see for instance, 'Meaning: A Project', p. 20; 'The Meaning of Paintings', pp. 6, 15; 'Meaning', p. 8.

78. *Meaning*, p. 129.

79. Ibid., p. 147.

80. Ibid., pp. 117–18.

81. Ibid., p. 109.

82. 'Meaning: A Project', unpublished lecture, p. 23.

83. *Meaning*, p. 109.

84. See 'The Meaning of Paintings', p. 26.

85. *Personal Knowledge*, p. 65.

86. See *Meaning*, ch. 7, 'Visionary Art', pp. 108–19, esp. p. 112.

87. Ibid., pp. 115–16.

88. Ibid., pp. 116–17. The original lecture is less grudging: 'its power to transcend this decomposition by new ranges of visionary experience has revealed us worlds of the imagination, and I accept the balance.' 'Visionary Art', p. 12.

89. Ibid., p. 112.

90. Ibid., p. 115.

91. *Saving the Appearances*, p. 131.

92. *Romanticism Comes of Age*, p. 20. Yet it is not so simple. Hugh Kenner in *The Pound Era* (London: Faber and Faber, 1972), pp. 105–6, 163, et passim, describes the preoccupation of modernism with etymology and the tensions of polarised energy. Some of his descriptions of Fenollosa apply well to Barfield. Also, Polanyi's indebtedness to the phenomenological movement, acknowledged especially in *The Study of Man* (Chicago: University of Chicago Press, 1958), p. 102, bears close resemblance to Barfield's appeal to the same body of thought in *Speaker's Meaning*, pp. 106 ff. The modernism of both men reflects in their study of history. An interesting, more oblique connection is by way of Marjorie Grene's appeal to the physicist David Bohm to develop Polanyi's ideas. See *The Knower and the Known*, p. 246. Professor Bohm is a favourite authority of Barfield's.

93. Polanyi uses this phrase throughout his writings. An example is, *Personal Knowledge*, p. 266. For further analysis, see my article, 'Michael Polanyi: The Augustinian Component', *The New Scholasticism*, XLVIII, 4 (Autumn, 1974), pp 438–63.

94. See *Personal Knowledge*, 'Dwelling In and Breaking Out', pp. 195–204.

95. Ibid., p. 199.

96. Ibid., pp. 279 ff.

97. Ibid., p. 405.

98. 'Faith and Reason', ed. Fred Schwartz, *Psychological Issues*, Vol. VIII, No. 4, monograph 32, 'Scientific Thought and Social Reality, Essays by Michael Polanyi' (New York: International Universities Press, 1974), p. 117.

99. Ibid., p. 130.

100. This is Marjorie Grene's conclusion: see *The Knower and the Known*, pp. 56, 61.

CHAPTER 7

1. See Ernst Cassirer, *An Essay on Man* (New York: Bantam Books, 1970), pp. 230–31; 119.

2. Albert Camus's term: see *The Myth of Sisyphus, and Other Essays*, trans. Justin O'Brian (New York: Vintage Books, 1955), p. 86.

3. Letter, dated 7 June 1977.

4. A comparison of their largely autobiographical war books, *Goodbye to All That* and *In Parenthesis*, soon reveals this difference. Or Compare Graves's polemical essays in, say, *The Common Asphodel* with those of Jones in *Epoch and Artist*.

5. I disavow an over-simple notion of literary composition here: authors do not first decide what their ideas are, and then write about them. I am attempting rather to distinguish key elements in a complex process.

Index